BEHAVIOR MOD

BEHAVIOR

MOD

by Philip J. Hilts

HARPER'S MAGAZINE PRESS
Published in Association with Harper & Row,
New York

"Harper's" is the registered trademark of Harper & Row, Publishers, Inc.

BEHAVIOR MOD. Copyright © 1974 by Philip J. Hilts. All rights reserved. Printed in the United States of America. No part of this book may be used or reproduced in any manner whatsoever without written permission except in the case of brief quotations embodied in critical articles and reviews. For information address Harper & Row, Publishers, Inc., 10 East 53rd Street, New York, N.Y. 10022. Published simultaneously in Canada by Fitzhenry & Whiteside Limited, Toronto.

Designed by Dorothy Schmiderer

Library of Congress Cataloging in Publication Data
Hilts, Philip.
  Behavior mod.
  Includes bibliographical references.
  1. Behavior modification. I. Title.
BF637.B4H54   158   73–18664
ISBN 0–06–122700–5

Contents

Introduction

We have become huge by our technology.

Our ears are huge: we can hear words spoken anywhere on earth, and beyond; we can hear voices and sounds from the past. Our eyes are great telescopes and tiny watchers among atoms; we can see the faces of dead men smile; we watch long-disappeared feats unfold again and again. Our hands are massive machines: we can kill a man at one hundred yards; we can crush a city at any distance; we can tickle minute microbes; we can fashion a hundred tiny circuits instantly.

No other people in history has been so enthralled by the practical. Doing it quickly, neatly, with the smallest effort is our greatest obsession. We have tools for every area of life from brushing teeth to controlling fertility, and these new means have splattered old values on the wall. They blast at the roots of our basic patterns of living. Still we make more tools, and faster.

But there is one sacred area, one blind spot, in which we have made no tools more effective than those used by Plato two thousand years ago. We have fumbled, groped, and guessed about what tools might work in this curious eye of the technology hurricane.

The sacred, undeveloped area is human behavior. Psychology in the past one hundred years has wrestled with behavior, searching for rules that might be useful. Some marvelous mythic treatments of man have emerged, like the Freudian three-tiered personality. But these designs have been no help when we have tried to change or control behavior. We still discard people like garbage when they act strangely, shutting them away in institutional cans until they die.

But our fascination with the practical, with tools, determined that eventually it would happen. Eventually technology would reach the area of human behavior. It has.

There are now hundreds of men and women around the country using the new technology of behavior. They are manipulating the behavior of people in businesses, prisons, homes, public schools. They can untangle a homosexual, dry out an alcoholic, toilet train a youngster in half a day, turn a delinquent into a scholar. They say they have just begun.

With technology, we have created a paradox for ourselves. While we feverishly mother our new tools, and continuously conceive more, we are at the same time sketching details into the nightmare of the clockwork man.

No technology is as useful as the one that will empty our prisons and mental institutions, teach us how to raise our children efficiently, allow us to free ourselves of bad habits. The technology of behavior offers this. No technology can amplify the clockwork-man nightmare more than one that can turn a man into a puppet. The technology of behavior offers this, too.

Victor Ferkiss of Georgetown University has said that it is "now theoretically possible . . . to control human personal and social development in a systematic way. Whether one has regarded previous situations as bondage or blind fate, as preferable or not, is beside the point. The point is that now a choice can and must be made. . . . The power exists. It may or may not be used or abused, but it is there. . . ."*

* *Technological Man* (New York: Mentor/New American Library, 1969).

Since Ferkiss made his comments five years ago, the choice he urges has been made, again and again. It's not been a decision made by governments, national, state, or local. Behavior control technology has moved the way any technology moves. It's simply been installed. The decisions have been made by lone individuals who have found the technology useful.

By now we should know that technology has a momentum of its own. On a morning not long ago, we woke up to find a monstrous atomic bomb in our backyard, and still we don't know the full effect the discovery has had on us. We woke more recently to find our air poisoned and our families rotting from new technology. Still we don't know how far it will carry us, or where.

The growth of behavior technology has not been well reported. This book is a first attempt to describe the burgeoning field of behavior control. Perhaps we can avoid the ambush of this technology, and not awake surprised to find our children carefully manipulated in public schools, to find licenses required for parenthood, to find employers who keep charts and graphs of employee behavior.

1. The Controllers

It is 11 A.M. The room is jammed with data books and papers; there are charts on the wall. The controllers are relaxed, talking casually to a visitor.

A noise from the TV monitor: a door opening, shuffling feet. The controllers look up at the monitor. The monitor is looking down on a young black kid as he walks into a little box of a room. The kid looks up at the camera monitoring him. "I want a Coke and a game on the bowling machine."

One of the controllers looks down from the monitor, checking a point sheet. Yes, the kid has enough points. "Okay, Jordan," he says to the kid. A button is punched. Another. A Coke drops in the machine, the bowling game lights up and whirs. The boy moves over to the bowling machine and presses a lever. . . .

This is a junior high school. Jordan is one of those kids who have labels hung by their names. Problem Kid. Juvenile Delinquent. Jordan has messed up the decorum of several of his classes. His grades are awful. The controllers watching him on the monitor are a group of psychologists, and they have a label of their own.

Behavior Modifiers. They're here to show that these down-and-out kids can be shaped up. That kids like Jordan can put out some impressive academic behavior and come on like those other kids, with the big glasses and brown brief cases.

Ogden Lindsley is peering into a little wooden box, monitoring the rat that is shuffling about inside. The rat looks at his fur, pees, then runs over to the lever that extends out from the side of the box. He jumps up and hangs there. Slowly the lever drifts down, triggering a switch. The rat has hit the reward point. A food pellet drops in the food-dispensing machine. The rat moves over to the tray. . . .

This is a Harvard laboratory. The rat is normal, and if left alone would look for food, clean his fur, explore his cage, scout for sex sometimes. Ogden Lindsley is a behavior modifier. He is trying to show that normal rats can put out some impressive behavior. Lindsley is developing a weight-lifting rat, a rat that will build huge shoulder muscles and walk around in the cage with other rats as if he's Charles Atlas at muscle beach.

Jordan the junior high student has been quieter this year. While last year he got three Fs and two Ds on his report card, this year the card shows A, A, C, D, D, and they're still shooting up.

Ogden Lindsley's rats lifted nearly three times their own body weight. "My God . . . *six hundred grams!*" says Lindsley.

Both Jordan and the rat have been on the receiving end of a new technology—the technology of behavior control. It began some seventy years ago. Then, just before World War II, Harvard psychologist B. F. Skinner added some important new principles. The new Skinnerian principles allowed a total control over the behavior of animals.

They started with lever-pressing—getting pigeons to press a lever for a reward. They found ways to control the rate and the style of lever-pressing, just by manipulating the way the reward was given. They worked on other behavior, getting pigeons to bob and weave in prescribed ways, getting birds to discriminate between colored disks, pecking at only the proper color. They soon learned they could get *any* kind of behavior from animals, quickly and efficiently.

Skinner himself got a pair of pigeons in a box to play Ping Pong. The ball was placed in the middle of a table, and as it rolled to one side of the table, the pigeon on that side pecked it, and drove it back across the table. The pigeons bobbed and shuffled to meet shot after shot, and could drive the ball quite hard and straight across. Skinner's movies of the Ping-Pong matches show the pigeons carrying on volleys of as many as six shots before one bird scored a point.

Other researchers got a pigeon playing a little bowling game, got a dog to make chess moves, got a rabbit to play a piano while a chicken danced to the tune on a nearby platform.

While they were pulling off the animal stunts, developing behavior principles for animals, the behaviorists hoped that their work would lead to a description of human behavior as well. In the late forties, Skinner, a failed novelist who had lived in Greenwich Village and had roamed Paris in search of material, wrote a novel depicting human behavior control. But the details of his controlled, utopian society were still vague.

It was about 1952 when the bridge to people was crossed. Dr. Ogden Lindsley, trainer of the weight-lifting rats and one of Skinner's students, was among the first to make the journey to human behavior.

They call him Crazy Og, and he's something of a legend among the behaviorists now. He is fifty years old, and his brief goatee and flaring mustache are gray. In the twenty years since he began the work, he has published papers that would make a pile reaching halfway up his long, thin legs.

His office is a tiny, cluttered room in Lawrence, Kansas. He is leaning forward in a squeaky swivel chair, pausing to search for the study, the graphs that illustrate an important point. He pokes through the rubble of ideas that is heaped on his desk and the floor around it. In a moment he finds the right paper, but has already gone on to another point. His blue beacon eyes look up. "Where was I?" In a way he is the image of the gray, respectable scientist, intense and a little absent-minded.

But he is also Crazy Og, looking younger than his years, one of this new breed of science activists, the behavior controllers. His face is tan, healthy-looking. And his hair! It's long and fine, billowing over his ears with a careful mod hair style that looks as if it were coifed in a fag salon for some young rock star. Crazy Og drives a yellow Mercedes, and will explain quite unscientifically how to prepare your head to hear thick acid rock on his big stereo system.

His turned-on life style fits the Crazy Og title. But he picked up the title for more than that. The man has run against the wind throughout his career, even in those early behavior control days under Skinner. If no one else would touch an idea, Crazy Og was out trying to pull it off. When those ideas caught on, Crazy Og was out in some other left field. And he rides his far-out ideas hard, carrying the mental mail on his own pony express of the mind with the Indians right at his back. . . .

Lindsley is up out of the skreeking chair in his tiny office. He is talking about the beginning in 1951. He was a graduate student and he had just dumped his field—electrophysiology—to be at Harvard with Skinner, this intriguing man who was being ripped for his manipulative ideas about behavior. The controversy excited student Lindsley.

"My first job as a graduate assistant under Skinner was to make the weight-lifting rat," he says. It was for a class demonstration to show students the power of behavior conditioning. "It was a real turn-on for the students. . . . In something like three weeks, I had three rats all pulling down something like 250 percent of their body weight. They developed huge muscles."*

---

* Lindsley had each rat in a box that contained a weight-lifting bar and a small food magazine. Each time the rat pulled down the weight bar, the bar hit a microswitch that would drop a food pellet in the magazine. In behavioral terms, the rat's weight-lifting behavior was reinforced, or re-

The turn-on of making weight-lifting rats wasn't just for the students. "I was a farm boy," Lindsley says. He grew up on a 365-acre farm in Rhode Island, and one year when he was a boy there, he caught some baby woodchucks.

"I tried to train them for the county fair. I had an awful time. They bit me and . . . well, I got them to do a few tricks, got them to sit up on their hind legs. But it was nothing like what operant [behavior] conditioning could do. . . . I never had such control over animals! I could make these rats lift . . . my God . . . *six hundred grams!* That so impressed me. . . ." The experience of total control was exciting, but already his mind was running far down the road.

"Working with people was always very much on my mind. I worked with dogs next because I was trying to get closer and closer to people," he says.

He had already done a little preliminary work on his daughter Cathy. She was raised in an air crib, an enclosed temperature-controlled, soundproofed environment for infants invented by Skinner. "At that time about sixty people had done that with their children. But nobody had put toys in there and put [behavior] recorders on them. Nobody had taken behavioral data out of it. I hung rattles, gave her buttons to push that ran lights, and gave her a switch to control her own lights, and then recorded all of that. We found that all the laws we found in rats and pigeons were true. . . ."

In World War II, Lindsley had suffered the shock of prison camp life, and when he started behavioral work only a few years later, his whole idea was to work with people.

"My whole logic in getting into it was that if this doesn't work with people, then it's some kind of animal put-on. I would have to leave it and go into religion or something. After being a prisoner, I wanted to help change people.

---

warded, with food. Any behavior that is reinforced is likely to be more frequent in the future. The rat pulled down the bar, got "reinforced," and began pulling down the bar more frequently.

"My plan was to give it five years, and if I didn't find any way to understand people better, or help people, that was it. I would leave operant conditioning for something that was appropriate to people," he says.

Those first years, just as the behaviorists were beginning to apply their ideas to people, were the roughest. "We were criticized by everybody. You'd go to a meeting and people would say, 'Hey, here come the pigeon peckers!' People would come up behind you and go 'Ditditditdit . . . ditditditdit,' which was the sound of the cumulative [behavior] recorders we used. Old buddies wouldn't even talk to me anymore. A real friendly one would tell me I was committing professional suicide." Most of the attacks, though, were still done as jokes, because many believed that the mechanical pigeon view of behavior wouldn't hold up with people.

At Harvard there was a small squad of believers called the "pigeon staff." They were mostly graduate students who were working in Skinner's pigeon lab. The Harvard faculty was mostly opposed to the Skinnerian notions of behavior, Lindsley says, "and the graduate students were caught in the middle, and some had to go underground. I was one of the graduate students who never went underground, and consequently my degree was held up a long time, and I was given low grades. . . . Like in [Professor E. G.] Boring's course.

"Boring would say, 'What is behavior?' He'd want you to say, 'It's a very complicated thing'; then he'd say, 'Some people say behavior is nothing but muscle twitches and gland squirts,' and we'd spend maybe three hours proving that it's more than that. Then he'd go around the table, asking, 'All right, what's behavior?' Each student would say, 'It's a complicated thing. . . .' Then he'd come to me and I'd say, 'Muscle twitches and gland squirts.' He gave me a B-minus."

Crazy Og loved the pressure, fed on the controversy. But still, he wasn't sure that the principles of behavior control would work with people.

"I always had escape routes. My plan was that if the thing

turned out completely haywire and I couldn't work with people, while I was trying to figure out how to get back to people in some other field, there was still one aspect of operant conditioning that hadn't been used—a way I could survive while figuring out what to do next. We could train animals with nothing but a reward: just find a reward they like, deliver it quickly, immediately, and *remotely*. We were never in the box with the animal. . . . I used to tell students that if there were funny evil people on the moon that radiate disease, all we had to do was parachute a food magazine in and we could train them from earth, using food as a payoff for behavior.

"So my plan was that if the bottom fell out of the whole thing, I would drop out of graduate school and try to get a job with Ringling Brothers. . . . Nobody had ever done anything with gorillas, except keep 'em in a cage, and they'd just do gorilla stuff. But nobody ever had a gorilla dancing or playing the piano or anything like that. And I thought, Gee, what a natural—all you gotta do is put a huge indestructible food magazine in there and you can stand outside the glass cage and make him do anything. . . .

"I'd try to get this job with Ringling Brothers, and if I had my degree I'd sell that, you know, put on this crimson hood of Harvard, and . . . *Professor Lindsley and Gargantua!* And out into the center ring we'd come, and Gargantua would run off all these behaviors. . . ."

Professor Lindsley didn't have to join the circus. People turned out to be as susceptible to the rules as gorillas. In perhaps the first experiment with humans, Lindsley worked with psychotics in a Massachusetts mental hospital.

For an hour or more a day, he put them in a room designed to imitate perfectly the Skinner boxes used to train pigeons and rats. The rewards dropping down in the dispenser included food, money, candy, and opportunities to reward another person.

"We got them doing different tasks. The simplest task of all was just to push a plunger; the most complicated of all was, I'd yoke two rooms together and the two would have to push their buttons simultaneously to get a reward. . . . They had to push their levers within 125 milliseconds of each other. They would stand there and kind of look at each other and say, 'Go! Go! Go!' "

So it was done; the work on people had begun. Lindsley worked with psychotics for several years, turning out hundreds of graphs of behavior. The graph patterns—those straight upward lines, the scallops, the jumping steps—matched the pigeon and rat charts.

The attacks on behaviorism kept up, Lindsley says. "People would say things like, 'What happened to Og?' 'Well, he went to the dogs, then he went nuts. It takes a psychotic to work with a psychotic.' It was a funny, negative kind of bar talk."

But from that time in the fifties, the beginning of behavior control with people, things moved fast. Others began working with people, starting with the psychotics because those were the only people behaviorists could get permission to work with. It later spread to retarded kids, inmates in prisons, delinquents in school, and others on the fringe.

In one experiment, the behaviorists worked with a young retarded girl named Sue. Sue couldn't speak in sentences, couldn't name objects; she could only vaguely imitate the sounds of others. She couldn't walk, and couldn't manage even the simplest exercises with her hands. She was tested for intelligence and she scored a zero. Sue's future was almost guaranteed: she would spend her life as a vegetable in some corner room of an institution.

The behaviorists began with language training. An experimenter uttered a word, and if Sue repeated it, she was rewarded with a piece of candy, a pat on the head, and a compliment. Gradually she learned to name objects for her payoff, then to speak short sentences to elicit the reward. But though she was gaining verbal skill, she still couldn't walk and her leg muscles were thin and atrophied. The behaviorists mounted a bicycle in a frame, and began to give Sue the payoffs for just sitting on the bicycle seat. When she was doing that regularly, they set up an automatic candy dispenser. Each five times she pedaled the bike wheel around, her candy would be delivered. When she was proficient at this, they set the device so it would deliver the reinforcement only after she had pumped the wheel around many times. The girl's legs were still very weak, and the pedals were made easy to push around. So the behaviorists' next tactic was to make the pedals harder to push, by small degrees. After a few months of this, Sue's legs had developed considerably and she was spending several hours a day pumping away at the bike, gobbling down the sweets.

The behaviorists continued shaping her behavior, eventually getting her to ride the bike by herself for no reward. Her verbal skills were developed. Finally, she was released from the institution with an IQ score that allowed her to attend public school.

Not all stories are so hopeful, or so innocent. In two California prisons, some ninety inmates were put in an aversive-conditioning program and given fright therapy to condition them not to commit acts of violence.

Each inmate was strapped to a table and injected with a drug called Anectine, which slowly freezes the muscles. First, the prisoner could not control his hands, then his arms went numb. His head lolled uncontrollably. Finally, for a few minutes, the prisoner could not breathe. He quickly became terrified that he was going to die of suffocation. He tried to struggle but was helpless.

While he was stricken with the fear of dying, the prison doctor demanded that he stop the bad behavior he had been putting out. Or else.

Or else he would be brought back for another terror treatment.

In the sixties, those years that gave us the ghetto riots, the women's movement, and other wonders of modern disbelief, behavior control spread away from the fringes. The controllers moved into regular classes in public schools, into normal homes, into businesses, and into the army. By the beginning of the seventies, it was a wild, blooming field in which no area of life was fenced off. The only limits to its use were those that it had faced all along, and even some of those resistances were dissolving. "Our major problem in working with people," Lindsley notes, "was not so much the method, or the people. It was the resistance of other people who work with people. Around people research and people therapy, there are these great hordes of special-interest groups with other techniques and they don't let you close to the people."

Along the way, the new technology was named "behavior mod" for short, and the practitioners were dubbed the "mod squad." Faced with a nearly continuous heckling from those outside the sanctum, and inspired by the regular, almost monotonous discovery "It works!" the mod squad developed a peculiar evangelism. Since there were no behavior mod degrees and no curricula that could teach the technology, the mod squad members were all converts from other fields who saw behavior mod working and were turned on by its efficient power over behavior.

Dr. R. Vance Hall, who is now working at the University of Kansas, is one of the leading converts. Hall is a small and friendly-looking man. With his clear eyes and open smile, he might easily be a troop leader in Norman Rockwell's boy scouts. Before behavior mod, he was a schoolteacher. "I was thoroughly frustrated by my inability to solve classroom problems. It wasn't that I was a bad teacher; I was a good teacher," he says. But like all teachers, he faced a few kids he couldn't help. There were no rules, no techniques that could do the job. Educators and psychologists only offered theories. "I got into psychology and there was nothing there to help. Finally, I stumbled on behavior mod."

Now, he says, "It's sometimes difficult to resist the Flying Jesus Syndrome. You know, swooping in and saving everyone." Hall's fervor is common among the behaviorists.

"I'm convinced absolutely that these laws of behavior are going to hold," says Dr. Leopold Walder of the Associates for Behavior Change. "It's like the revolution in physics. We are at the beginning of it. There will be some new developments, but Newton's gravity will still get you to the moon." He sounds as if he feels a little like Sir Isaac himself.

And Dr. Roger McIntire of Maryland University declares, "You can't stop something that works. The history of science has always been that way, no matter whether it's the Salk vaccine or the atomic bomb."

There are now mod squad platoons in every major city in the country, hundreds of behavior modifiers around the nation. Any of these missionaries can recite the behavioral catechism for you:

Psychologists, they say, have been poking about in the back rooms of the mind for a century, trying to find the basic rules of behavior. They have tromped about in people's fantasies, lifting up the rugs of the psyche to see what would crawl out. Sure enough, all sorts of things have crawled out, and the psychologists have named them all. But after tagging all the mental beasties with names, the psychologists were lost. They had as many sets of labels and theories as there were psychologists. None of the theories were practical; they could not straighten out people's problems, turn on delinquents, relieve homosexuals who wanted to change their stripes.

The mod squad gave up the search through the back rooms of the mind. Ask them about the beauties of the mind, and they simply shrug—as in the case of the young man who went to a university psychologist to pour out all the nightmares he'd been having for weeks, all the dreams he had carefully recorded. He talked passionately for twenty minutes, then sank into his chair. The psychologist looked at him blankly. "I'm sorry you had some bad dreams," he said, "but I'm a behaviorist. I don't know anything about those things."

Digging through the rubble of childhood won't help you change problem behavior, the mod squadder says. What they want to know is: Can you count it? What will it look like on a graph?

The whole approach, as Lindsley puts it, "is a very heavy trip." If it is true that psychotics and others with behavior problems can be saved, can be resuscitated, what are we to think of the good doctors who for years have been making Swiss cheese of people's brains with their electroshock therapy? Childhood memories, deep-seated neuroses that were supposed to be altered with the shocks, have got nothing to do with the problem, the behaviorists are now saying. So the modern shock techniques, which have always sounded a little like something out of a sixteenth-century torture manual, are just old-time butchery after all. Not only the shock treatments, but the rest of modern treatment begins to look pretty crude if the behaviorists are right.

One story told by behaviorists compares behaviorism with an old psychology view. A behaviorist working in a mental hospital took a patient and picked out a behavior he wanted to add to the patient's repertoire. For demonstration purposes, he decided to try to get the patient to start carrying a broom around the wards, wherever he went. So every time the patient went near the broom or picked it up, he was rewarded. Later, he was rewarded for holding the broom, still later for toting it around.

Then the behaviorist called in a psychoanalyst and innocently asked, "Say, we have this patient who keeps carrying around a broom all the time. What do you suppose is the cause of that?" The Freudian doctor did a little probing of the symptom and began to explain. "Well, of course it is a phallic symbol and has to do with the patient's relationship to his father in childhood. . . ."

While much of psychology may look silly at best and barbarous at worst when compared with behaviorism, at the same time, what lies behind the doors opened by behavior control? First, the behavior control field has no shortage of tales of crudity. Whenever one man, Freudian or Skinnerian, is put in charge of another man's behavior, there are bound to be abuses.

But perhaps the most important ethical problem with behaviorism is a subtle one. Since Freudian psychology is more a mythology than a technology, though many abuses have been created, its use has been limited. But behavior control is too effective to have this innocence. As we will see in another chapter, while schoolteachers have had few effective tools to enforce the homogeneous everyone-sitting-quietly-with-hands-folded-doing-their-work approach to children, we did not have to worry too much about the teacher turning out robots. Since the teacher is ineffective in controlling behavior, much deviance is assured. There will be creativity, geniuses, iconoclasts, actors, and doubters. But what will happen in schools when teachers begin to use behavior control, and are able to enforce homogeneity? The behavior modifiers' criticisms of other brands of psychology are completely justified. Their own work shows some earlier theories to be laughable at times. But regardless of the merits or validity of the points of view, how systems of psychology are used in society is also important. The behavior modifiers in this are no better than their predecessors, so far. Their certainty about their own ideas has led them to be overzealous in their application. Just as the Freudians did, they have begun to go far beyond what their science tells them. They find themselves, for example, making essentially political decisions about what kind of behavior in public schools is acceptable and what kind is "misfit behavior." The important ideas behind behavior modification have been violated and abused by this kind of action. So it is no longer behavior modification. It is, by any name, the rigid enforcement of arbitrary norms of behavior. Freudian or Skinnerian, John Stuart Mill would have applied the same phrase to it: "social tyranny."

The roots of the behavior control movement, of course, go back further than Ogden Lindsley, than B. F. Skinner, than Pavlov's pioneer conditioning work with dogs in the twenties.

We can go back as far as philosopher René Descartes in the early 1600s for Skinnerian notions of behavior. Some engineers and architects in Descartes's time had constructed Disneylandlike moving statues as garden amusements. A visitor to one garden would unknowingly step on a hidden treadle, activating a statue of a huge leering Saracen, which then emerged from bushes brandishing a sword. Descartes marveled at how well these statues could imitate humans and frighten strollers in the garden. Perhaps, he said, the statue responding to a signal in the environment was something like human behavior. Descartes was a religious man, and he didn't carry that idea too far, likening man to the garden robots. But he did speculate that some human action was governed by will, while other action was involuntary. His idea that some behavior, like pulling a scorched finger away from fire, was involuntary and could be looked at in the same light as animal behavior was an important step.

Out of this dual view of human behavior came two distinct ways of studying psychology. One, the mentalistic approach, has dominated the popular notions of psychology. This school of thought described the roots of behavior as deep and obscure. On the other hand, reflex behavior, since it was limited and did not threaten the view of man as a deep and mysterious creature, could be studied in the same way as the movements of a stone—under physical laws.

Psychologists could study all of rat behavior without looking for a soul, without looking for childhood causes, without searching for symbolic mysteries. With humans, they had limited themselves to studying only reflex behavior this way. Behaviorism crossed that boundary. In behaviorism, all of man's actions could be viewed the same way a rat's behavior might have been viewed by Descartes. The behaviorists are now saying that animal behavior and human behavior are very similar, and neither the rat nor the man is in control.

This view of man's behavior was first set out clearly by John B. Watson, a psychologist born in South Carolina in 1878, who has been unofficially named the father of behaviorism. Watson dispensed with the mentalistic view of behavior, and in 1912 outlined the new science of behaviorism. "Behaviorism . . . was an attempt to do one thing—to apply to the study of man the same kind of procedure and the same language of description that many research men have found useful for so many years in the study of animals. . . ."[1]*

With that, the tone was set for a technology of behavior. The mind, the consciousness of people, was no longer "a definite nor a usable concept," Watson said. Human activity was to be handled as animal activity was. It's just behavior.

* Source Notes begin on page 229.

These are the assumptions underneath the work of behavior mod. Like any technology, it cannot simply be plugged in and turned on to solve problems. It carries with it a set of ideas that have been heresy until now.

The behavior mod squad has done its best to defang the issue. As Dr. Leo Walder put it, "In the beginning, we were very brazen. We went into these meetings and talked about humans in terms of pigeons and pecking. We didn't know a nice euphemistic language for it. But we've learned."

In Kansas City, for example, behavior modifiers have been supercautious recently. A few years ago, before the current behavior mod projects in the city and the public schools got under way, some behavior mod worker spoke loudly, with the wrong words. He turned off a lot of people. So the present behavior mod workers blanch at the words "behavior mod." They've picked some new words to describe their methods: The Responsive Teaching Model. They emphasize the positive—how much better the children are learning, how much more effectively teachers can deal with problems—and skirt the mechanistic-man issue.

But the mod squadders themselves have no illusions. They buy the new vision of man the manipulated. More than that, they live it. . . .

Dr. Richard Malott, Ph.D., is sitting in a bare room in Kalamazoo, Michigan. He is leaning back in his chair, with his feet propped up on a bare Formica table. He is wearing heavy motorcycle boots and a checkered shirt.

A wide leather watchband is strapped around his wrist. On the top is a watch, and on the two sides are small behavior counters. Rolling down his chest is a great, wide brown beard. He's talking about the life of behavior mod.

"Then I came to Western Michigan [University]. . . . It was a fantastically supportive environment for thinking-behavior," he says in slow, spaced-out tones. That phrase, "thinking-behavior," is common mod squad affectation. It's not just thinking, eating, sex, studying. For the mod squad it's thinking-behavior, eating-behavior, sex-behavior, study-behavior.

"When I came here, it was the first time I came in contact with the subculture that analyzes the world, themselves, and everything they did in terms of behavioral principles. . . ."

Western Michigan, with half a dozen well-known behavior modders and a legion of students and graduate students into behavior mod, is only one of several behavioral centers. At the campus bookstore in Kalamazoo, alongside the usual beer and football T-shirts, there is one that reads: "Better Living Thru Behaviorism." There is a textbook on sale (written by Malott) that looks like a Superman comic book.

Con Man, the black-and-yellow title declares. "Con man" is short for contingency management, another phrase used to substitute for behavior mod.

Malott is talking about the students at Western Michigan, and begins to stroke his beard. He stops. He reaches for his wrist counter and clicks off one beard stroke.

"I'm counting beard strokes. I was very heavily into beard stroking; ended up pulling hairs out of my beard. . . . I got it under pretty good control for a while. My wife is one of the main sources of motivation for eliminating this behavior. . . ."

The other counter on his wrist, he says, "I use to eliminate aversive behavior, aversive comments to other people. You know we have a long history of reinforcement for developing skilled putdowns of other people. Negativity. It really has broken my negativity, brought it way under what it was. There are some situations, like with colleagues, that I got predictably negative. There are other situations . . . after you've been married for about five minutes, the major form of interaction is bitching at each other. I would say we have virtually eliminated that from our marriage. Really beautiful . . ."

He calls it "my clockwork marriage." They've got little behavioral systems designed, with piles of graphs, for the full gamut—making dinner, doing dishes, getting ready to go out, writing letters, weight control.

"It's not a cold, mechanical, uptight thing," he says. "We just set up procedures to eliminate much of the aversive bullshit that people have. . . . Many of these procedures tend to become second nature. For example, we put a contingency on me that I had to close the shower curtain when I take a shower. We have all these rules written down, and I know if I don't do it, something bad will happen, but I don't know what because I've forgotten. So I do it. My old lady used to leave drawers and doors open. We specified that if she'd do that five times, something bad would happen, like she'd have to do the dishes. Most of that stuff now is under pretty good control. . . ."

Behavior mod is an encompassing technology. Since it deals with human behavior, which is always going on around us, it is an immersing technology.

The mod squadders keep graphs on themselves, their children, their friends. They analyze politics, government, and laws by behavioral principles. The world is a different place, with a different set of boundaries, structures, and meanings, for the mod squadders. As Skinner says it, "We are concerned . . . not merely with practices, but with the design of a whole culture."[2] Skinner drew the blueprints, and the mod squad now has the carpenters and masons at work. For a society obsessed with efficient tools, with getting results, the neat systems of the behaviorists will be hard to resist.

2. The Ideas

A fictional Galileo, created by Bertolt Brecht, once talked with a monk from a poor peasant family. They spoke of science, of the idea that the earth is not the center of the universe.

Said the humble monk: "My parents are peasants in the campagna who know about the cultivation of the olive tree, and not much about anything else. . . . They draw the strength they need from the sight of the trees greening every year anew . . . from the little church and the Bible texts they hear on Sunday.

"They have been told that God relies upon them and that the pageant of the world has been written around them, that they may be tested in the important and the unimportant parts handed out to them.

"How could they take it, were I to tell them that they are on a lump of stone ceaselessly spinning in empty space, circling around a second-rate star? . . . What comfort, then, the Holy Scriptures, which have mercifully explained their crucifixion?"

Galileo replied: "Shall I lie to your people?"

The little monk: "We must be silent from the highest of motives: the inner peace of less fortunate souls."[1]

Science must have passed this place a hundred times. Science has always answered the monk the same way: Peace is not as important as the facts. And science moved on, passing another monk, giving the same answer, and moving on.

It's a human tradition to ascribe mysterious inner causes to things unknown. At one time, a burning tree showed that the tree god was angry. Men used to believe that when a ball rolled down a hill, some inner property determined how fast and far the ball would move.

Perhaps it is fragile man's respect for the unknown that causes this attitude. Or perhaps it is just that we have only recently learned, and not got used to, the idea that all the world is a flow of activities dependent only on each other. No props, no inner demons, no control. Just a great flow.

This is the behaviorist's view of behavior. It is a flow, controlled by the bounds of the banks, the rocks in its path, the depth of the channel, the trees that sometimes fall in its way. There is no "inner controller" here. No personality structure, no "real person underneath."

This may be a step forward for science, and it promises to deliver us a huge chunk of technology, whether it is welcome or not. As Galileo told us that we are not at the center of the universe, Skinner tells us we are not so human as we thought. We behave by the same rules as the animals.

We now know something about the technological society, and its unsettling impact on man. Imagine now the post-human society in which technology is extended to the direct control of human behavior. There is a great crop of benefits to be harvested from the ability to change behavior efficiently. But we should be cautious. In order to choose the side of Galileo or the monk, we must know something about behavior mod and why it works.

About forty years ago, the bits and pieces of a technology of behavior were scattered in the works of several men. A few important tools were still missing. It was in 1938 that B. F. Skinner pulled together the bits of theory, and added the necessary tools.[2]

The first requirement of science is a system of measurement.

Physics and chemistry have unique means of measuring change. Their work depends on them. But in psychology, there had not even been agreement on what should be measured. Some said we should measure ids, some said measure ink blot fantasies. But even the psychologists who created grand self-contained theories of man offered no yardstick to measure the things they believed were there.

When the behaviorists abandoned the search for will and other mental events, their job was made easier. They looked only at behavior, physical action, so at least they were dealing with things that could be seen and heard.

Skinner found that the most important feature of behavior for the scientist is how often it occurs. Frequency was his yardstick. A man's action that is judged normal when it occurs only occasionally, such as singing, could get a guy put away if he did it too frequently. In looking at psychotics, when each bit of behavior is counted up it becomes clear that some of their actions are normal. The normal bits of behavior simply don't occur often enough. Some bits of psychotic behavior are odd, and those occur too often. A psychotic acts crazy *often enough* to be given a label. Watching President Nixon on television last year, I saw him scream at and shove his press secretary in public. This was a rare action, and it attracted some attention. If it happened quite frequently, the man would be out of a job.

We decide that people are normal, neurotic, or psychotic on the basis of behavior we have seen or heard. But we have treated people by ignoring behavior ("It's only a symptom"), and asking instead what is in their thoughts. It is more logical to count the bits of behavior. Then if a man waves his arms in the air too much to be judged normal, we can try to reduce the number of arm-wavings. To zero, if necessary. If a man can't sell enough vacuum cleaners because housewives say he's not amiable enough, then he needs to increase smiles rather than delve into his childhood.

This idea of measurement, in one stroke, eliminates any need for guessing and fancy interpretation of urges and complexes in order to deal with behavior. Once you start counting behavior, you can put it on a graph and watch it change. Efforts to change it can be checked and tested.

Another step taken in Skinner's 1938 book clarified the problem of reflex and voluntary behavior. The study of reflexes had moved along quickly after Pavlov, and some scientists believed that most human behavior could be explained by the stimulus-response idea—that a stimulus in the environment triggers each bit of behavior. Pavlov's dogs were conditioned to salivate at the sound of a bell. They salivated when a meal was presented, a bell was rung every time the meal was brought, and finally the dogs salivated just at the sound of the bell. Researchers found that many human fears were conditioned the same way, by association, and figured that might be the way most learning takes place.

But Skinner demonstrated that reflex conditioning accounts for only a small portion of human behavior. E. L. Thorndike, a contemporary of Pavlov, had written about a law of effect. He said that instead of responding to a stimulus, animals act to get a response from the environment. They behave to elicit rewards. Skinner showed that this idea was correct through his laboratory work, and said it accounted for most behavior.

Once a system of measurement had been devised, and it was clear that behaviorists should be studying voluntary behavior, the road was open. The problem then was to take the experimental notions and see how much behavior could be explained and altered by them. Skinner laid out the rudiments elaborated in the next three decades:

Behaviorism abandons the idea of personality. "John is a mean and disruptive child in school" is a nearly meaningless statement for a behaviorist. Teachers and educators have found this statement of personality useful, because it has provided an excuse to throw in where technique fails. Educators have said, "This is what the child is like. I've tried to help, but there is something wrong with him." Psychologists and doctors follow up the educators' comments with tests, and determine that the child is hyperactive, has learning disorders, or is dyslexic. These terms are only slightly less helpful than "mean" or "disruptive," which the teacher used. All this ends up with no help for the youngster.

The behavioral substitute for this hassle begins with the statement that behavior is controlled by the consequences immediately after it. Control the consequences and you control the behavior. An illustration of this rule may be found in a tale recounted by Western Michigan's Dr. Jack Michael.

Several grizzled old veterans recovering from bouts of cirrhosis had been sent to a rehabilitation center for physical therapy. Their bodies were shot from the illness and a dissolute way of living.

"It is quite common in the rehab situation that when these people should do their work and their exercises, they often don't," Michael says. "Even though it's very important to them, they can't bring themselves to do it. It's like people who can't quit smoking cigarettes."

The crew of old men spent their time in the rehab center sitting together, lobbing complaints back and forth. They were doing very little exercise.

"The therapist was an attractive young woman who wore a nice starched white uniform. She was rather buxom, and really cute," Michael says. "She would come over to an old guy who was sitting down complaining. 'Come on, Mr. Jones, let's do your walking on the parallel bars.' Then she'd take him by the arm. She didn't exactly cuddle up to him, but there was enough contact that it had an erotic significance for an old man."

She guided him over to the parallel bars. He grumbled. She soothed. A few walking exercises were coaxed out of the old fellow. The sexy therapist then left him to exercise while she went to help another patient. The old man quickly stopped work, and hobbled back over to his buddies.

"This scene was natural. It was the old practice of the squeaky wheel getting the grease," Michael comments. Except that from a behavioral viewpoint, the squeaky wheel theorem is all wrong. Behaviorist Nancy Kerr made some adjustments in the therapy situation. She told the therapists never to make contact with the old gentlemen while they were complaining or lounging about. Only when one got up and made a move in the direction of work was the therapist to come over and chat. Later, only when they were doing exercises was the therapist to come over, help out, and generally offer herself as a consequence.

"The effect was almost miraculous," Michael says. "Pretty soon they were working like crazy. Eventually there was a note from the physician saying that the therapist was coming home exhausted every night. The men were working too fast, and he wanted them to slow down a little bit."

The payoffs had simply been switched from payoffs for complaining and lounging to payoffs for performance. The old men didn't have to know about the rewards shifting on them; they simply reacted to the current consequences.

In behavioral terms, any event that comes right after a bit of behavior and makes the behavior more frequent is a reinforcer. (The young lady's attention was a reinforcer for the old men: first it reinforced complaining and not work; then it reinforced work and not complaining.) A reinforcer is almost the equivalent of a reward.* Dr. Vance Hall's examples of reinforcers in action are "a hungry animal will learn to do a trick, if each time it does the trick, it is reinforced with a bite of food. A pupil will be more likely to study on future occasions if each time he studies his lessons, the teacher reinforces him with her attention and praise."[3]

In order for a reinforcer to be most effective, it must be delivered immediately after the behavior. The longer the behavior

---

* Reward and reinforcement are not exactly the same for several reasons. What is a reward to one may be anathema to another. Also, behaviorists are now discovering that behavior may be supported by consequences that no one would consider rewarding. For example, they have found that under certain circumstances, a monkey will press a lever *in order to get* a painful electric shock. Getting the shock will make him press the lever more and more, strange as that may sound. So the behaviorists simply define a reinforcer as "any consequence that increases the probability of the behavior it immediately follows."

and the consequences are separated, the less effective the consequences will be. If you have wondered why prison sentences are so ineffective in dealing with criminals, this is it, say the behaviorists. It takes a lot of learning for most of us to shun immediate rewards for the greater long-term benefits. This learning has apparently broken down in criminals. The criminal act is so distantly connected in time to the confining consequences that the consequences are simply ineffective.

Behavior modifiers are fond of pointing out that in the natural environment at home, school, or work, consequences are often delivered in exactly the wrong way. In one classroom, an eleven-year-old boy, who was being tutored in several subjects, had developed a habit of arguing with his tutor over the correctness of his work. When the teacher corrected him, the boy refused to look at his work, declaring that there was nothing wrong with his answer. A yes-there-is-no-there-isn't exchange usually followed. Temperatures rose on both sides. The tutor tried to be patient, to explain, to understand the boy's problem. That patience turned out to be the problem itself.

When the situation was analyzed behaviorally, first a graph was kept of how often the boy disputed with his tutor. It was two or three times every half hour. Next, the tutor was told to correct the boy's answers only once. If the boy questioned her correction, she should simply ignore it, and pretend to be busy with something else. After two sessions, the boy gave up arguing.

Sharon Jones, a behavior mod student who was guiding the tutor, wrote in her study, "The tutor had been inadvertently reinforcing Mitch's arguing behavior by responding to his contradictions. . . . When she withdrew this reinforcement, arguing quickly extinguished."[4]

Behavior can be increased or extinguished by manipulation of rewards. But it is important to notice that the rewards we have seen so far have been delivered after *every* correct action. The behaviorists call it continuous reinforcement, and use it as a technique to change behavior in the short term. But what happens after a student has been conditioned with continuous rewards to study more? The student's career will go beyond that teacher, and that year.

Skinner found that behavior being supported by continuous rewards will stop abruptly when the rewards are pulled out. He also found, however, that shifting from continuous to intermittent rewards will keep the behavior going. The behavior will continue at a high rate, even though the rewards have become infrequent.

This discovery, and what followed from it, boosted behaviorism from lab work to practical science. Behaviorists could now explain how behavior was maintained in the real world, where rewards are not doled out as lavishly as in a Skinnerian lab. A lot of behavior can be supported by few rewards. Skinner went a step further. He found four basic ways that rewards could be given intermittently.* Each of these elicited a unique pattern of behavior from animals. They controlled how fast and hard an animal would work, and when the animal would pause to relax.

In a VA hospital in Coral Gables, Florida, some experimenters worked with drunks.[5] They put a patient in a room with a drink dispenser, a shot glass, and a lever. It was not long before the dried-out drunk pressed the lever to see what would happen. When he did, a nozzle squirted his shot glass full of his favorite drink. Quickly the man grabbed the glass and imbibed the liquor. He pressed the lever again, grabbed the glass, and imbibed. But soon the lever didn't respond to one press. He had to tap it three times before the glass filled. As soon as he was doing that regularly, the nozzle quit pouring for three taps. He had to press seven times to get his swig. By the end of a twenty-minute session, the experi-

---

* The four are: Fixed Ratio—getting the reward after a set number of actions. Variable Ratio—getting the reward after a number of actions, but the action that will produce the reward varies; it may be the sixth or the sixtieth. Fixed Interval—the reward comes after a specified amount of time has passed; e.g., after ten minutes of lever-pressing, the next response gets rewarded. Variable Interval—also based on the amount of time passed, except that the time is not fixed. Again, it may be after six or sixty minutes.

menters had the man rapping out 120 lever presses for each shot.

When the man was brought back for another twenty-minute session with the lever and the shot glass later in the day, at the rate of 120 presses, he was spending a great deal of time pressing the lever for very few drinks.

The man had gone through a simple conditioning procedure. First he got continuous reinforcement. Gradually he was shifted onto a schedule called by the behaviorist a Fixed Ratio 120—that is, 120 actions per reward, with the rewards coming every time on that fixed number. Not that the drinker was counting. He wasn't. He just rapped away until the juice poured out.

In the natural environment, say the behaviorists, this is the way things are. We get paid off only occasionally for our actions. A lot of behavior can be supported by a few rewards, as one experimenter showed when he got a pigeon to respond reliably on a schedule in which the reward was delivered only once every twenty-thousand pecks. The bird had to hammer away nearly all day before he got his handful of grain.

The pattern of behavior put out by the Coral Gables drinker was predictable to the behaviorists. People and animals both deal with that kind of reward schedule in the same way. It is an all or nothing sort of response. The drinker zipped through the required lever presses, then took his drink, then paused to relax for a moment. When he started again, he zipped through quickly, swallowed his drink, and paused again.

The experimenters could have got the man to eliminate his relaxed pauses and press the lever at a steady, high rate. For that, they would simply have changed to a Variable Ratio schedule. This one is the bane of all gambling addicts. The whole procedure is the same, except that the drinks would not be delivered on the 120th press. They would vary. Sometimes the juice would pour out on the tenth press, sometimes not until the two hundredth.

For the behaver, one act is just about as likely as another to produce the reward. So he keeps trying. On a slot machine, the gambler knows the damn thing has got to spill coins after a while, but he doesn't know just which yank will make him rich. The characteristic response is a steady output of behavior.

There are two other basic schedules of reward, which also elicit predictable responses. Of course, in the natural environment, most activities are maintained by combinations of schedules, and these are modified by competing interests. But the difference between intermittent and continuous reward is important.

Don Whaley and Richard Malott have pointed out that children are taught social skills quite early. Parents expend great effort and pour out large amounts of reinforcement, delight, and praise whenever a child first begins to master a new skill. The parents' enthusiasm, however, wanes after a time. Gradually, each new item of skill is taken for granted as a part of the child's repertoire. Reinforcements for the skill get thinner and thinner. "Social graces are soon reinforced by other people in the world," Whaley and Malott say, but "never on the rich reinforcement schedule provided initially when the behavior was conditioned. It is maintained on the intermittent reinforcement which comes naturally from social interaction."[6]

What at first looked like a simplistic reward approach to people became more reasonable after Skinner delved into schedules that maintain behavior. With a few basic patterns of action, an infinite variety of behavior can be produced. In addition to the schedules, Skinner added to behaviorism another pair of concepts learned from animal work: discrimination and generalization.

In certain circumstances, an action normally rewarded will be punished. Being able to discriminate between the two is important.

Keller Breland, a behaviorist noted for his wild tricks with animals, has demonstrated how discrimination can be built up. He stood in front of a target. Aimed at him was a pistol (loaded with a cork). A trained chicken held in its beak a string that was attached to the trigger. While the pistol was aimed at Breland in front of the target, the chicken stood still. He waited. Breland stepped aside. The chicken instantly fired at the bull's-eye.

Breland's chicken had been rewarded, first, for pulling the string that fired the gun. When this was well conditioned, Breland taught the bird to discriminate between an open target and a Breland-covered target. He could do this by rewarding the bird for pulling the trigger when the target was clear, and punishing the bird for firing the cork at his nose.[7]

Although discrimination is a common-sense concept, it is seldom manipulated. One Kansas schoolteacher has found it very useful in getting instant quiet from a roomful of youngsters.

The teacher conditioned the youngsters to expect a reward for quietness when that silence followed immediately after the room lights were switched off. He began by rewarding them every time after the lights went out, but soon the rewards did not have to come every time. The children learned that switching off the light was a cue, or as the behaviorists put it, a discriminative stimulus, for quietness. Now, any time quiet is required in the classroom, such as after a game, the teacher just flicks the room lights off and on. A sudden quiet descends on the room.

The mate to the principle of discrimination is the principle of generalization. Instead of reacting to the differences in two situations, we are conditioned to react to their similarities. Pigeons that have been taught to peck at large black circles will also peck at small black circles, and even at circles of another color.

By manipulating this concept, experimenters have discovered that there is perhaps less of a mental gap between man and animals than we have thought. We have previously believed that only man was capable of learning concepts, of dealing with such an abstraction as "idea." But in 1964, two experimenters set up an experiment to teach a pigeon the concept "man."[8]

As Whaley and Malott said, "Plato defined man as a two-legged animal without feathers. Sly Diogenes then picked the feathers from a chicken and brought it to the Academy. . . . The Academicians realized they would have to change their definition. . . ." No one has yet come up with a set of rules that will define the concept "man" so that there are no exceptions that can be made. Still, we all know the concept and can easily choose between man and nonman every time.

The pigeon in the experiment was trained to press a key while looking at a picture of a man. The experimenters showed the pigeon many pictures of a man, and rewarded the bird every time he pressed the key for "man" when one was present in the picture. He didn't get the reward when there was no man in the picture.

After some time of this training, the experimenters brought in a whole new batch of photos. In these, sometimes the people were obscured by objects in front of them, sometimes they were close, sometimes distant. They were in various states of undress, and were in many different postures. They were of different colors and races, they were sometimes alone, and they were sometimes in large groups.

"The concept of man is a very complex concept and, to my knowledge, this is the first attempt to teach such a complex concept to a lower organism," say Whaley and Malott. "The birds, however, mastered the discrimination rapidly. In fact, occasionally when the birds appeared to make mistakes, the experimenters looked more closely and, obscured in some corner of the picture, there would be a human. The pigeons were about as good as the experimenters at detecting the presence of humans in the picture."

All the principles we have looked at, and a few others, are the ideas upon which the technology of behavior has been built. With these tools, behavior becomes a quite malleable thing. Some behavior can be planted and shaped up out of nothing; some strong and frequent behavior can be knocked off. Once a bit of behavior has been shaped up, it can be maintained with very little attention to it. It can be faded into a person's repertoire so that it is supported naturally rather than by an experimenter.

All these operations can be used on a person *without his knowledge or consent.*

Even though they have worked with them for years, behavior modifiers are still impressed by the power of these techniques. Behavior modifiers all acknowledge that they can be used kindly or cruelly. These issues will be taken up again later, but it is important to note here that, as the behaviorists say it, "It is reinforcing to use behavior mod. People may use it out of altruism, or a lust

for power over others. But it works. The satisfactions are enormous."[9] They have no doubt that their technology will eliminate
the more vague attempts to describe or change behavior used in
other branches of psychology. The behavioral technology grew out
of a laboratory science, and depends heavily on hard data. The
results can be easily read. Few other systems of psychology have
even attempted to offer data to back up their claims and theories.

The one system of psychology that has dominated public thinking, the Freudian, has attempted continuously to escape from the
burden of proof. Freud himself vigorously and arrogantly refused
to have his ideas and "cures" tested. In fact, he counseled his
followers not to promise anything to patients except very long
treatment (years!), very expensive treatment, and quite uncertain
results.

To examine this idea further, we should look at a case study in
psychoanalysis, one conducted under Freud himself. It is called the
case of "Little Hans."[10] Hans was five years old and afraid of
horses. Since the case took place in the early 1900s, Hans's fear
was interfering with his ability to walk in the street. The fear began
when the boy was out walking one afternoon with his mother. A
horse pulling a van slipped and crashed to the ground near the
boy.

The boy's father, a psychiatrist, and Freud worked on the case
together. At first, they didn't know about the incident in the street
that kicked off the boy's fear. They didn't know this simply because they didn't ask. They *assumed,* once the symptoms appeared, that the fear stemmed from deep psychic developments of
the boy's earlier childhood. (It may seem absurd to delve deep into
the past of a five-year-old, but that was the Freudian approach.)

So the pair began a search for relevant material in the boy's
experiences. The Freudian method, of course, does not dictate
looking for just any material. Only sexual material.

In digging, these men came up with such items as: At the age of
three Hans showed "a quite peculiarly lively interest in that portion of his body which he used to describe as his widdler. . . ."

At three and a half, his mother once found him touching his penis. On another occasion, his mother told him it was piggish to touch his penis, and Hans said that he didn't understand this; he thought it was fun.

This, of course, was stuff of great significance. Hans's father had decided that sexual overexcitation was at the base of the real problem, and the fear of horses was "somehow to be connected with his having been frightened by a large penis." There was no penis involved in the fear, and the boy had never been frightened by one, but that didn't daunt the psychoanalysts.

Freud suggested that the boy's father should lay it all out with the boy. He should tell the boy "that all this nonsense about horses was a piece of nonsense, and nothing more. The truth was, his father was to say, that he was very fond of his mother and wanted to be taken into her bed."

When the boy was confronted with this stuff, he tried to convince his father that it really was horses he was afraid of.

The story only gets stranger after the psychoanalysts discovered the falling-horse incident that started the fear. After learning about it, the father and Freud ignored the main event for a detail:

In recounting the horse story, Hans mentioned the item that "horses wear in front of their eyes and the black around their mouths." The horse's muzzle must be important, concluded the psychoanalysts, because the boy's father had a mustache. The horse must represent the boy's father, because of the similarity between a muzzle and a mustache. The father told the boy "that he was afraid of his father precisely because he was so fond of his mother."

The boy's phobia gradually waned during the year and a half of this whole treatment ordeal. Freud noted at one point that while the treatment was not progressing at all because they couldn't convince the boy that he was only afraid of his father, not horses, the phobia still seemed to be going away. When it did go, Freud claimed a cure. He was proud of it.

Alongside this—and such other marvels as primal-scream therapy, group encounter, and the games-people-play approach—it is little wonder that behaviorism has grown so quickly. The principles are simple and forthright, the results are testable and based on facts.

There are a few cases in which the old notions of psychology have crossed the path of the behavioral approach. A woman in a mental hospital who had for three years spoken bizarre psychotic nonsense almost entirely was one of those who was seen by both sides.[11] During the three years, the woman's problem had been poked and probed many times by observers and psychiatrists. One psychiatrist said she was "a delusional patient who feels she must push her troubles onto someone else, and by doing so she feels that she is free." After pulling this bit out of the air, he could not help her any more than the cleaning woman could help her.

The woman's aggressive and bizarre conversation became so annoying to those around her that other patients began to beat her to keep her quiet.

The nurses and attendants around the hospital paid attention to her when she spouted off. They tried to understand sometimes; other times they mechanically said, "Yes, I understand." Whaley and Malott add, "Such attention, which is normally reinforcing, is particularly so in the bleak environment of the back ward of a mental hospital."

When two behaviorists attempted to help her, their procedure was to instruct nurses and attendants to ignore the woman when she spoke nonsense, pay attention to her only when she spoke normally. The woman's behavior was measured before treatment. Ninety-one percent of her talk was psychotic outbursts. After nine weeks of the simple procedure, she was speaking rationally more than 75 percent of the time.

It is interesting to note that during the last three weeks of treatment, the woman got some bootleg reinforcement, as the behaviorists call it. She began talking to a social worker who didn't know about the treatment, and who listened to her bizarre speech. The patient later told one of the nurses, "You're not listening to me. I'll have to go see Miss —— again because she told me that if she could listen to my past, she could help me." During this period, the woman's bizarre talk increased.

When Brecht's Galileo tried to impress on the little monk the truth in his new theories, the monk replied only that old ideas would die, and some peace die with them. Science is passing that way again, and the conversation of Galileo and the monk has been repeated in an altered form perhaps a thousand times on the subject of behaviorism. "If by 'machine' you simply mean any system which behaves in an orderly way," says B. F. Skinner, "then man and all the other animals are machines."[12] That will not go down easily.

But even while Galileo and the monk spoke, the new ideas they spoke of were spreading. So are Skinner's principles rapidly being applied to almost every conceivable human problem.

---

3. The Children

In the offices of the Institute for Behavioral Research, director
Harold Cohen sits with his back to a large photograph.

The faded picture shows Cohen's father wearing a wrinkled
dirty apron. His mother is wearing a worn baggy dress. He was a
fishmonger. She was illiterate. The pair stand in a doorway, close
to each other. They look stern, and unspeakably tired; they are a
single frame from a distant, immigrant America. To these people,
children were the center of life. They were redemption from too
many years of soiled, fish-stinking aprons. The children were sent
to school and, with the grace of God and years of saved nickels, to
college.

Harold Cohen was one of these children. Now he is sitting in a
large black executive chair, in another city and a different age.
"The Charles Dickens family is gone," he says. "Even a single
kind of family is out. Some children have grandma at home, and
some have never seen grandma. Some have a hometown, some
move every two years. . . . When I was a kid, who moved?"

In the photograph, the father's hair is clipped short, and

straight. Harold Cohen's hair is long, and gray-flecked muttonchop whiskers run down to his cheekbones. He is talking about change, about breakdown. The breadth of kids' lives is so much greater, he says, the chaos is so complete, saved nickels and public schools won't do it anymore. The face and the guts of society have been changed by radical surgeries, while public schools still use the old castor oil bottle, adorned with a new label.

Harold Cohen's faith is like his father's. It is with the children. He talks about the need to install effective tools in a chaotic society, saying that democracy requires a lot of options. It begins with the children, he says; they must get the tools first. He believes he has found the tools and a way to deliver them: he's a convert to behavior modification.

He sinks down in his big black chair, folding his fingers over his belly. "I don't like to talk about behavior control; those are bad words," he says. He is sensitive about the attacks on behavior mod because he has encountered a lot of them. He consoles himself with the words etched on a plaque over his desk: "At every crossing on the road to the future, each progressive spirit is opposed by a thousand men appointed to guard the past."

Cohen says, "I'm a romantic. I grow orchids; I have a big picture of my parents over my desk. . . ." Behaviorism is not something mechanical and sinister; it is "just like gravity. There are laws there, and we just work within the laws. After all, God was the first behaviorist, with his 'Thou shalt's and 'Thou shalt not's. We are just trying to make it science."

The kind of idealism that his father might have had about the future and the children, Harold Cohen has also. "I think we are about to bring America to the point that it works," he says. "The schools could be the center for preparing America. . . ."

The schools are a unique environment. By law, all children must attend. They must be there five days a week, seven hours a day, for ten years. The society expects the school and its teachers to alter the behavior of each child. A bagful of new skills must be learned, and much social behavior shaped. Short of a laboratory, the behaviorists could not expect a better set of circumstances for their work. Besides the prolonged and easy access to the children, parents are brought into the work with meetings and counseling. The police and courts are wired into the system when behavior becomes a problem. Local politics often center on school issues. The schools, in short, are the ideal arena to begin Skinner's "remaking of a culture."

In the beginning there are the words. Intelligence, knowledge, teaching. The old definitions are vague, inaccurate, or wrong, say the behaviorists.

On the matter of intelligence, behaviorists have found that IQ labels are mostly nonsense and clearly cruel in the way they are applied. Behavior modifiers have altered the IQ of many children, not by five or ten points, but by twenty, thirty, or forty points.

Harold Cohen says, "Some administrators find it useful to diagnose a student's IQ and describe the child as basically poor material," in order to explain their own failure to teach him. "The attempts to correct the present school system generally start by testing, classifying, and grouping the youngsters. We tend to accept nineteenth-century concepts of genetic behavioral limits. . . . This national practice permits intellectual discrimination, for it uses past performance . . . to predict a diagnosis that the brain of the tested individual is limited. This is the most insidious kind of discrimination."

And teaching? James Johnston, of Georgia State University, writes, "It seems that whatever is done by a teacher to or for students is commonly accepted as teaching . . . *Now* whatever a teacher does to a student is called teaching only if directly measurable and desirable changes occur in the student's behavior." In other words, teachers will have to perform to deserve their title. "It is likely that some of our most cherished methods (like the centuries-old college lecture) may not deserve the title teaching, because they do not produce the appropriate changes in student performance," Johnston says.[1]

The process of education is changing behavior. It is shaping students to use words. Even high-level college courses reduce down to this: a student has "knowledge" if he can speak or write accurately and without hesitation about a subject. We have thought that writing and talking about a subject were only *signs* that knowledge has been acquired. But Skinner says, "We need not view such repertoires as 'signs' of knowledge, but rather as knowledge itself."[2]

The mod squad questions even the most basic of assumptions. In a paper delivered at a behavior modification conference, Donald Baer of the University of Kansas laid out what the squad thinks about children: "We argued that a child was, *essentially,* a collection of behaviors, some of them organized into classes, like imitation or grammar, some of them separate, individual, independent responses. If a child had a problem, the fundamental nature of that problem could be nothing more than two lists of behaviors: certain desirable behaviors that were too low in rate; and certain undesirable behaviors that were too high in rate. . . ."

The behavior mod work in schools began with the throwaways: delinquents, the retarded, the brain-damaged, the hyperactive.

Dr. Henry Pennypacker of the University of Florida tells a tale to illustrate. Several years ago he worked with a young boy who doctors said was a hopeless case. He didn't talk; his activity was a flurry of pinching, biting, crying, and destruction. He was diagnosed as autistic.

"The father called me up and said that he had a son, five years old, and he had already spent forty thousand dollars and been all over the country with him," Pennypacker says. "The last place they had him was at Johns Hopkins. They told him there to put him in an institution and forget him. The father told me that before he did that, he wanted to try everything possible.

"I told him that I had never worked with humans. I worked with monkeys. But we had some ideas and we'll try these things.

"So we talked awhile, and we approached it the way we did then. We asked him, 'Well, what's bothering you most that your son does?' He talked about all the symptoms and all the diseases.

Then he said, 'I guess the thing that really gets to us is that he bites his arm. When he bites it, he tears pieces off it, it bleeds. We just can't stand that.'

"We told him to go home and count how many times the boy bites his arm," Pennypacker says. "We showed him how to use a chart. We talked to him a little bit about how we view behavior as largely a function of what happens after the behavior. Then we put in a little change procedure," says Dr. Pennypacker, drawing on his cigar.

"We asked him what would happen if he really bit his arm terribly much. Well, he couldn't use it. Okay. Let's see if we can rig the environment in such a way that when he bites his arm, he can't use it. He said, 'Why don't we tie it behind him?' Beautiful.

"So he gets a little thong, ties the kid's arm behind his back for two minutes each time he bites it. That's what the boy gets as a consequence."

The boy's father drove from Jacksonville to Gainesville, Florida, every Thursday night to go over the charts at Dr. Pennypacker's home. "We saw that the number of times he bit his arm came down in the first four days," Pennypacker says. "Then it leveled off. Now you contrast that with, say, a physician treating this. He would probably say, 'Well, how is it this week?' 'Oh, it's much better.' 'Good.' Now, what the chart told us was that it had indeed worked, but that something was still supporting it. It leveled off.

"So I said, 'Tell me what you do when he bites his arm.' 'Oh,' he says, 'it's the most terrible thing! The poor little guy. He comes up, he bites his hand, he holds it out for us to tie, and then he says, "Sugar pop." We take him in and give him a sugar pop. It's the neatest thing, because he never used to say sugar pop.' "

Dr. Pennypacker stops again to draw on his cigar, letting the point sink in. "He's biting his arm now about once every twenty minutes for sugar pops. I said to the father, 'Let's think this thing over. Do you really want to stop the arm-biting?' He said yes. 'Don't you think the sugar pops have something to do with it?' 'Oh, they probably do,' he says. 'I never thought of that.'

"So now we tried five minutes behind the back and no sugar pops. Zap. Zero. In five days. The first time in four years the kid went the whole day without biting his arm. That just blew the guy's mind.

"Over the next hundred and ten days, it went on occasionally, but it wasn't much of a problem anymore. So he asked us if we could forget about the arm-tying. We told him, 'Okay, just forget about it. Make sure you don't pay attention to it anymore.' In the next two days, the boy tested his father out by biting his arm, then tested his mother out. They didn't pay any attention. Then, bang. It was gone completely."

Dr. Pennypacker and the parents started in on the boy's other behavior problems. They built up his speech from a sound uttered every hour and a half to talking at least every twenty minutes. They got him to stop his tantrums, which had been exploding about ten times a day. Every two or three minutes he had been pinching himself and everyone around him. That was stopped. The boy couldn't sleep at night unless he was in his parents' bed. He was gradually shaped into sleeping alone. He was also introduced to basic school subjects, and he performed well.

"Six months after we began working with the parents," says Dr. Pennypacker, "they brought him to the office of the pediatrician to whom they had been taking him for physical evaluations. The pediatrician came into the waiting room. He said, 'Where's Brian?' The quiet little kid was sitting in the office reading a magazine. The doctor asked, 'Didn't you have an autistic child, too?' The parents said, 'Well, here's Brian.' "

When the pediatrician found out how the boy's behavior had been changed, "There was talk about practicing medicine without a license, and about filing a formal complaint," Pennypacker says. "I responded that I would welcome that, because I could file a counter complaint asking to see their data. . . . That's as far as it went," he says, "but I was a little bit scared for a while."

Dr. Pennypacker, relaxing in his huge living room, runs a hand through black curly hair and gives a tug at his brief goatee. He is talking about working with labeled kids, and says that many people are fast reaching the conclusion that special-education classes must go. The labeled kids are dumped in these classes, and never again have a full chance.

"Here's the way I see it happening. You get a little kid. First grade. He comes to school with one of these 'learning disabilities.' The kid will look like all the other kids for the first few weeks of class. He will then begin to not progress as rapidly. The teacher, well-meaning soul, will start giving more and more attention to him. And—there's no way to avoid it—that attention will most often come contingently on his failure. So, by about December, she has him spotted as a problem. He has spotted a way to produce her attention. So he remains a problem.

"This much is sort of traditional. Now the terrible thing happens. He will get evaluated. He will get labeled. And the teacher will say, 'Oh-oh, there's nothing I can do for him.' She won't give him as much attention anymore. So he engages in more and more curious behavior to produce the attention that he had been producing by just not achieving. By the third or fourth grade, you begin to get truancy. You get cherry bombs going off in the toilet. I think this pattern repeats itself over and over again. Not to mention the fact that if the kid is thusly labeled, the responsible adults in the environment, quite accidentally and quite without meaning to, will functionally deprive him of just the things he needs the most.

"If we have a six-year-old who doesn't read too well, the normal reaction of the teacher and the parent will be to arrange the environment in special ways to help him read. If that same kid doesn't read too well and is called dyslexic, 'There is something the matter in his head so he *can't* read.' Can't read? The tactic is to remove him from the reading environment, because that might be frustrating, or threatening, or upsetting. So what we functionally do is deprive him of the very opportunity he most needs. This just compounds itself until, in fourth or fifth grade, he's in deep trouble socially and academically. Small wonder he drops out of high school!"

Pennypacker is suspicious of the label "dyslexic." It refers to some sort of brain damage, though no one has ever found that it really exists. One symptom that supposedly results from this damage is the inability to perceive right from left: for example, a dyslexic child cannot tell the difference between small *b* and small *d*.

"I have worked with any number of kids who are supposed to have this disorder, and I have never seen it fail that we can get rid of that thing in about a week. They can't tell *b* from *d*. Granted. We simply ask the question: What *can* they tell the difference between? Most of them can tell the difference between red and green. We color *b* red, and *d* green. We attach names to them, 'bee' and 'dee.' Then we just slowly fade out the color. In about a week, they are telling *b* from *d*. Now what happened to the perceptual disorder?"

Another supposed disorder that the mod squad has often found to be phony is hyperactivity. One experimenter told of a wild and disruptive child who threw all his classes into an uproar. Except music class. The youngster was diagnosed hyperactive. The behavioral experimenter wondered about the music class. He found that the boy was able to sit more quietly in music, attending to the teacher more often. The kid just liked music. So first the boy was sent to the music room to spend some time. Then he was told that he would have to have a pass to get into the music room. He could earn the pass only by quiet and work in his other classes. Gradually the amount of work required was built up. The boy's hyperactivity slipped away, as he worked for his music payoff. Again, the experimenter asks, "Where did his physical disorder go?"

In one Oregon case, a nine-year-old boy had not been able to move past the second-grade level. He spent most of his time misbehaving: talking, pushing, hitting, pinching, squirming, and staring around the room. He would sometimes get up and shove his desk around the aisles. Behaviorist Gerald Patterson set up a small light on the boy's desk, and told him that it would flash every ten seconds if he was sitting quietly doing his work. For each flash, the boy earned a penny and an M&M, payable at the end of the lesson. The other kids in class would be paid off with a share of the booty if they did not distract the boy when he was working. After ten days of conditioning, he was misbehaving about 5 percent of the time. That's about average for normal children.

William Brown, director of Maryland's Anne Arundel County Learning Center, has a considerable disdain for some traditional psychologists. He runs an entire school for hopeless kids, the ones thrown out of public schools and not yet sent to jail. He is familiar with the practice of labeling kids. He pulls out a thick file on a twelve-year-old boy. The boy had been shuffled from school to school, but his records were slow in following him. Each school psychologist had an opportunity to diagnose the boy's problem on his own. The first thing diagnosed was his learning difficulty. It was decided that he had physical learning disorders and was a borderline mental retard. At the next school, the psychologist decided that the boy was hyperactive and had some kind of speech disorder. They began giving the boy dope to straighten him out. He downed Ritalin daily. At the next school, of course, he had no such problem; here he was "extremely phobic," afraid of school and of people.

The diagnoses were the fantasies of the psychologists, Brown says. "They described the boy with phrases like 'poor self-concept' and 'he is phobic.' They mean nothing."

Finally, the boy was brought to the learning center. "His father brought him up to the door, and the boy was kicking and screaming every step of the way," says Brown. "His father was trying to understand him, relate to him. He told his son, 'If you will please just try it at this school, I'll do anything.' "

The father would drop the boy off at the learning center and go on to work. But the boy would escape the center so quickly he sometimes arrived at his father's office only a few minutes after his father. There, the father would try to be understanding and not send him back right away.

"It took us a few days," Brown says, "but we finally convinced the father that he was maintaining the boy's behavior by giving him attention and love every time he displayed bad behavior." Brown convinced the man to change his approach. The son was put on a reward schedule, earning a successful-day card for each day he came to school at the center and stayed all day. At the end of each week, he could turn in the cards for cash. Forty cents for each card, and a bonus if he had a perfect week.

"This is how much the boy usually got in allowance, but now it was made contingent on his behavior," Brown says. "We had planned that after he started coming to school regularly, we would then start giving additional rewards for work done at school.

"But we didn't have to. As soon as we started the card system, the boy came every day and worked. He's getting good grades now. As soon as daddy didn't maintain the bad behavior, the rest took care of itself."

The stories go on—there are thousands of them—depicting the remaking of behavior among the fringe kids. Every kind of problem, from talking out in class to the rejuvenating of human vegetables, has been attacked.

A long tradition in handling human behavior is ending quickly. The medical approach to behavior problems, which flourished in the nineteenth century and grew to become a social horror in our own, is giving way. We cannot assume anymore that children who seem retarded, who seem to have obsessive behavior, who seem to have brain damage, are suffering from some diagnosable diseases. We can no longer weed them out of the system, giving them up as defectives.

The old models used in special education have failed. They were, and are, fantastically expensive flops. The recognition of this fact has been slow because very little was expected of these programs. After all, what can you do with a kid who has an IQ of 20? What can you do with a frantic, hyperactive, destructive child?

Much can be done. The movement to change our nineteenth-century systems has begun, and already several state legislatures are redrafting education laws.

After a change in the Texas laws on special education, the

Houston Independent School District has designed and is now installing a massive plan to rescue the special-ed children. It entails a huge teacher-training project, setting up behavior resource labs in 170 schools, disbanding some one hundred special-ed classes, and establishing six new appraisal and treatment centers. The plan is designed to keep the kids with problems in the schools and in regular classes while the problems are worked out.

There is no way to estimate how many schools are now using behavior mod with problem kids, but it is certainly thousands in the United States. It was in the early sixties that the mod squad first started working with these kids, and the work has spread steadily. It has only been in the last few years that the mod squad has got its ticket to work with normal children and normal problems. The squad had developed a truckload of tricks to short-circuit bizarre behavior and plug in normal, cooperative behavior. This work was on very difficult children, and required some rigid control. It did not emphasize academics.

When they started working with the normals, they were still using the heavy control techniques. The teachers and administrators who invited the squad into schools were pleased with this. They are generally a frustrated bunch, and would have been pleased to get *any* clearly useful tools in class. Besides, teachers are usually judged by the orderliness of their classes. Schools have never before been able to measure teaching ability by student performance. The tests are too vague, and there has been the assumption that some kids are just poor material to work on. But an orderly classroom you can see and hear. Reprimands and compliments flow easily to a teacher on the subject of order.

All these things came together, and the first tools the mod squad offered in teaching normal children were those to modify troublesome behavior. Some of the techniques were aimed at single students, some at whole classes.

In one group procedure reported from a Michigan elementary school, the target was noise. An experimenter first gauged the noise in the class with a meter; it was about fifty to fifty-five decibels. Much too noisy. The teacher brought a timed buzzer into the room and read an announcement to students:

"A timer will be set at ten minutes and be allowed to run to zero, at which time the buzzer will sound. Each time the buzzer sounds, you will receive two extra minutes added to your gym period, and a two-minute break to talk, ask questions, sharpen pencils, or whatever before beginning the next ten-minute period." Now the catch: "If, however, you become too noisy at any time during the ten-minute period, [the experimenter] will blow a whistle to let you know, and reset the timer back to ten minutes. . . ."

From the moment the buzzer-clock-whistle system was put into effect, the noise in the classroom dropped to about thirty-eight decibels. This becomes impressive when you know that without any students at all, the empty room registers thirty-six decibels. "Control and suppression of sound levels can be accomplished in a regular elementary school classroom," the experimenters said. "While the additional gym time as well as the two-minute breaks may have been reinforcing for most students, it need not have been so for all." When some of the students said to hell with the experiment, and started disturbing the quiet, other kids took over the teacher's job. They threatened the noisy child, made angry faces at him, and waved their arms for quiet. The children also got angry with special teachers and the school nurse who occasionally came into the room, raising the noise level slightly. The kids simply were not tolerating any noise; they wanted the payoff.

The same experimenters worked in another classroom, which had been in continuous chaos. In this one, noise was not the only problem. The children spent a great deal of time wandering around the class while the teacher worked with small reading groups in the back of the room. The experimenters started with the same procedure here, just dulling the din in the room. After a short period of that, the teacher announced that for every five minutes of quiet, the children would earn an extra three minutes on their gym period. But also, another timer would be set in the room. This one went off at unpredictable intervals. If any student was caught out of his seat when this buzzer went off, he had to write his name on the blackboard and lose five minutes of gym.

Even while the room had been quiet before this new buzzer, the children ran up a cumulative total of between one hundred and two hundred times out of their seats during some forty-five-minute periods. After the new buzzer was installed, it dropped to about twenty.

The experimenters concluded, "The technique used here for control of out-of-seat behavior is a simple one that a teacher alone could easily operate or could allow a student to operate. Its effectiveness with these relatively young students implies possible wide application. The present data further suggest that it can be gradually discontinued without loss in effectiveness. . . ."[3]

It is interesting to note that in these experiments, no candy, money, or artificial reinforcers were used. The kids were being reinforced by their own behavior—things they wanted to do. The principle behind this was discovered by David Premack, a California behaviorist, and is often used to control whole classes at once. Essentially, the Premack principle states that given any two behaviors, the stronger one can be used to reinforce the weaker one. Freelance behaviorist Lloyd Homme, one inventor of programmed instruction, tells a tale by way of example. He was working with three three-year-olds. "The amount of control exercised on the first day can be summarized: none. One child was running and screaming, another was pushing a chair across the floor (a rather noisy chair), and the other was playing with a jigsaw puzzle. Once our scholars determined that punishment did not follow these activities (the rate at which this discrimination was made must have set a new indoor record), the response to the verbal instruction 'come and sit down' was to continue running and screaming, chair-pushing, and so forth. . . ."

Homme, after the first day, had little doubt that running and screaming was a stronger behavior for these kids than sitting quietly and working on books.

So, he says, "We made engaging in these behaviors contingent on the subjects' doing a small amount—very small at first—of whatever we wanted them to do. A typical early contingency was merely for them to sit quietly in chairs and look at the blackboard. This was followed immediately by the command, 'Everybody run and scream now!' This kind of contingency management put us in immediate control of the situation. We were in control to the extent that we were able to teach everything in about one month that we could discover was ordinarily taught in the first grade."[4]

Another common technique used for controlling groups is the token system. One of the more elaborate uses of the token approach has been exemplified in a program directed by Harold Cohen. In a suburban Washington school, some eighty problem kids punch a time clock as they come into school every morning. From that moment, each activity is monitored and charted on a student activity log. The students tote their bared souls around on these charts all day. They contain the day's academic output as well as "appropriate and inappropriate" behavior.

For math and English, the students work in study centers at a battery of teaching machines. They push through self-paced chunks of work, and rack up points each time they pass a short unit quiz with 90 percent or better. Good behavior also earns them some counters, while disruption and inattention bring fines.

The payoffs for the kids are set up in a "reinforcement area" in a blocked-off hallway. They can buy a few minutes of freedom to sit and talk with friends in the lounge. They can also purchase Cokes, candy, and games on a bowling machine.

When the behavior target is a single child, the control is made a little easier because the controller can take advantage of a kid's personal enjoyments and fears. In one experiment, a first-grader who talked too much in class was offered the opportunity to play with a magic slate for five minutes after each half hour in which he didn't talk. Another boy was reinforced with the chance to earn tickets to a pro football game if he showed up for school on time. Still another wanted to play basketball with the principal. He could, if he behaved well. In most cases, no tangible rewards are required, especially in the lower grades. The teacher's attention and praise, when it is consistently applied to the desired behavior, will do the job. One study is worth quoting briefly, because it is an example of the possible abuse of control to be discussed later in this chapter.

The subject was a nine-year-old boy. The teacher felt he did not "attend to his assigned work enough." She felt this prevented him from achieving. During a half-hour period when the children were supposed to be quiet and working, the teacher recorded the boy's behavior. Every three minutes she watched him, marking a plus if he was attending, a minus if he was not. She then was to apply praise whenever the boy was "attending." The boy's rate of "attending" rose from 9 percent to 50 percent of the time. This may be an example of the control syndrome that some teachers and mod squadders have fallen into. What they wanted from the child was academic performance. But what they ended up controlling was "attending behavior."

Teachers with behavioral tools say they have found it easy to deal with the normal range of problems. A few researchers have gone beyond the usual boundaries.

One nine-year-old girl who had a long list of "disorders" attached to her record was enrolled in a class that met every day. She started vomiting in class, at first only rarely. But it built up until it was almost daily. Not only was she vomiting, but she picked some regular targets: she was sick most often all over the teacher's desk and the table at which other students were sitting. The teacher tried drug therapy. It was no help; the vomiting continued.

Each time the girl vomited, she was taken out of class for the day, and was attended with care. A crew of behavior mod experimenters decided to find out if the vomiting could be controlled by contingencies. The teacher was instructed to ignore the vomiting (except to clean it up). The girl was not removed from class after being sick.

At first, the vomiting increased. It increased so much that in one class of an hour and a half, she vomited twenty-one times. But then it started dropping off. By the end of thirty days, it was gone. To be certain that it was the attention that had been supporting the girl's vomiting, the experimenters again put in the old contingencies. They had to wait about fifty days before the girl vomited again, and as soon as she did, the teacher attended to the girl again and removed her from class. The girl quickly started her vomiting schedule again, and vomited on twenty-three of the next fifty-eight days. Then, again, the experimenters instructed the teacher to leave the girl in class and remove her attention from the vomiting. Over the next thirty-four days, the vomiting decreased gradually, and disappeared.*

Behaviorists have also found that the playground need not be off limits to teachers. Playing can be conditioned as easily as other behavior. The notion that children play naturally because it is fun doesn't hold up. One boy who was excluded from playground games and who hadn't developed the simple physical and social skills necessary to fit in was aided by some behavioral techniques. A teacher at the child's preschool watched him during play. He wandered aimlessly about the play area, avoiding the games of the other children, such as climbing on the monkey bars. In the first nine days that the teacher eyed the boy's actions, he rarely went near the monkey bars, and touched them only once. The teacher plugged in a little attention when he was near the bars, and pulled out the plug when he was playing alone. The teacher paid off each gradual approximation of climbing the bars, and at the end of the treatment the boy spent 67 percent of his time playing monkey. The teacher moved on, shaping up other playing skills in the boy's meager repertoire.

One of the new fads in the mod squad is the venture into

---

* The procedure used here to be certain that it was the attention that was causing vomiting is used in almost all behavior mod experiments. The common organization of an experiment is: one period of observation and counting the behavior, followed by a period in which the new contingencies are put into effect. This is followed by a period in which the old conditions are restored. Then the behavior is again changed. Nearly all the cases and anecdotes noted in this book followed a procedure similar to this.

creativity. They enjoy hacking away, chip by chip, at the province of the old mentalists. Creativity, they are now saying, really may be a behavior and be controllable. You can elicit it, or douse it.

In one of the early experiments with creativity several years ago, block building by young children was the target. The researchers prefaced their paper on the work with the note that defining creativity is not easy.[5] They accepted the definition of "behavior not previously shown by the youngsters in block building." New and different structures were the key.

The experimenters played with blocks enough before the study to figure out that there were a limited number of forms used in any construction job. They identified about twenty of them, including: fence, ramp, pillar, post, tower, arch. In each construction the children made, the experimenters photographed and counted the number of different forms. This gave them a form-diversity score. The children, without any reinforcement, ranged from one to nine different forms in each construction. Most of them had less than five. Then the teacher "remarked with enthusiasm, interest, and delight every time a child arranged blocks so as to create a form which had not appeared previously. . . ."

The kids' form scores jumped up to between ten and twenty different forms per construction. The children in the study, who had been identified as "poor block builders" before the experiment, were easily shaped into architects of originality.

One of the clearest features of the mod squad's work over the past ten years has been the avoidance of using punishments. The tool has always been in the basic science, but they have been reluctant to use it and have preferred positive reinforcement systems.

This bias probably began with Skinner, who said in 1953 that using punishment might cause side effects difficult to control. Punishment, he said, was a blunter tool than reward.[6] Also, his philosophical writings promised that the great value of behaviorism in the modern world would be the elimination of a lot of the punishing and coercive control that now go on.

The mod squad created a problem for itself, however, in the way it uses the word "punishment." It is used to mean nothing more than a consequence that decreases the behavior immediately before it. It is not necessarily shouting, inflicting pain, or imposing something unpleasant. It is *anything* that decreases the preceding behavior. But when the mod squadders mentioned punishment, immediately mothers conjured up gory images. Explanations didn't help a lot sometimes.

Recently, the mod squad has lost some of its timidity. Lab work has shown that Skinner's worries about side effects were mostly groundless, and a few inoffensive punishers have been found effective.

One is called "time-out." The idea is to remove a child from the situation in which he can get reinforcement. If he is misbehaving in class, he may be getting some payoff for his bad behavior. In the time-out, he would be removed from the class and put, for example, in an empty room for five minutes. This is an old idea, of course. But the mod squad applies it very carefully. The offense must be specified carefully, and the punishment must come consistently and immediately.

Kansas University's Vance Hall described another procedure that points up the difference between the conventional view of punishment and the mod squad's punishment. One teacher complained that a seven-year-old in her class cried and whined and complained of stomachaches when he was assigned arithmetic and reading work. The little incidents occurred at a rate of about five per study session. After the sixth day of counting the behavior, the teacher put five colored slips of paper on the boy's desk. Each one had his name on it. She told him that each time he whined and complained, she would take away one of the slips. There was nothing else involved, just the teacher picking a piece of paper off the boy's desk. But that was enough. Within a few days, the complaining stopped.

There is very little that is new about the punishments the mod squad uses in schools. Most are as old as schools. But the difference is that behaviorists deliver them systematically, according to a given set of rules. They are not applied whenever a teacher feels tired or frustrated, as is the usual practice.

Some of the new converts to behavior mod are, however, not very familiar with the rules. A few have found that behavioral terminology can serve as a cover for cruelty.

A state-run school for the retarded in Miami that had a history of cruelty to children picked up some behavior mod techniques in 1971.[7] They set up a token program in one cottage, which housed some twenty retarded youngsters. Tokens could be earned for good behavior and for work. They could buy nights out, dinner at a hamburger stand, and other goodies. But the doctors and staff seemed more interested in punishment than in dispensing goodies.

The crime that the doctors and staff thought was most heinous, and perhaps the one they enjoyed punishing the most, was masturbation. One boy caught masturbating was taken out of his room, brought naked into the common area of the cottage, and forced to masturbate in front of all the staff and residents. The staff ordered the other youngsters to shout and call the offender names so that he should be properly ashamed. This procedure was carried out several times on different boys, to the apparent delight of the staff. A similar punishment was meted out to boys who had been caught in homosexual activity.

Another grievous offense, the stealing of a few handfuls of Cracker Jacks from the kitchen, was also punished severely. The log of treatment kept by the staff betrayed the joy with which this boy's punishment was executed. The entry was filled with exclamation points, underlines, and capital letters. "Thief caught red handed!! . . . NATURALLY HE FORFEITS ALL TOKENS AND NOW HAS ZERO. He is not to earn any until further notice—HE CAN'T SINCE HE IS ISOLATED FROM THE OTHER BOYS—NO JOBS, NO APPEARANCE, NO NOTHING!!!"

The boy's punishment took several forms. First, everyone in the cottage was ordered to stop using his name, and instead to call him "thief." The staff and a doctor decided that his stealing Cracker Jacks was "girl's play" so they ordered some girl's bikini underwear and forced the boy to wear it. Further, the culprit was not to eat meals with the group. He had to beg for his food, and then was required to sit on the floor, alone, to eat it. He was also banned from the most favored activities around the cottage—playing ball and washing cars—"since they are male jobs," the log says, "and since his girl treatment begins."

The unfortunate child was later caught again in the kitchen, this time taking a handful of sweetened cereal. He was beaten ("35 licks," says the log) with a paddle that was a half-inch thick. He was tied down with leather straps, but not in his room. He was tied in the bathroom. The staff further suggested not allowing him to eat regular food. They suggested a twenty-four-hour diet of sweetened cereal, knowing that he was diabetic and that a high-sugar diet would knock him into a coma. One staff doctor stopped the diet before it could go into effect. The log did not record whether the boy was cured of his enjoyment of Cracker Jacks and sweetened cereal.

The punishment for fighting in the cottage was another one apparently enjoyed by the staff. Two boys who were caught at it were forced to take a bite out of a bar of soap and chew it until "it made suds in their mouth." The staff punisher boasted in the log, "I refused to let them rinse their mouths out for ten minutes. . . ."

Other punishments included forcing a boy to lie in a urine-soaked bed, bathing a child with gritty kitchen cleanser, locking some youngsters in their rooms for up to six hours, and refusing to feed others.

The program in the cottage was called by an appropriate behavior mod name: "achievement group." Of course, very little in the program had any relation to achievement, and the techniques were only very crude behavior mod. But the Florida case is not the only one in which behavior mod words have been used to cover abuses, both mild and severe. As one observer put it, "The words of behavior mod allow some cruel teachers to feel scientific and detached. It allows them to carry out punishments with no feeling."

Paul Graubard was a problem kid in school. He learned much about discipline in the public schools by being on the rough end of it. He dropped out when he was fifteen, before finishing high school. So perhaps it was to be expected that years later, when he got into behavior mod, he would take an unusual approach to problem kids.

Graubard was sensitive to the injustice in schools, and to the absurd labeling of any kid who is slightly off the "normal" mark. He was disturbed, he says, at "seeing individuality and creativity suppressed in 'exceptional children,' who were expected to conform to the rules of the dominant culture. These children are often the tragic victims of our society. Under the mantle of 'helping,' society has stigmatized these children with labels such as 'mentally retarded,' 'psychotic,' and 'schizophrenic.' They have been subjected to the loss of privacy, to public ridicule, to involuntary detention in training schools and hospitals, and to loss of prestige and privileges."

The public schools have always been severe with and intolerant of unusual behavior. But with behavior mod, there is some clout to that intolerance. The literature of behavior mod is filled with the cases. The clients of the behavior modifiers have been the school administrators and the teachers. The client says let's eliminate talking in class, that's what gets eliminated. They don't like kids who argue with teachers, then arguing with teachers gets sliced away. The kids don't sit still enough for the teacher, the behavior modifier will get them to sit still.

But Paul Graubard had been on the other end of this business. When he got a contract to work in the Visalia, California, school system, it began with the usual approach: There are these disruptive kids. . . .

The plan was to shape up some of the kids who had been

identified as troublemakers. The school he was to work in was known for its tough discipline and rigid teachers, and the rigidity was "compounded by racism and class bias," Graubard says. When Graubard got a good look at the situation, he changed the tack.

"We decided not to try to shape up the kids, because we could almost never satisfy these teachers," he says. So quietly he set about to work on the other half of the equation. The teachers became the targets; the students became the modifiers. The disruptive youngsters were taught behavior mod—how to control the behavior of their teachers. The teachers, of course, were not told what was going on. All they knew was that these disruptive kids were attending a special class.

Graubard and Visalia psychologist Harry Rosenberg took seven students between twelve and fifteen years old. They had been nominated as the worst behavior problems in the school. The psychologists brought them into their secret lesson for one class period a day. "We took it from a straight power point of view," Graubard says. "We told the kids we would give them a certain kind of power over their teachers. They liked that idea." The goal was to make the most punitive teachers more warm and open, and each young behavior modifier was assigned two teachers to work on secretly.

One of the techniques used on the unsuspecting teachers was called the "Aha phenomenon." When a teacher explained something the child already knew about, the youngster waited until the teacher was finished with the full lecture. Then he would meekly raise his hand, and even though he knew the material, he would ask the teacher to please explain it again. The exasperated teacher would start back at the beginning.

Then, about halfway through the explanation, the youngster halted the teacher. His face lit up. He smiled. "Aha!" he said. *"Now* I understand!"

Invariably the teacher felt a sense of achievement and a little more warmth toward the youngster. "I know that when I was teaching," Graubard says, "when I could see a student get a point, it turned me on immensely. Teachers don't get much of this."

In their top-secret classroom, the little behavior shapers were taught two sets of techniques: those designed to stop bad bits of behavior by a teacher, and those designed to increase positive behavior by a teacher. "When a teacher hollered at a kid, instead of glaring back, we taught the kids to break eye contact, to stare at the ground and look sheepish. We taught them how to avoid any hassles," Graubard says. They were also taught to respond to teachers' patient explanations with such items as "Gee, that's interesting." The kids practiced nodding their heads at the appropriate moments, how to make small talk with a teacher, and how to compliment a teacher's work tactfully.

"There was one kid we worked with named Willy. Willy was an immense child. Just huge. He looked like a tackle in professional football, and he scared the shit out of some of the teachers," Graubard says. "His problem was that he didn't know how to smile. His smile came out more like a leer." The psychologists spent hours in front of a mirror with Willy teaching him how to smile innocently and how to talk amiably with teachers.

A few times, the kids' sweet-talking backfired. "Sometimes we had to use a tape recorder with a kid, and practice those things, so he wouldn't sound like a con artist. They had to sound sincere." How do you teach them sincerity? "By teaching them to be *successful* con artists," Graubard says.

Dr. Rosenberg says that the psychologists worried about the "straightforward manipulation" carried on by some of the youngsters. "We told them they would lose credibility after a while if they were always insincere. But praise, even when it's insincere, is effective. In the end, we figured that if the kids could achieve the same goal through this technique rather than violence, we were ahead."

After their guerrilla training, the youngsters went into classes armed with small golf counters in their pockets. They had been taught to keep an accurate record of a teacher's bits of positive and negative behavior. The psychologists' final graphs, after nine weeks, showed that the number of positive contacts between the young behaviorists and the teachers rose from eight to over thirty. The negative contacts dropped from about twenty to zero.

Another experiment Graubard worked up in a Visalia classroom was on the matter of noise. "One of the most basic issues of teacher-pupil interaction is the complaint that children are too noisy," Graubard wrote.[8] "Our approach was not to attempt elimination of the noise problem by producing more quiet children. Rather, we wanted to promote teacher readiness to accept the children's spontaneous noise level."

The experimenters surreptitiously monitored the noise level in four classrooms. These were the classrooms of four quiet-freak teachers, who had done a good job of keeping the children silent. The average noise level in all the classes for a week was thirty decibels.

Then the program began. The teachers' supervisors were given a program of reinforcement. They went to the teachers to praise them for the job they were doing in their classes. They particularly emphasized how much they were impressed by the teachers' tolerance of noise and free expression by the children. After a little of this praise had sunk in, the supervisors asked each teacher's permission to use her classroom as a model. The teachers were told that visitors would be brought in to see "how much freedom of self-expression and behavior a good teacher permits." The visitors included the superintendent of schools, who also praised the teachers for their tolerance.

Over a period of five weeks, these teachers who had been forcefully maintaining quiet in their classes became exponents of open classes. The decibel levels rose in their classes from thirty to forty-five, to sixty, and finally to a nearly seventy-decibel average.

The experiment shows that teachers are quite as malleable as their students. "Teachers can change, and change quite radically," Graubard says.

In two other studies in Visalia, Graubard worked with retarded kids. He taught them some techniques to change the behavior of the normal kids who had snubbed and abused them.

In the conclusion to the four experiments, the psychologists wrote:

"Socially deviant groups can readily change the behavior of those groups who generally exercise the most control over them. . . . The program that was implemented in this school also shows that it is possible to diffuse power, even political power, in a way that is not usually available to those from minority groups. Currently, establishment groups, such as teachers, normals, and high status children, retain control over the power structure within the schools. It has been demonstrated that this control may be neutralized. . . ."

Graubard and Rosenberg are now looking for other schools in which to continue their experiments. Excited by the possibilities, Graubard adds, "We're diffusing knowledge and power. I want to build that right into the curriculum . . . with a behavior-shaping class in every school!"

His work underscores both the power of behavior mod and the abuses he counteracted. A breach in the ranks of the mod squad has already opened over the issue. What behavior should be shaped, and in whose hands should the tools be placed?

The behavior mod establishment (it has grown its own little academic hierarchy) says that there has been emphasis on the control of problem behavior because that was the easiest target and teachers wanted it. One pair of researchers noted that the *Journal of Applied Behavior Analysis,* the field's establishment journal, between 1968 and 1970 had among scores of projects only one study that questioned at all the ideal that silence and lack of movement is the ideal classroom behavior.

A few of the mod squad establishment confess that the argument "The teachers wanted us to" is weak. The other standard defense—"The technique itself has no values"—is also weak. As one outsider said it, "That's the old Wernher von Braun argument. My rockets just go up. Who cares where they come down?"

Richard Winnett and Robert Winkler, in a somewhat stiff scholarly article in the *Journal* (No. 5, 1972), said, ". . . behavior modifiers have used their procedures to serve the goals and values of the existing school system. If the existing school system had adequate goals and values, this would be admirable, but if the critics . . . are even partly correct, then behavior modifiers are doing education a considerable disservice. . . . It appears that behavior modifiers have been the instruments of the status quo, unquestioning servants of a system which thrives on a petty reign of 'law and order' to the apparent detriment of the educational process itself. What is, perhaps, most disheartening is that our procedures seem to work, and thus make the system operate that much more effectively."

Besides slicing out "problem behavior," behavior modifiers have worked to increase such items as "on-task behavior," "attending behavior," "study behavior." In other words, docile children.

The largest group of mod squad rebels is led by Ogden Lindsley. With a few dozen other behaviorists, he is out laying siege to the behavior mod establishment. Yes, behavior mod is rigid and will produce robots, he says. That's because the behavior modifiers have forgotten their basic science. When the Skinnerian principles are used properly, they free our children from control. Skinner's rules can put the children in charge, he says.

In his little Kansas office, he is rummaging through a briefcase, pulling out charts and data. He begins by saying that behavior mod started out with the very advanced work of Skinner, and has been slipping back into the Watsonian behaviorism of 1900.

In the animal lab, he says, Skinner did not record the behavior of the rat. If a rat was supposed to press a lever, it was the movement of the lever that was recorded. The early behaviorists never recorded the rat lifting his paw up to the lever and pushing his paw down on it. The only thing recorded was lever movement.

"A lot of people have forgotten that in the animal lab we didn't record the *pressing* of the lever. We recorded the *effect* of the animal's motion. We put him alone in a room and recorded the movement of the wall," says Lindsley.

He is just warming up. "Okay, what does that have to do with current applications? We've drifted back to Watsonian behaviorism. People sit in the classroom and record whether the kid is engaging in study behavior! Not did he learn anything. That would be the effect. We've got people recording eyes-on-page! So we've got highly diligent, studious-looking classrooms. That would be like somebody looking into the rat box and recording paw on lever."

Lindsley pauses, reflects a moment, then dives in again. "The layman knows this! I can remember being in study hall in North Kingstown High School in 1938 or 1939, and being forced to read a civics book. I was really being 'on-task.' If you looked, you would say, 'Isn't Ogden a diligent student!' But inside the civics book I had this spicy detective novel. 'His hand slipped up the silken thigh to the soft white flesh. . . .' "

In reverse, he says, "I could have been staring at the ceiling and trying to do square roots in my head!" It's against all the Skinnerian principles to require everyone to behave the same way, Lindsley says. You deny the learner the opportunity to perform in his own best way. The early Skinnerian had more respect for rats than the behavior mod squad now has for people!

"We never told a rat how to press a lever! We rewarded him for doing it his own best way. We rewarded the effect," says Lindsley. With kids, it's the learning, the academic achievement that should be the target. Not quietness or "study behavior."

"You know the Fosbury Flop?" Lindsley asks. "The guy who goes over the high jump bar backward to set a world record? Well, if his coach had been like current behavior modifiers, he would never have let him approach that bar any other way than the way the coach thought was best.

"If you record 'How well does the cello sound?' then you can get a Pablo Casals. He holds the cello some bizarre way. If you pay attention to how you must hold it, then you may not get Casals. You are not letting individual differences occur."

Lindsley has whipped out another batch of charts. Besides all this basic-principles stuff, he's going to prove that there is no relation between learning and "looking like you're studying." He picks up the chart of one boy.

"Okay. Math facts correct. You'll notice here when he is being observed attending to task more and more, he produces less correct answers. Now, when he is attending to task less and less, he is getting the same amount correct." He moves to four other children. "If we take four special-ed children and put all their 'percent of time on-task' on the chart . . . then we compare that with their increased work . . . there is just no relationship at all!"

So the mod squad is just on some kind of power trip: Performing behavioral surgery to keep kids quiet, and nearly totally ignoring the main thing—learning, academic performance. But again, it's not the Skinnerian science that is turning kids into robots. In fact, claims Lindsley, Skinnerian science can free the kids. Here Lindsley begins his heavy trip:

We should respect kids as much as we respect rats, he says. The rats recorded their own behavior. A machine automatically counted every time the rat pressed the lever. So why not have kids chart their own behavior?

"If you've got a nation of self-recording people, you've got a much less expensive system than if you've got a nation of people being monitored by machines or other people. And you also solve this whole manipulation business. If you offer the system to the people for self-control, you completely by-pass this whole powerful manipulation thing. . . . In traditional behavior mod, the charts belong to the experts, or the teacher, or the manager. We give the charts to the children. We only make suggestions when the children's attempts to change their own behavior have failed. And that's not very often."

The chart is a turn-on for the kids, Lindsley says. It is not uncommon that a kid will improve his skills just to see the line rise on his chart, just to know he's improved.

The issue of control breaks down into a few parts: Who records the behavior, who puts it on the chart, and who uses the chart to decide what behavior will be changed? "We try to put all those in the hands of the students," Lindsley says. The farther away from the student those things happen, the more manipulative, rigid, and misplaced will be the results.

Of course, using the Lindsley approach, the former school power syndrome is broken up, as in Graubard's study. Not only would the teacher find it difficult to exercise authoritarian means; the kids could stop her.

"Here's a chart," Lindsley says. "A twenty-five-year-old teacher, and the behavior manager is an eleven-year-old girl. Sixth grade. The child recorded teacher tantrums. What they were was the teacher getting angry: 'We can't have this nonsense in here anymore!' The kids call them tantrums. We asked [another adult] to describe them. He called them 'brief moments of overcommitment.'

"This is the kind of thing that shows what happens when children design their own change procedures. They are very creative and effective. Each time the teacher had a tantrum, the girl got up out of her chair, walked around it once, and sat down. Was it effective? In two weeks, the tantrums were gone. Just as good as any cattle prod or anything else," he says.

In another classroom, the kids wanted to get more praise from the teacher. They thought he wasn't complimentary enough. So, "They made up a cardboard sign that read: WE LIKE PRAISE. They just put it on his desk. It was there all the time.

"He was praising five or six times a day. [A student] put the sign up, and he went to forty or fifty a day, immediately. That was for five weeks. When she took the sign down, he leveled off at thirty per day. So the total effect was, he was praising six times as much after it was over," Lindsley says.

And so Crazy Og is off into another rebellion, this one against the behavior mod establishment. He is not alone in this one. Many of the mod squad are idealists, and were converted to behaviorism from other disciplines because they had a chance to do some real good for people. Now they often find themselves allied with the establishment procedures and values from which they escaped. So, in the behavior mod literature, in seminars, in conferences, in conversation, the doubts keep popping up.

"As long as we patch up the system, the system is going to stay the way it is. What we're doing now is letting teachers get lousy training in schools . . . or no training, and the result is a school or cultural system which maintains trivial or stupid behavior on the part of the kids. . . ."

"Often the psychologist, like other scientists, sees himself as totally uninvolved in [power relationships]. But whether the psychologist is concerned or not, the growing use of contingency management in our society most often is in the service of our present elites and further entrenches them. . . ."

"A quiet, controlled, docile classroom may not only be unnecessary, but destructive."

These are the comments from the mod squad. But it is not yet the prevailing view. It may not ever be if the current behavior mod practices become entrenched.

The final irony of it is the life of John Broadus Watson, the father of behaviorism. John Watson was a lousy student in school, and a troublemaker. But very creative. His rebellious bent later served him well when he announced the birth of a science of behavior even before he had all the facts. We must wonder if John Watson would have been an accountant or a bank teller or a bureaucrat if he had gone through a behavior mod class. Could he have been shaped into normality?

4. Families

"In that brave new world which science is preparing," wrote B. F. Skinner in 1945, "the young mother has apparently been forgotten." That was the great controller himself writing for the *Ladies' Home Journal.* Skinner and the ladies' journal may at first seem like an odd pair. But Skinner has always had a utopian cast of mind, a quite detached idealism. He has spent many words working out the little kinks of ordinary life. The squishy-soft and smiling idealism of the 1945 *Ladies' Home Journal* seems in the same league.

So Skinner made his first public offering of behavioral work in a women's magazine. He suggested to the little mothers a super Skinner box for children: "A closed compartment about as spacious as the standard crib."

The gadget was a large box with a glass window on one side. Its temperature was carefully controlled: "crying and fussing could always be stopped by slightly lowering the temperature." It was also soundproofed: "We are never concerned lest the doorbell, telephone, piano, or children at play wake the baby. . . . soundproofing also protects the family from the baby."

Skinner, always the scientist, made a number of interesting discoveries about children through the use of the box. He acknowledged some criticism. "Mechanical dishwashers, garbage disposals, air cleaners, and other labor saving devices were all very fine, but a mechanical baby tender—that was carrying science too far! However, all the specific objections which were raised against the plan have faded away in the bright light of our results. . . ."

So behavior mod in the home began. The great shaper has never been bashful about it. He's never listened to critics: it's part of the theory, you see. If you pay attention to them (reinforcement), they will get worse and louder. Some of the mod squad have picked up on this posture, and there are a good number of righteous young behavior shapers stomping around now.

Skinner himself was not sure that the masses would ever get the point about behavior, and he has always imagined some philosopher-king behaviorists at the controls. But now the mod squadders are talking about training parents, and believe that behaviorism can go the whole distance:

"When we license parenthood, behavior mod will be very important," says Dr. Roger McIntire of Maryland University. He is sitting in a narrow office, with his feet propped casually on his desk. The light from the window halos his blond hair. He's a clean-cut young man.

He talks about abused children, about population control, about letting people without training raise children. "Society is going to see the folly of that," he says. "We are *going* to license parenthood. You know, the main reason we have never licensed parents is: on what grounds would we license them?" There have been so many competing theories about the proper way to raise children; fads come in and recede like waves.

"But behaviorism will show that there are principles for raising children. We ought to have certain abilities before having a child," McIntire says.

Underneath the curls of his hair, a scenario for licensing parents has already sprouted. "I can tell you how it might happen," he says. "We have only one step to go and we will have a semipermanent contraceptive. It would exclude ovulation and have no side effects. We might give these out freely to twelve- and thirteen-year-old girls."

It would ensure disaster-free teen years for many young girls, ease the oppressive problems of illegitimacy, and help control the population boom. The contraceptive would stay in effect until a doctor neutralized it with, perhaps, another pill.

"If you have a pill that would unlock the procedure, then you would get a doctor who would say, 'Any fool can see that in this particular case, this young girl shouldn't have a child!' The girl asking the doctor to unlock the contraceptive might be fifteen years old, from a large welfare family, unmarried, diseased, whatever. The first doctor to say, 'No, you can't have your contraceptive unlocked,' will certainly have a good reason for saying it.

"There will be some circumstances in which it will be clear that the doctor shouldn't," says McIntire. "Then the debate will begin. This is a very serious thing, people will say; we ought to lay down guidelines on this. . . ."

Enter behavior mod. When the experts are laying down the guidelines on just who should have their contraceptives unlocked, he says, someone will bring up the subject of education, of parent-training. Certainly people should get *some* training before rearing children. After all, we license people to drive cars. How much more important is raising a child. Statistics on child abuse will be paraded, and the crime statistics will be walked down the runway for display. Someone will start to talk about medicine.

Medicine, runs the argument, was once practiced by any old grandmother who could amble out to the woods to pick herbs. After the principles of medicine were discovered, we began licensing the users of medicine. We required education for doctors, nurses, paramedics.

So it will be with parenthood, says Dr. McIntire. The idea's time will come. "After all, fifty years ago, who would have guessed that America would have a peacetime draft?" he asks. The notion of conscription used to be abhorrent and contrary to the essential idea of American democracy. We bragged about our voluntary army. But the draft was installed, and maintained for thirty years. Now it is accepted, and the all-volunteer army is the controversial and experimental concept. And what about abortion? Even Huxley would have had a hard time putting that in his brave new world and earning belief.

"Really, the most important course in college should be child-rearing. It should certainly be over and above English and math," he says. Principles of child-rearing would almost certainly be more useful to most students than calculus. Think also how useful good parents are to society, he says.

McIntire has put his provocative arguments in a modest proposal for licensing. He argues, "What about the rights of children? . . . Today, any couple has the right to try parenting, regardless of how incompetent they might be. No one seems to worry about the unfortunate subjects of their experimenting.

". . . those who oppose a parent-licensing law usually do not oppose the discriminating policies practiced by adoption agencies. . . . our culture insists on insuring a certain quality of parenthood for adopted children, but if you want to have your own, feel free. . . . The times are changing. With the population problem now upon us, we can no longer afford the luxury of allowing any two fools to add to our numbers whenever they please."

And finally, ". . . for our safety and well-being we already license pilots, salesmen, scuba divers, plumbers, electricians, teachers, veterinarians, cab drivers, soil testers, and television repairmen. . . . Why, then, do we encounter such commotion, chest-thumping, and cries of oppression when we try to protect the well-being of children by controlling the most crucial determiner of that well-being, the competence of their parents? Are our TV sets and our toilets more important to us than our children?"[1]

McIntire's views are shared by a number of behaviorists, and they estimate variously that in something between ten and fifty years, we will have licensed parenthood. "You just can't stop something that works," McIntire says. "The history of science has always been that way, no matter whether it's the Salk vaccine or the atomic bomb."

The ideas of some behaviorists about the licensing of parents tell us much. These scientists have no intention of confining their ideas to the laboratory. They are impatient. Even though their theory and proofs still have given us little and incomplete information about man as a behaver, they are ready to abandon the long perspective of science to meddle in social policy and politics. McIntire does not suggest licensing because of the fullness of his understanding of children, families, or the social fabric. He starts with the political questions: Why licensing is necessary; why it is logical and good social policy. After setting up the case with political opinions, he then offers his behavioral knowledge as a way out. It can be useful in training parents, in deciding who is a fit parent, he says.

Licensing parents does not follow from the things learned in behavioral experiments. Shaping school children into being quiet and docile is not dictated by a science of behavior. These are political acts. Dr. Thomas Szasz, critic of the psychiatric establishment, has pointed out that psychiatrists often act as a kind of gestapo in an undeclared war against people they have decided are misfits. The mental hospitals are the POW camps in the war. Some psychiatrists, he says, pretend to authority on the subject of behavior, while in fact they have little better information than the rest of us. Their authority is used to make essentially political judgments about other citizens.

The behavior modifiers are susceptible to the same misuse of power, and try equally hard to enforce their own political and social beliefs on others under the cover of degrees, titles, and white lab coats.

The Skinnerian school of psychology is coming to power in America. Its numbers and influence are growing in the established groups of psychological society, such as the American Psychological Association. The behaviorists fully expect that some of their popularity, being faddish, will deflate in ten years. There will be reforms and retrenchments. But they are confident that their basic assertions will become accepted and dominant. What should be feared in this coming to power is not the ideas coming out of the labs, but how the behavior controllers extrapolate those ideas and attempt to enforce the extrapolations on others. The theories may be important and useful, for example, in counseling families. But this involves no social policy schemes, just advice.

Leopold Walder looks like a Jewish Ben Franklin. He is not unpleasantly on the plump side; the shiny dome that is the top of his head is surrounded by a wreath of long hair, curly and black. He wears thick glasses. He is not a well-known behavior modifier. Not like Crazy Og Lindsley, perhaps the best known of the mod squad, or like Vance Hall or Harold Cohen, whose work is known and often quoted. Walder is, as he says it, "a small-town psychologist." He lives in Greenbelt, Maryland, and walks to work. He is a free-lance behaviorist, moving from project to project, and keeping up a private practice. His specialty has been families.

He came to behavior mod late in his career from traditional psychotherapy. His earlier work is now a joke, like the Rorschach tests he used to give that he now calls "those stinky ink blots." Walder starts from the usual ground zero for behaviorists: he dismisses mental events and psychological "illness."

"My assumption is that *everybody* is normal, behaves normally. You may not like the way they behave. It may be undesirable. But they are behaving according to the same laws as anybody else. They learn to do something. You don't like it? Then you teach them better. You teach them something else."

Walder sits in a straight-backed chair in his spare and small office. The man is absolutely certain that behaviorism has got The Law. His arms are folded across his chest, and he laughs a little. "But still, today, there are many people who belong to an earlier culture! They say, 'Well, how about his insides? How about his feelings and so forth?' My general response over the years has been: We'll fix the behavior first. If there is some problem left, we'll work on that. Generally, when we fix the behavior, the other stuff goes along with it. Or it wasn't there in the first place. What I suspect these people are talking about is other parts of behavior that also get fixed in the process of fixing the behavior."

He pauses for a second. "Sometimes I figure there are no insides. But most of the time I say, 'If there are, it's not my business. I know *my* insides, and that's all I know. I don't know yours. I don't know my client's.' "

Walder started working with families in the early years of the behavior mod movement. He started with a parent-teacher training project in 1962. He learned then what the mod squad has found again and again to be at the core of family problems: Payoffs for behavior are delivered exactly backward.

Walder was a psychological counselor for an elementary school. "The typical thing was that the child behaved in some undesirable way. When he does that, he wakes up the environment around him, and the environment responds to him. Then, if he starts behaving in a desirable way, the environment goes to sleep. This situation is often helped by a label attached to the kid. 'Hyperactive' is a popular one.

"So what I would have the parents and teachers do is observe what he does and what happens right after he does it. You didn't have to be very smart to say, 'Well, why don't you switch things around? Go to sleep when he's behaving bad, and wake up when he's behaving better!' Miraculous cures and all that sort of stuff. I went from a long waiting list of problems to no waiting list. I'm pleased to say that I ran myself out of a job. That's what it's all about. . . ."

The mod squadders each must have run and rerun this scene about backward payoffs a hundred times. Gerald Patterson wrote it this way: "Perfectly reasonable parents can *accidentally* teach their children all kinds of problem behaviors and not even notice they have done it! Perfectly lovely parents teach their children to have a temper tantrum every hour! Others train their child to whine and cry each time he is asked to go to bed at night! . . . the child, on the other hand, trains his parents to nag, scold, and even spank him! These are certainly not the parent behaviors of his choice. . . ."[2]

McIntire tried it this way: "The satisfaction of the child's needs and wants has always been the parents' role. And the child's role has always been to adjust his behavior to obtain these satisfactions from his parents. Usually he does this by pleasing his parents, but he may have to make them angry, embarrassed, or simply tired before they give in and provide him with the things he wants. . . ."[3]

Skinner himself thought parents couldn't learn The Law. He said, "I despair of teaching the ordinary parent how to handle his child. They spank him when he does something wrong, instead of praising him for doing something right. They have no idea of the proper use of reinforcement. I would prefer to turn child-raising over to specialists." In *Walden Two*,[4] of course, he did just that. Babies were raised in a child-shaping center run by a squad of detached, objective specialists.

But the mod squad, the children of Skinner's labors, are not so radical and brazen as Skinner. They have begun writing Dr. Spock-style advisory books and pamphlets for parents. They have begun hundreds of parent-training workshops. They have devised special techniques to teach parents The Law. Leo Walder has run some of these parenthood classes, and has come up with a behavior-shaping charades game to put across the idea.

In a group, one parent was "it." The others passed a piece of paper among themselves. On it was written some behavior they were to shape up with reinforcement. Each time the target parent did the right thing, the others clapped once. For the target parent, the object of the game was to earn the most claps.

"We might start out with a very simple one, like just getting the person to turn his head in one direction. We might get the person to speak while walking around the room. Or we might build up a long chain of behaviors like having the person take a piece of paper and a pen, signing his name, and passing the paper to somebody," Walder says.

Despite Skinner's worries, the mod squad have found parents

easy to teach. In fact, Walder discovered that when he showed them how to "design" (his word) their children, they got excited about "the fact that an 'expert' was finally saying that they could and must do something for their own children."

The mod squadders, parents themselves, know the relief of having something to use that works on kid problems. Dr. Donald Pumroy, Maryland University, who commonly applies behavior mod to his own children, related one problem he had with his twenty-month-old son. The boy often woke up in the morning earlier than his parents, and started calling out to them from the next room. The Pumroys were roused out of bed every day in the dawning hours to go quiet the boy. At first, they went into the boy's room and told him it wasn't time to get up yet. But their admonitions didn't last long; a few minutes after retreating to bed, the Pumroys heard their son crying out for mommy and daddy.

Most parents would continue to respond to the boy's yelling out every morning, and would thus pay off the early-morning demands. Reinforced, the boy would increase his vocal reveille.

The Pumroys set up a behavioral plan. They decided it was all right for the boy to call out when he wanted to get up. But they didn't want him to call out before 8 A.M. First, they started graphing the youngster's crying-out behavior. They let him call out from the time he woke until 8 A.M., counting the number of calls. Then at eight o'clock, they went in to pick him up.

In the first few days, the boy cried out several hundred times before 8 A.M. arrived. On the fourth day of the plan, the Pumroys installed a small light in the nursery room where the boy could see it when he woke up. It was turned on from another room exactly at eight o'clock.

From that point on, the parents didn't respond to the boy's crying until the light was switched on. The boy might cry for many hours, but he got no response until eight. As soon as the light went on, however, the Pumroys responded to the child's first call. They immediately went in and picked him up.

The Pumroys' graphs showed that after several weeks of the light training, the boy had learned the routine well and no longer called out before eight. As Keller Breland had done with the pistol-shooting chicken, and as Skinner had done with pigeons, the Pumroys did with their first child. He was simply taught to discriminate between appropriate and inappropriate time to call.

One problem that has always puzzled, frustrated, and angered parents is toilet training. Dr. Spock devotes several pages in his book *Baby and Child Care* to the difficulties of the situation. It is a "major project," which can take from several weeks to months to accomplish, and sometimes becomes a real struggle to get the child to give up his "possessive" feeling toward his eliminations.

Behaviorists have found, of course, that toilet training can be a quick and simple operation. Dr. Nathan Azrin, who worked first with retarded adults and later with retarded and normal children, says that the job can be done in half a day. Easily. And that's not just the toilet training; that's teaching the child to use a potty chair, carry it into the bathroom, empty it, flush the toilet, and replace the pot in the chair. *And* to take complete responsibility for any future elimination accidents.

Dr. Azrin, who works at Anna State Hospital in southern Illinois, is another convert to behavior mod. He was once "one of the most dogmatic Freudians there was," he says. "I went around telling everybody what the *real meaning* of everything they did was. When they itched and scratched. Their gestures. Everything. And God help them if they had a dream!"

It didn't take him long to realize that all that stuff was pure fantasy. "You know, my grandmother actually told better stories, but she just didn't have the reputation Freud did."

Azrin's approach to toilet training is to make it a very intense and reinforcing experience for the child. "From the time the child starts the training to the time he is finished, he is going to be very, very busy. There is scarcely going to be any time when he is not doing anything.

"The first problem is to get the level of urination up from only once every three or four hours. We give him lots and lots to drink.

Not all of them want to drink, so we have developed procedures for getting them to drink. There are four different ways: first, imitation—you have the mother or the trainer go take a little sip of the thing, so he realizes it's all right to drink; second, you let him taste it, put the cup to his mouth and let him taste it; third, you can give him some salty foods, or at least dry foods, like Fritos corn chips, potato chips, or cereal—anything that is dried-up food; fourth, you give him drinks that he really enjoys, his favorite drinks. You give him a drink every few minutes. That's an awful lot for a child, and it leads to a lot of urination. So he's gonna be urinating every half hour.

"But he hasn't yet urinated, so how are you gonna teach him about it? We use imitation. We take a doll, a doll that can wet, and make sure it has pants on it. We use the principle that a very effective way of learning is by teaching. So we have him teach the doll how to toilet properly. We have him teach the doll how to go to the potty chair, have him teach the doll how to lower her pants, to raise her pants, to wipe herself, to take the pot out of the potty chair, to carry it all the way to the toilet, to empty it out in the adult toilet bowl, to flush the toilet, to bring back the potty, and reinsert it in the chair," Azrin says.

The motivation for a child to pull off all this behavior comes from the teaching of the doll, and from approval. "You give your approval in many ways. Both verbally and nonverbally. You praise him, tell him, touch him. You applaud, you hug him, you smile. And everything is in an overemphasis kind of way—you smile very broadly, you laugh when he does something right. You don't just say, 'That's good'; you jump up and down, you pick him up, you applaud and you clap. You give him candy and drinks."

For a child as young as two years, it is not just a matter of giving instructions and he will carry them out. The instructions and guidance must be carefully executed. "You give him an instruction, and if he doesn't understand, you break it down, be more specific. You've told the child, 'Pull the dolly's pants down.' The kid looks up at you. He's never done it before. So you break it down: 'Move your hand toward the doll . . . put your hand under the pants . . . now put your other hand on the doll . . . now under the pants . . . now push down . . . push down with the other hand. . . .' You've broken it down. Suppose he doesn't do it. It's because he doesn't know how, he is confused, the words are new to him, he just doesn't feel like it. The rule is that within a second or so after you give the instruction, you give gentle manual guidance. You take your hand over his and gently start moving it. . . . When you feel his hand moving, you loosen the pressure of your own. You never do it for him, you don't guide him any more than you have to. And there is no scolding. You never show anger. Never!

"So it goes on this way, and maybe halfway through, you want him to go to the toilet, the urine may be building up. Get him to sit quietly on the potty chair. Give him a big approval for sitting quietly. If he does urinate, you give him all this approval, you have him carry the pot to the toilet, and have him flush and all. You yell, 'God, you did it! That's wonderful! My goodness, just like daddy and mommy!' You jump up and down, like the whole world's changed for him. If he doesn't urinate, you only let him sit there for ten minutes at the maximum. This is not a sit-and-wait procedure. You do it a few times, and by the third or fourth time, he will have urinated.

"The procedure also has something built into it for what you do after training, because anything that involves learning also involves forgetting. You expect pretty much what you'd expect any normal adult to do if he has an accident. You expect him to clean it up himself. It's his responsibility. He must take his wet pants off, he must bring them to the hamper. It's all been done with the doll, when the doll had an accident, so the kid knows what is expected. A good part of the reason children have accidents is that the parents take the responsibility for cleaning it up."

Azrin adds, "The reaction of the mothers is something we were totally unprepared for. I never realized it was such a massive problem. People seemed to accept it like the measles—it was just something inevitable. Kids—you have to change their diapers. A frequent comment we get now is: 'God bless you. Someone at last has been paying attention to the problems of mothers.' So here is this big area that involved so much time and concern; family problems and nagging; ruining relationships; the mother ashamed of the kid; the kid feeling guilt-ridden and persecuted; the mother making demands that he couldn't possibly meet. I never realized the problem was that big!"

This is the kind of work that behavior mod does best—helping people work on the nuts and bolts of behavior. It is a long way from the grand social schemes of many behaviorists. Nate Azrin is one of the few behavior modifiers who claims no interest in remaking society or its various institutions.

One other problem Azrin has worked on is bed-wetting. His solution is particularly interesting because there has been a dangerous practice developing among doctors in the matter of bed-wetting. It is part of a larger trend among doctors who seem captivated by the idea that minor behavior problems can be stopped with dope. As behaviorists found with hyperactivity, bed-wetting can be dealt with more quickly and effectively with a little training than with bludgeoning drugs.

The drug that doctors have been prescribing to stop bed-wetting is Tofranil. It is normally used to treat severely depressed adults, and has never been proved to be effective in stopping bed-wetting. In some cases placebos—plain sugar pills with no medication—have done as well. The FDA has refused several times to approve the drug for use on children's bed-wetting, but doctors have continued to use it. The side effects from a normal dose include: hypertension, nightmares, nausea, vomiting, headaches, some cases of enlarged thyroids. In one drug company test it was reported that nearly one-third of the children given the drug suffered these side effects. If an overdose of the drug is accidentally prescribed, as it has been in a few cases, the results are worse: severe brain damage and possible death.

Says Dr. Azrin, "It takes one night. Many of the procedures are the same as for the toilet training. But we also use this gadget, the

bed alert, that signals the parents when the bed is wet. . . . Have
him practice getting up out of bed and going to the toilet. This is
often a big part of the problem. They are scared of the dark or
something. We have them practice inhibiting. You bring them to
the toilet and say, 'Okay, now can you wait? Can you hold it?
Let's see how long you can hold it.' You get them to hold it as long
as they can, and then see if they can hold it till the next wake-up
period, an hour later. We wake them up every hour to see if they
have to go. . . . If they have to, we have them practice going to
the toilet. Then we practice the inhibiting."[5]

Besides the more mechanical problems of behavior in the home,
there are those disruptive bits of behavior. When a child in a
family has a problem, Leo Walder says, there are two approaches.
"You can work with the parents, who have the most power in the
environment of the kid. Or the second way, which is really fool-
hardy, is you can talk to the kid alone. The kid has some power;
he is not zero power. Sometimes you *can* get him to change himself. But there are severe problems with this. In traditional therapy
you take him into a nice room, where you're nice and peaches-and-
cream to the kid. There you can get him to behave in new ways.
Then you hope that what he learned in this training session will
occur out there in the world. He may try it and get clobbered. Or
he may not try it out at all. . . ."

If you want to get the most effect from your therapy, he says,
you must go into family therapy. This is a very popular idea now,
and therapies other than behaviorism, he says, "have enough going
for them that they may accidentally bump into the right solution.
At least they have the right characters there: the family." But
often other therapies bring fresh disasters to the troubled family.
"I have witnessed some of that," Walder says. "They ruin their
own opportunities. They let people punish each other—yell and
scream and express themselves. Part of my business is patching up
some of those families. Part of those family therapies is where
each person says what he thinks and feels, and so somebody says,
'I hate you!' Then, 'I hate you, too!' And off we go!"

One Washington mother whose third son had continuous behavior problems asked for help. The boy, Peter, kicked people, threw frequent temper fits, threatened his sister, hit himself, and tore his clothing. He had been tested at a clinic, and the doctors labeled him hyperactive and possibly brain damaged. In visits to the home, the Washington mod squadders counted the number of bits of disruptive behavior. During the two or three hours a week they spent in the home, the experimenters found that the boy's disruptions varied from eighteen to 113 per hour.

The mother was instructed to begin employing three possible consequences for the boy's behavior. In the first, she was simply to tell Peter to stop his disruption. In the second, she put him in his room and locked the door. The room had already been cleared of toys and other amusements so the boy could not play during the punishment. When the boy was put in his room, he was to stay there a minimum of five minutes and was required to be quiet before he could come out. In the third procedure, the mother was to deliver attention, praise, and affection for some appropriate talking or playing.

When the contingencies were employed, the disruptive behavior dropped quickly to a range of one to eight problems an hour. The experimenters also noted that the disruptive behavior the boy still committed lacked punch.

The disruptive behavior "frequently lacked components which had been present earlier, such as facial expressions, voice qualities, and vigor of movement that typically constitute angry behavior," the experimenters wrote.[6]

Perhaps the most popular technique for the home is the token system, in which children earn privileges or allowance money for regularly completing jobs such as making beds, cleaning the bedroom, reading, washing dishes, and sweeping the floor. This system, of course, is a very old one, probably used effectively before history recorded parental techniques. The difference with behavior mod is that the system is more careful. Charts of behavior are kept, and the rewards are delivered consistently.

Dr. Henry Pennypacker believes that behavior mod will have

done its job on society if some behavior charts and a few rules can be put in the hands of most parents. "It should be an accepted part of life, like reading the gas meter on the house, or using a thermometer to take your temperature. There was a time when granny put her hand to your forehead and said, 'It feels warm.' Now people measure it accurately without even thinking about it."

It is, so say the behaviorists, simply another bit of technology moving into the home alongside the dishwasher, the TV, the little adding machine, the aspirin bottle, the Band-Aids, and the thermometer. But it is the first bit of home technology that applies to behavior.

Children who have grown up with pieces of technology learn to use them early. So it has been with the children of the mod squad. Behavior-shaping between parent and child need not be a one-way proposition. Ogden Lindsley related an incident of a child trained to use a behavior chart in school. The boy had a problem at home: he got upset because his father cussed and swore too much. So the boy began charting the frequency of his father's swearing. After he began charting, the boy simply told his father about the chart, and said that he was sharing the swear chart at school each day. The father zipped from ten per day to zero.

The Sturm und Drang between parent and child is only half of the hassle in family life (not forgetting half of the enjoyment). Putting two people, two minds, two bodies into the marriage blender and expecting a creamy smooth milk shake is somewhat optimistic, though that is the idea our love-romance culture-pushers have been selling for years. The mod squad has produced some analyses and remedies for couples' difficulties, too.

Dr. Shlomo Cohen, of the National Children's Center in Washington, D.C., described one of his little programs to help a couple. The pair fought often, mostly because they didn't talk about the little remarks and actions that irritated each one about the other.

Dr. Cohen set up a system under which the two could communicate the little things without quarreling. Each person was given twenty cards, ten white and ten yellow. On the white cards each partner had to write a specific action of the partner that was pleasant, and the time and place it occurred. On the yellow cards each partner had to write specific actions that were irritating. The cards had to be given to the partner when they were written, and all the cards had to be traded during one week.

With the cards, the pair communicated better the little pains and pleasures, leading to agreements and trades of behavior. For example, the two got angry at each other for being late. He picked her up late from work, and she was never ready to go places on time. So when he was late, he was required to buy her flowers. If she was late, she was required to refrain from shopping for a week.

One of the most irritating actions was for one of the partners to turn away from the other and refuse to talk. To combat this, the two decided that when one of them shut up in an argument, the other was to count to ten, out loud. The silent partner was required to come back with a rebuff before the ten-count ended, or face the consequences: singing, solo, "The Star-Spangled Banner."

The pair made agreements for a variety of situations, and eventually drew up a book of agreements. What they developed, in the end, was a rudimentary marriage contract.

Another marriage-straightening process has been developed by Dr. Azrin. Like Lindsley and his crew, Azrin is not a reinforcement freak. His marriage-fixing system is not a straight reinforcement procedure, like so many behavior mod cases. The straight reinforcement approach, he says, is like going to fix a car and saying, "Well, I'm going to use the wrench approach. Or I'm gonna use the hammer approach. Or the soldering-iron approach . . . You're not going to go very far that way."

The first effort in Azrin's five-week marriage-saving program is to get the partners looking at facts, and communicating them. Most couples come in thinking that their marriage is a series of bloody battles in a lost war. They are really looking for confirmation of the disaster and a way out.

Azrin starts them off by asking them to make a list of the things that each is doing for the other. They start out dissatisfied with each other, and unaware of the things each does for the other. For the woman, for instance, "You ask her how her marriage is and she says, 'He doesn't love me anymore. He doesn't talk to me.' And the sex part of it . . . She says, 'He's using me as an object, a sex object.' Now, with the women's lib thing, the household responsibilities are bigger than ever. She wants him to start doing things, she wants him to clean the dishes and to wax the floor. If you ask him, he says he is doing a fantastic amount! She says, 'He ain't doing nothin'.' The same thing is often true with children. He says he helps take care of the children. She says, 'Hell, he doesn't even know their names.' These are completely different perspectives on the same event," Azrin says.

By making a list of the things each partner is doing for the other, Azrin creates an awareness of the reciprocity. "Once you've got them talking civilly to each other, I tell them that virtually any fantasy they have is capable of fulfillment." He asks them to visualize the perfect marriage and the perfect partner. Then he says they can get it by using a simple compromise procedure.

"Any and every desire can be and will be at least partially satisfied by your partner," he says. The reaction he gets to this is disbelief. For the men, who have mostly a lousy sex life on their minds, the reaction is: "You've got to be kidding! She would never do *that*. The cold fish!"

Azrin gets the troubled twosome to make lists of the things they want in each of ten areas of life: "care of the children, household duties, sex, communication, money matters, social activity, and whatnot. You get them to talk about the things they like rather than the things they don't like. Even if they criticize, you teach them to criticize the specific things they don't like and not the person. . . . They start off saying, 'Well, he is just no good!' If he says, 'Let's give it a try,' she says, 'Yeah, I bet you will!' So the whole thing has to be turned around.

"We teach them this positive-statement procedure. Look for the positive part of it. So if he says, 'Let's give it a try,' and she doesn't trust him, instead of saying, 'Oh, I bet you will,' add a positive statement before the reservations. That is, 'I like the idea that you're trying, but don't know if I believe you.' It's telling him the same thing, but it's commenting on some part of it, however trivial, that you really like. The women say that's the best part. They say that's just the greatest. No more of this constant nagging and criticizing. No more of the guy just walking in the house and saying, 'The floor's dirty.' Men say that! Now he's got to go and say, 'Gee, the house looks great! I wonder what happened to the floor?' That's all right!" Azrin says.

He goes on, "You've got to have this whenever you make a critical comment. You don't like the peas. They were burned. Then you're gonna say, 'Gee, that meat was so delicious. Was there something wrong with the peas that made them burn?' "

Once the communication system is wired up, then comes the Big Trade, the procedure that can get you what you want from any situation. "We change the all-or-none kind of expressions into expressions of frequency and duration. 'I wanna go out to dinner,' she says. '*I don't* wanna go out to dinner,' he says. Well, once you change it into *which place* you go out to dinner, *how often* you go out to dinner, etc., then there is a way you can work it out. When you talk about all or none, you're dead! . . .

"They go over each item in the list of things they want, and they find a way of getting it. If what he wants is to go to parties where certain of his friends are, and she doesn't like it, then you teach him there are strategies of compromise. She says, 'Well, yeah, I'll go every two months.' He says, 'That's not enough. I want to go more often.' The counselor asks if she would agree to stating something else. 'Well, maybe I could do it once a month. But no more.' He says, 'Well, shit, that's all I ever wanted!'

"Or it could be duration. She might say, 'Okay, I'll go, but we won't spend more than an hour, if I say to go home.' Or qualitatively: 'Okay, I'll go, but don't ask me to talk to those people.' So, by breaking everything down into its dimensions, it turns out that you can find a solution to just about everything," Azrin says.

"If it's something they haven't tried before, it's the old idea of reinforcer sampling. Try it, you'll like it! Just try it, but as soon as the reluctant one says he wants to leave or to stop, you stop. It could be a novel sexual posture, or a social occasion, a new place to eat. Anything. Once they sample it, they often find out they like it. Or if they don't like it, they often reach a compromise as to duration or frequency."

Over the five weeks, the couple builds up a book of agreements for each of the ten areas of difficulty. Throughout the procedure, the couples take daily readings of the positive and negative feelings about their marriage and all its parts. Not surprisingly, they are hugely successful.

For Azrin, the distinctive and important thing about the mod squad workers is their scientific posture. They pay attention primarily to data, to what works. Unlike the Freudians and others, "the behavior modifiers abide by the outcomes of what they are doing. They're looking for results. If anybody says, 'These encounter groups work fine,' they will say, 'Okay, show me the data.' Whatever biases I had before will disappear when I see the results. When anybody tells me they are going to use a procedure and don't show results and don't abide by them, don't compare it with other things, they haven't earned the right to be heard. Like I said, my grandmother gave me more exciting suggestions about how to change things, and she also didn't require outcome data. . . . The thing about behavior modification is not that it deals with just behavior or reinforcement. That isn't the thing. It's that these are people who abide by outcomes."

Another, older, branch of behaviorism has also tossed its tokens into the marriage game. It is the stimulus-response behaviorism of John B. Watson. Watson conducted several experiments on an orphaned infant, and found that the only natural fear he had was of loud noises. All other fears, then, must be conditioned somehow. The baby was found to be fond of white rats, and he was allowed to play with them quite often. He enjoyed feeling their fur and watching them move. Then Watson decided to try to condition the baby to fear the rats. So each time he reached for one of the furry creatures, Watson, standing nearby, slammed a hammer against a piece of metal. The racket was unnerving. It was not long before the frightening noise and the furry rats were paired in the baby's mind. He became afraid of the rats, would whimper and try to crawl away from them. He now had a rat phobia. Even though Watson's experiment was short, and the noise was never again made to be connected with the rat, the baby's fear did not fade. It was permanent. Furthermore, the infant was afraid not only of rats, but of all furry animals. Watson, not wanting to be cruel, eventually cured him of his fear.

That experiment and cure stand at the beginning of the growth of a practice now called behavior therapy or desensitization. A good number of fears and dislikes can be dealt with by calling on the stimulus-response idea. In marriage, most of the fear and trembling comes in bed. A huge number of normal people have difficulty with sex because of fears.

Barry McCarthy of American University has made a specialty of unbending sex problems with a behavioral approach. He describes the plight of one woman in her forties. "She had never been orgasmic by any means. She had been married twenty years and had four kids. Her first intercourse was on her wedding night. It was a disastrous one. Her husband was much too fast and much too rough. Not only broke the hymen, but broke a blood vessel. She bled all over the goddamn place and they had to take her to the emergency room.

"A bad beginning . . . but basically these were good people, their relationship was good. The sex problem was a problem of bad practice and lack of knowledge. This is what is the problem with most people. Masters and Johnson say that 53 percent of couples have one kind of sex dysfunction or other. I believe that. So this couple had been having sex for twenty years, had several kids, but they really didn't know anything. They hadn't talked about it, they hadn't talked about that wedding night experience, they hadn't talked about much of anything," McCarthy says.

He met with the couple once a week, assigning them sex home-work during the coming week. In the first week, she was given a manual entitled "A Self-Exploration Program for Women." It contained a set of exercises for the woman to feel her own body, and to explore it carefully. The exercises gradually move the woman toward manual masturbation. "Spread the vaginal opening with two fingers and notice the color and texture of the interior," says the manual. "Feel the warmth and dampness. . . ."

While the woman was thus exploring in the first week, the husband was instructed to masturbate. When in bed together, they followed a careful program of nongenital touching. This also is laid out in a manual: "Hold your partner's feet and caress them with your hands. Notice the length of the toes. . . ." This activity goes for every part of the body except the main areas. Partners take turns, according to the manual, being "pleasurer" and "pleasuree."

McCarthy explains that the whole process is gradually building up skills, and doing it in a relaxed, positive way. During the second week, the woman learned to have orgasms during masturbation. When in bed together, they had moved up to slow, careful "genital touching." Still no attempt at intercourse. The third week, the pair masturbated together. "Then, from that, by about the fourth or fifth week she became orgasmic with his touch," McCarthy says. "Then it became harder because learning to become orgasmic during intercourse is harder. They didn't learn to be orgasmic during intercourse while the therapy was going on, but did a little later. A lot of this stuff takes practice."

The therapy is short, running from a few weeks to three months. After that point, the skills have been taught and the couple can practice on their own.

In the end, the mod squad's arsenal is a fascinating, attractive bunch of technology. Any average Mrs. Smith in Iowa probably didn't see or read *A Clockwork Orange*. Skinner means nothing to her. She is not likely to feel intellectual anguish at being classed a determined creature, as some have, like writer Stephen Yafa:

"With great persuasion [Skinner] shows us how, when, and why we are controlled in our daily lives. Nobody, of course, wants to hear; it is like learning that you have several million body lice building nests in your armpits *at this very moment.*"[7] The average Mrs. Smith is not likely to think *that* way about it. But by God, when she can get George to quit smashing her dishes when he gets angry, she knows she's got something. Getting that kind of power by pulling such slender and delicate strings in the environment may echo the feelings of the first guy who figured out that pulleys allow a very little man to lift a great hulking weight. So easily! And it was there all the time, right on the tip of your affection!

Most of the mod squadders want to hand over the tools to Mrs. Smith as quickly as possible. They resolve all the questions of control by proposing to dole out their power to the people. They do not want to develop a mystical corps of controllers to handle the whole show, the way the Freudians did.

But at the same time they are saying this, they are talking about big-scale social reform. Licensing parents. Behavior mod classes in the schools. And one tactic, which is likely to come on very fast, uses day care centers. It is the natural extension of the movement to free women by putting their children in centers. Jack Michael of Western Michigan University describes it:

"It is very difficult to take kids away from parents now," he says, thinking of abusive, chaotic, cruel families. One behaviorist has used a tactic to take children from "parents who are very ineffective. In a sense, we can get rid of the parents' control over the kids in a way that will be socially acceptable," Michael says.

"With the day care center, for instance, on a free basis you arrange it so that the mother can, if she wishes, at no cost to her, bring the child to the day care center, which is staffed with public funds of some sort and run on a behavioral basis. She brings the child there, and leaves the child there during the daytime. They'll feed the kid, take care of him, and train him to whatever extent is needed. And if the mother doesn't pick the kid up, you will point out, 'Mother, you're supposed to pick the kid up at five o'clock;

however, if something happens, we recognize that your life is difficult, with your job or something. If you don't pick the kid up by five o'clock, or by six o'clock, then you can simply pick the kid up in the morning. You can leave him overnight. We have overnight service in case the parent can't get back.' Well, most ineffective parents will simply begin to leave the kid there. The kid will be in the control of the agency. . . .

"You know, the completely disorganized mother who has no husband in the home, has eight kids, and is out hustling to get dope, and stuff like that, simply won't make it back. So the kid, for most of his young life, will be in fairly good hands. The mother may occasionally get a lot of guilt feelings or something, and go and take the kid out. But increasingly, particularly with the younger kids, who require the most care and are most likely to be mistreated, a mother will be likely to unload that kid. That kid might very well, then, get a satisfactory infant experience. . . .'"

This reform tactic allows behavior modifiers to help children who would otherwise have a disastrous beginning of life. That is clearly a positive step. But the mod squad, while seeing the good, is naïve about the problems of power and politics presented by this tactic. The psychoanalysts, too, were naïve about these problems.

Imagine, for example, the tactic extrapolated just the way the psychoanalysts' extrapolations became real. Imagine the day care centers becoming great bureaucratic inns for thousands of children. The state as parent.

Bureaucracies are notoriously bad at watching out for the welfare of people. Think of the mental hospitals, jails, housing where the government is slumlord. The government as caretaker is rigid, punishing, dull, and at the mercy of politicians with clout.

There is a zealous optimism underneath a proposal like this one, and it is much like the optimism that pushed the great disastrous Freudian reforms on us. Both sorts of proposals stem from a considerable naïveté about politics and power. Behavior mod, now reforming the reform, seems drawn into the same errors.

Perhaps Dr. Szasz, author of *The Myth of Mental Illness,* has the explanation. It is that we are living in a "therapeutic state" in which we want to, need to, revere our doctors the way previous generations revered priests. He says, "For nearly twenty years now I have been writing about the fundamental similarities between the persecution of heretics and witches in former days, and the persecution of madmen and mental patients in ours. My view is that just as a theological state is characterized by the preoccupation of the people with religion and religious matters, and especially with the religious deviance called heresy, so a therapeutic state is characterized by the preoccupation of the people with medicine and medical matters, especially with the medical deviance called illness. . . . We thus persecute millions—as drug addicts, homosexuals, suicide risks and so forth—all the while congratulating ourselves that we are great healers curing them of mental illness. We have, in short, managed to repackage the Inquisition and are selling it as a new scientific cure-all."[8]

The mod squad is fast slipping into the role. Roger McIntire points to a few items: "Ayllon and Azrin's new book *The Token Economy* reports successful reinforcement of attendance at religious services. . . . counter conditioning studies claim success in treating a 'cleanliness obsession,' 'frigidity,' and 'sexual deviations.' . . . counseling literature deals with the *problem* of promiscuity. . . ."[9]

Dr. Daniel Robinson of Georgetown University recalls listening to a cure report in a lecture by an eminent neurologist. "The patient was a 'depressive type,' an inveterate homosexual, and, in the words of the speaker, 'a knight of the open road.' When shown a heterosexual stag film, the patient was overcome by revulsion. However, after a few [pleasurable brain stimulations], he reported a feeling of great well-being and asked to see another such film. At this second showing, he enjoyed the benefits of . . . stimulation during the film and, under these conditions, began to masturbate. Sure enough, he soon agreed to accept a prostitute procured by the medical staff and 'performed quite satisfactorily' with her.

"After the lecture, the speaker was asked if the same procedures would have been undertaken had the patient been a successful homosexual businessman. No; in that case, where the individual's 'adaptation' to social expectations was 'satisfactory,' some more conservative therapeutic methods would be provided. . . ."[10]

The day care center reform is a particularly striking thought because it seems an echo of something we have heard before. Skinner's *Walden Two* had collective parenting. And yes, Aldous Huxley had it in his *Brave New World*. In fact, the point Huxley was making is the same that Skinner and the mod squad are making: Science can indeed make a happier, more orderly world.

Huxley, however, went on to say that this is precisely why science frightened him so. It works, and does not leave enough room at the edges of normal for unhappiness, deviation, sin, experience.

So Mrs. Smith ought to get relief from an angry husband, more help around the house from an errant child. She should go ahead and accept delivery on the super new Mod Squad behavior–washing machine, and put it alongside her miracle blender. But when they come knocking on the door with the blueprints for a marvelous new dome to shield us all from a troubled society, she should throw the bums out. If she had the facility, she might put it the way Blake did:

"Let us pray always for individuals. Never for worlds. . . . The general good is the plea of the scoundrel, the hypocrite, and the flatterer. . . ."

5. The Corporate Controllers

In the seventeenth century, when a man went hunting in the Massachusetts woods, he prayed that he would come back with an animal draped over his shoulder. The hunt, like all the man's life, was in the hands of God. Hunting should be profitable; if it was not, then the man must be a sinner, in God's disfavor. If the prey was too quick, or the citizen's aim a little high, he had best be on his knees repenting.

Business and religion were melded in that America. A man's nearness to salvation could be measured in gold coins, yards of silk, and acres of land, for God blessed good men with prosperity. Sinners were the poor and inept.

The alloy that came from mixing the base metal of profit with the fine ore of the spirit was made into the steel bones of America. America grew on this sturdy frame: life was plain and hard, not mystical; profit was revered, not shunned; hard work earned both money and salvation.

So America's businessmen became heroes.

When psychology became a profession, and esoteric theories of mind and personality grew large in thought and literature, businessmen were perhaps the least affected by it. It didn't do much for the quality of their ball bearings, and didn't change the color of that last figure on their balance sheet. Psychology was a little mystical for these plain heroes. They might have looked for, but could not see, the phantom id along the rows of die cutters and lathes in their dingy factories. Taking it seriously would require spending money and time, for which the businessmen, too often, got zero results.

Even now, with theories of psychology grown and matured, businessmen find little use for them. A salesman who could use some knowledge of people and how they work finds only contradiction and vagueness in psychological theories. The American Management Association recently did a survey of top management in business. The managers felt that there were many business problems that could be relieved by an effective psychologist. But only 3 percent of the managers had used psychologists. And that 3 percent did not seem to be sold on their effectiveness. They used psychologists only sporadically and on tiny problems.

It was left to a few practical young businessmen to dip the first toe into behavior mod. Edward J. Feeney was twenty-two years old and just out of college when he took a job as freight agent with Emery Air Freight Company. It is the biggest air-freight outfit in the world and has offices all over the globe. Feeney slipped into the sales department early, and in 1960 he tripped across his first piece of behavior mod when he heard about a programmed instruction technique that could teach effectively without a teacher. He didn't use it, but his interest was piqued. In 1966, by which time Feeney had become assistant vice-president for sales, he was assigned to set up a sales training program. "I was kind of reluctant to do it. I was never impressed by anything I had ever done before. I wasn't impressed with anything I had ever seen anybody else do. None of it seemed to work. You didn't seem to be able to get the behavior change. When you did, it didn't last."

Feeney went to take a behavioral course in training at the

University of Michigan, and discovered that "you *could* have a training program that had an impact. It's like building an engineering plan that is very precise as to the behavior change that you want. You could not only design a program that would specify the behavior you want in very precise terms, but you could actually predict it and get it. Enlightenment!"

Edward Feeney's office is now in an impressive executive building in Wilton, Connecticut. The grounds have curling pathways, trees, and a private lake.

Feeney is vice-president for systems performance; his office is large and comfortable, with a great brown desk in the center. Behind his desk, Feeney looks an impressive young executive. He is forty-five, looks thirty-five, is wearing a striped sports coat and a brightly colored shirt. He seems to have an excess of energy: he bobs, weaves, and swivels in his chair, pops up to make a chart on his easel. When the rest of him is quiet, his hand taps the desktop.

Feeney's conversion to the mod squad began with the dawning of the notion that everybody's training program was talking about motivation, attitude, and self-image—things difficult to measure, which may not be the problem anyway. "Visualize this report being given to top management: Our self-image went up 5 percent last month, attitudes improved 8 percent . . . and now a few words about the bankruptcy proceedings. . . ."

Feeney counts behavior in dollars. If employees are using a money-saving container only 45 percent of the time, or the customer service department makes return calls on only 70 percent of the complaints, Feeney finds out quickly how much that behavior is costing Emery. Then he fixes the behavior.

He places stress on picking which behaviors to change. "In our company, we must have eighty thousand behaviors we exhibit. The trick is to find those dozen or two that are really crucial; the ones that, if you were to improve them, would give you a huge performance improvement in that whole area. We look strictly at the outputs of behavior: forget the idea of happy and unhappy about workers. Look at the outputs. When you look at it this way, there isn't a hell of a lot of value to many of the things a corporation does. The man doesn't fill out a form. So what?"

In his first behavior mod project at Emery, Feeney worked with the idea that listening to a customer's needs is a top priority for salesmen. If the salesman knows what the customer wants, he can hit him with the right information and start the right pitch. "We tape recorded sales calls. Other companies say you have to listen to what the customer's needs are. But they don't spell out exactly what those needs sound like," says Feeney. "So we take the tape recorder into our training program. We sit the salesman down and let him listen to one short sentence. Then we ask him, 'What was the customer's need there?' We go on up through longer sentences, conversations with multiple needs, different types of needs. They would get immediate feedback if they got it right.

"For example, a customer says on the phone, 'Do you serve Saint Louis?' You don't know what he means by that. He may mean that there was a shipment there last week by us that we handled badly. He may mean that a shipment was mishandled by a competitor, or he's got a shipment sitting on the dock ready to go, or he's putting up a new plant there next month. That's a stimulus for a probe. Instead of saying, 'Yes, we do,' and then going on to something else, the salesman says, 'Yes, we do. Why did you ask?'

"It's amazing when the salesmen go through the program. A brand-new salesman, never made a sales call before in his life! They go through the program and then go out with somebody who's an expert. The expert comes back just kind of shaking his head because this new guy is exhibiting all these behaviors that even our best salesmen are not doing."

Stirred by his first success, Feeney dug a little more deeply into behavior mod. He went to see a film of the mod squad shaping up autistic children. "I looked at that and thought, Well, a company is not unlike a mental institution. I think that'll work. I'm gonna try it!"

One of the first chances Feeney got to try to slap some behavior into shape came in the customer service department. "We are a nationwide, worldwide air-freight company, we're the largest in our field, but we charge a rate that is most often higher than our competitors'. To get that kind of rate, we've got to provide a pretty good service." Emery was getting too many complaints and not dealing with them well.

"We did the thing most companies do. We had run an audit. A management member goes out there, and runs through, tells them what they are doing wrong, and writes up a long letter. There was a flurry of self-justification, some activity, and finally whatever improvement is made lasts about two days. Six months later, somebody else goes out there, and it's the same thing all over again. Nothing seemed to work.

"We went out to some offices and started by defining the output behavior. 'Customer service' is a nice term, but what does it mean? We defined it: such things as messages answered between offices, phones answered without the customer getting a busy signal, call-backs to customers if you can't answer their request immediately. Then we began.

"On messages answered between offices, we asked people what percentage of the time they were answering it within sixty minutes. Well, they didn't see too many yellow pieces of paper around, they wouldn't hear too many complaints, they had a good crew of people, so-called well-motivated, whatever that means, they had a good supervisor. So they figured, 'We're answering 95 percent of all the messages within sixty minutes.'

"People in business are very bad observers of themselves. They tend to overestimate their performance. Not only do they not know, but they overestimate. And they strongly believe that they *do* know! It's kind of a potent combination."

Feeney had the customer service people go back and measure what it actually was. It turned out to be 45 percent.

That was true of *all* the offices.

Feeney handed out little charts to the customer service people, and asked them to measure their performance regularly, and to compare it with their starting point of 45 percent. They handed in their charts to the supervisor, who passed it on up. Then they installed the reinforcements.

Feeney gave the supervisors a list of ways to react to the workers' performance. They were supposed to deliver positive comments whenever a worker handed in his chart. Even if it went down, they were to find something to reinforce. If it went down, they could be pleased that the worker measured it, or that the worker handed it in on time, or that he did it without prompting.

"Then we asked a key question: What reinforces the supervisor? When he handed in that report, you had to be there with the reinforcer. And similarly, all the way on up. I would reinforce the regional office. I would call them, write a note, pass it around to other offices. 'Boy, that's a big improvement!' "

Feeney now slips out of his chair. He's up at an easel, stroking a huge sheet of white paper with a black marker. He sketches out feedback, figures, charts. He's playing sales trainer. "Now, we've put in those two changes, feedback and reinforcement. What do you think might happen? Just those changes without any more money or vacations?"

"Well, umm, it might go up to 90 percent?" says the interviewer turned student.

"That's a very good guess!" says Feeney, spreading a little reinforcer and hyping it with a little smile. "It went to 95 percent! Good. Now, how long do you think it might take to get up there?"

"Very quickly. Umm, maybe in a week?"

"Exactly!" reinforces Feeney. "It was instant! In fact, in about 80 percent of the offices it went up to 95 percent in the first hour of the first day!"

Interviewer-student now asks the tough question. "Just about any kind of change will have an immediate effect. But can you sustain it?"

"That's the question. If you keep up the feedback and some consequences, it will keep going. For example, when we started

this thing in New York in 1968, they were at zero. *Zero* percent.
Nothing was going right. And they didn't know! Now, I go back
there; in fact, I was down there just last month. They are up at 99
percent. And they know exactly what's going on, exactly how
they're performing!

"You know, in most organizations, the feedback is *all* negative.
'Here's what you're doing wrong, buster!' It's a big difference with
reinforcement. People say that's Mickey Mouse stuff. That's not
the way to train people; you've got to do it by discipline. A good
kick in the butt!" But, Feeney adds, "There's nobody that I can't
win over with the results. The stuff works."

Feeney confesses that the job of installing behavior mod has
been difficult at times. People resist. He is careful not to violate his
own rules of behavior in selling the stuff. It's the soft, positive
push. "Oh, there are at least eight hundred objections people have
brought up to this stuff. One example is the time I gave a talk
down at a regional office, an office where they had quite an attendance problem. I talked about that and the advantages of reinforcing people for just coming to work. I said maybe a supervisor
ought to stand there on a rainy day and as people walk in, say, 'I
really appreciate the fact that you came to work today, particularly
today, because it's a bad day. Our performance is always better
when you're here.' Then you give them some evidence of that.

"That line struck one guy as utter nonsense. This was an office
where the people were being exceptionally well paid. The guy got
beet red from here on up. Finally, he exploded. He said, 'You
mean to tell me you should *reinforce* people who are getting *so
well paid?* They ought to *want* to come to work!' He was really
hostile. I said, 'Let me ask you this: if you tried this, and it
worked, would you continue to do it even if you felt people didn't
deserve it?' He thought about that for about five seconds, and you
could see the wheels going around. He said, 'Yeah, I'll do it if it
works.' "

Feeney set up an experiment, it worked, and the angry man was
converted.

Feeney's best-known coup with behavior mod was a loading-dock project. Emery was well known in the air-freight field for one of their packing procedures, called containerized shipment. Essentially, it meant putting a number of smaller packages headed for the same destination in one large container. The procedure saved time and much money.

When the men and supervisors on the dock were asked, they thought their performance was good, and figured that they were using the larger containers about 95 percent of the times they were called for. A quick measure of the real situation showed that they were wrong. They used the containers only 45 percent of the time.

Training was not the answer, Feeney decided, because the men on the loading docks knew how and when to use containers. But they were getting no feedback on how well they were doing, and the bosses never took notice of their performance.

So the company passed out check lists to the dock workers. The men kept track of their own performance, and thus got immediate feedback. Bosses tacked graphs of performance up on the bulletin board so everyone could watch the action. At the same time, the bosses began applying positive reinforcement to the workers: praise and recognition for performance improvement.

Container use jumped from 45 to 95 percent in offices throughout the country, and in most cases the increase came in a single day. Since the experiment, the procedures have been installed as permanent parts of dock work, and the high performance has been maintained for several years. The company has saved more than three million dollars.

Like any good mod squadder, Feeney gets amazed and upset by what goes on in the natural world. It's all backward! They're out there punishing the hell out of people, paying off all the wrong things!

Salaries, among the biggest of all payoffs, are continually mishandled. "I don't know of any that are designed right," says Feeney. "There are one or two salary increases a year. They are not dependent upon performance. The amount of performance improvement is not related to salary increase. For example, if one manager did an outstanding job he may get a 12 percent increase. A guy who does an ordinary job gets a 9 percent increase. The other guy may have a 50 percent profit improvement! There is just no relation to pay.

"Bonus systems are too predictable. The Christmas bonus: you know when it's coming. I would make all these rewards unpredictable. You wouldn't know when they are coming, or how much they will be. I'd have a slot-machine-schedule kind of reinforcement. . . ."

So here is Skinner's gambling addict, and the pigeon who pecked twenty thousand times for one handful of grain. Work addicts.

"You might have some kind of minimum amount of salary. Enough to get him through. And the rest unexpected. They wouldn't know when it's coming. But the payoffs would be high-frequency. Suppose a subordinate comes in, and I ask him to prepare a plan or something. Maybe he's reluctant to get started. When he walks in here with a plan, I say, 'Hey, here's twenty-five dollars.' Bang! Unexpected. Maybe the next time it will be a hundred dollars."

Feeney is ready to install an experimental plan like that at Emery. There is one small task that freight handlers on the docks have to do that just doesn't have any reinforcing consequences. After the workers do it, they enter it on a computer. So Feeney plans to make the computer a giant one-armed bandit.

"We would program the computer to come back with an answer. One time it would be: 'Thank you very much, your entry was successful.' Another time it would be: 'You just won five dollars!' Or maybe fifty dollars. It would be very unpredictable. Well, I just *know* they couldn't wait to get to the damn machine and get those entries made!"

Another big problem with the world as it is, Feeney says, is that people can be very punishing to their subordinates. And *their* superiors are punishing to them. The wheels of companies are often greased with a great flow of threats. Workers do their work because if they don't . . .

Emery has often run into this situation, and it sometimes gets out of hand. Feeney himself has worked on eight cases in which the company was ready to fire a supervisor.

"Here's one case. You know, you can rubber-stamp most of this. Before they even call I know what it's going to be. The guy is punishing to his subordinates. He'll criticize people, yell at them. We try to identify the stimulus that comes in and the response he makes to it. Usually it's when something goes wrong. Then he yells. We try to shape that gradually."

Feeney is working on the boss of a guy who's about to be fired. The problem is usually not the worker, he says. The worker can be shaped up. But the problem is the boss's punishing and misperception of the subordinate's work. First, they point out to the boss that the worker can and does improve. But he's got to watch for it. And he's got to reinforce the good work and the improvement. "He's got to reinforce the good things when he sees them. They are occurring, but he's not seeing them." The boss has also got to let the worker know what improvement is. He's got to let him know *exactly* what's expected.

"Maybe just after the guy's exploded to one of his people, if he comes in to the boss and says, 'I goofed,' that's an improvement. Before he might not have recognized that that was wrong.

"Maybe the next time he comes in and he also knows what he *should* have done. Or maybe even just asks for advice. The guy is having daily discussions with the boss. He's getting reinforced when he does things right. They are reviewing any situation in which the guy got irritated, what was his response, and what should he have done. First, we just kind of reinforce talking about it, and talking accurately, admitting he did it wrong, accepting responsibility.

"We work him up through these levels of improvement. So then, given a situation where he is irritated, instead of him blowing up, he follows the reinforcement model. That is, find out what was *good* in the problem area. State the goal. Reinforce the good they're doing. Measure it, and so forth. It just works *all* the time. . . .

"Tell the man what you *want* him to do. And deal in positives.

Before, any time this guy came in and said, 'I just blew my cork and yelled at this guy,' the boss would say, 'For crissakes! You shouldn't be doing that! How many times have I told you not to do that!' Now he knows that isn't the way to handle it."

Feeney says that almost all the behavior shaping that goes on at Emery comes down from on high. Top management zips in to straighten out the workers. But he hopes that eventually he can hand the tools over to the low-level workers to do some of their own shaping. "I taught an agent-clerk how to reinforce another office for sending her messages on time. To make call-backs to customers in ninety minutes, she had to get answers from other offices quickly. They weren't doing it.

"I asked her, 'Have you ever tried to change anybody else's behavior?' She said, 'Yeah, I wrote a note to the manager in the other office: "Here's a message you didn't answer, I sent a third request, and you didn't answer it." ' So I asked her how they reacted to that. 'Very badly. They complained to my manager that I shouldn't be writing directly to them.'

"I gave her some theory about positives and negatives. So then, when she got an answer from this other office, even if it was on the second prompt and it was delayed, she would drop them a note: 'I appreciate the answer on the second request. That helped.' Next she reinforced when she didn't have to prompt twice. Finally, if she got it within two hours, she would say, 'I got it in two hours. That's good. That's pretty prompt. If you could get it within an hour, that would be very helpful to me so I could meet my standard.' Pretty soon she had it under control.

"Then," says Feeney, "I went over to the other office. The guy there says to me, 'Boy, are we really doing a good job of answering messages! We keep getting all these messages telling us what a good job we're doing!' I asked how the girls react when they get a message like this. 'Oh, they jump right up and answer this.' "

Unlike many others caught up in the mod squad phenomenon, Feeney is not naïve about power and behaviorism. He knows the tools can and will be misused, sometimes stupidly, sometimes cruelly. He reluctantly recalls one company that got hold of the tools. The company was losing a lot of money. The executives were upset. The orders went out: do something, goddamn it, or else! The supervisors immediately leaped on a problem that irritated them. Absentees. Now this company already had more than 99¾ percent attendance, a great record. But the supervisors were really bugged by the no-shows. So they installed a behavior mod program. It worked. They shaved the already tiny percentage down even further. "That's ridiculous!" says Feeney. "To get it down to one-tenth of one percent! What would you save? A nickel? Nevertheless, one top man in the company said that his managers' heads were on the rack if they didn't straighten out the damn absentee problem."

Feeney didn't start out cynical. When it first really came across to him that he had some powerful tools, he was anxious to pass them along. He got a lot of other people going on it. "But then I got feedback on what they did. It was just not good. They do things I clench my teeth at! I would never do that!"

This, of course, is the bottom line in any accounting of the business of power. And it's the thing most often missed by the academic-minded mod squad. People sometimes use power in bizarre and terrible ways, and society is enormously tolerant of this abuse.

Businesses that have used behavior mod in some form are legion, and among them are some of the biggest: General Motors, Bell Telephone, Warner-Lambert, Wheeling-Pittsburgh Steel, Questor Corp., and several major airlines. The spread of behavior mod has been quick, but not as obvious as it has been in some other fields. Businessmen have not published their results as often as psychologists and educators. And the businessmen are more acutely aware of the public relations problems of behavior control. So they use it, but don't call it behavior modification. They give it a fancy name, and mix in some other management principles when they use it. But the principles have spread just the same.

Businessmen have reacted to behavior modification proposals with much reservation at first, according to some who have lectured on behavior mod. Though philosophical grounds are often cited, most objections are made simply on a practical basis. The businessmen don't believe that it could possibly work as well as they are told. Mod squadder Dr. Karen Brethower says, "I try to begin teaching behavior mod with a pilot project because people tend not to believe the extent to which they can succeed." Feeney does the same, and reports that it is fairly easy to get somebody hooked on behavior mod by demonstration.

One of the first businessmen hooked was Daniel Grady, a division manager for Ma Bell in Michigan. He began injecting the stuff into the mainstream of the telephone business as early as 1965. Since then, he has run dozens of programs in groups ranging from twenty to 1,800 workers.

One of his big projects involved getting people to come to work. Michigan Bell had one of the poorest attendance records in the Bell system. Some of the Michigan offices ran as high as 12 percent absent on the average. In Grady's division, it ran about 7 percent, still several points too high.

"We started the project in one office of about thirty people, the office that had the worst record—about 12 percent." The 12 percent included both the common absences of one or two days and the more prolonged absences caused by serious illness and injury. Grady decided to concentrate on just the common variety, which was three-quarters of the problem. Before the behavior mod plan, he says, "we started with all the crappy stuff you always do to make people happy. Was it because it was in the inner city? We found that it wasn't. Was it because the office was dirty or uncomfortable? No. None of that has anything to do with whether people come to work or not. . . . Well, I suppose there are extremes, like if you worked in a coal mine full of rabid bats. . . .

"But we found that the difference between good offices and bad offices on attendance was: what the boss expected and whether that was transmitted to the operators; and how frequently the boss told them they were doing well."

For the first part of the problem, they just set standards and told the operators, " 'We expect perfect or near-perfect attendance, missing only a day or two a year, but not every year. Those are the ideal standards.' Eighty percent of the people said, 'I didn't know that.' All but 2 or 3 percent didn't argue with the standard," Grady says.

For the problem of reinforcement, Grady says he "looked at what was said to the people when they did or did not come in. We had worked it on a monthly basis. If you came in every day for a month, the boss spent fifteen minutes with you to say you were good. Or, if you didn't come in, to say we have to do something about it.

"It was supposed to be once a month, but it varied a lot. Sometimes it was only once every two or three months. Then we figured, why not make it easier to be successful? So we used a weekly record instead of a monthly record. The chat about performance at the end of the week was not to exceed fifteen seconds. The objective was to tell them how good they were. We figured it would be hard to get negative in fifteen seconds, and hard to stay positive for fifteen minutes."

Setting standards, keeping charts, and giving praise as a payoff worked smoothly. "In three months it went down from about 12 percent to 5½ percent. And one interesting thing that happened was that the boss who was involved went on vacation for a week during the program, which meant that the feedback and praise stopped. So did the results. For that week, it popped back almost to 12 percent," says Grady.

Grady's division is still using that sort of system, and absenteeism is running about 4½ to 5 percent. He intends to get it down to 3½.

Grady notes in passing that positive reinforcement doesn't wear out. People never seem to tire of hearing good things about themselves. If anything wears out, he says, "it's the boss. Bosses tend to forget to do things sometimes." He also finds that money, though a powerful payoff, is too difficult to deal with to be valuable in a behavior mod business program. First, there is the matter of unions, which tend to frown on messing with salary schedules. Also, there can be some strange distortions caused by money. An example he cites is one large retail chain that is manic about profits. They have a large number of cash incentives for their sales workers. Grady says the system gets good performance in an area where there is tough competition from other stores. But where the competition is slack, the employees are "taught" to be devious by their incentives. They sometimes will refuse to put items on sale when the company authorizes a sale. That keeps the number of dollars sold up. They will also scrap their service departments to cut costs. They will arbitrarily jack up prices on some items for a quick cash gain. They will purposely not cooperate with other salesmen.

Grady is convinced, therefore, that there is just no need to reach for bigger payoffs like money. Praise and warmth are quite effective in themselves, he says.

In another of Grady's efforts, he tried boosting productivity. One of the measures he used for productivity was: how many information calls are handled in ten seconds or less. In one of his offices, the figure was 9 percent. "We decided to put an effort in there to see if we could move that. Essentially, we started by just telling the operators that there were ways we could handle some of our calls—like calls to the police department and other frequently called numbers—very quickly. That is, by memorizing the numbers, quoting them by what we call confirmed memory. There is a list of frequently called numbers in front of the operators. The customer wants the number for the police, so the operator quotes the number from memory, and she puts a marker up under the number to confirm that her memory is right. You're maintaining the quality of the quoting, and at the same time getting it out quickly." That little skill, plus a lot of feedback on her performance and positive comments from the boss, jumped the figure from 9 percent of calls finished in ten seconds to 19 percent finished in ten seconds. It took four months to double the rate.

Sometimes, says Grady, it's not easy to get bosses to make a lot of positive comments and ignore little errors. "Bosses are pretty well trained to be nit-pickers and fault-finders. At least they are here. We don't really have a training program called nit-picking and fault-finding. It's called problem solution, which means nit-picking and fault-finding. It is almost a superhuman effort sometimes to get people not to do that. . . ."

In his years of behavior mod, Grady has put together a number of rules for successfully modding employees. There are five guidelines: One is being ready to aim higher, work harder, expect success from what you're doing. That's "achievement orientation." Second is target-setting. You must set goals and they must be quite specific and measurable. Three is feedback, letting the workers know *exactly* how they are doing. Grady comments that having this one without number two is a hell of a nifty system for continuing mediocrity. Number four is positiveness. If you've got the others going, he says, this one is crucial. If you're setting goals and aiming for them, but also are rough or punishing with the workers, you are going to have a disaster. "It can be horrible," he says. "I have seen people learning to cheat, lie, sandbag objectives, go hide in their shell, or quit. You can push performance down with negativity."

Item number five is: Establish a managerial philosophy. Under this item he's got another long list. He figures that a good way to test whether you really know what you're doing and what you want is if you can write it down succinctly.

This philosophy list reflects the sharp optimism of behavior mod. It points up the malleability of people and problems. Number one on this list is "Excellence is a natural thing." He doesn't believe in the good guys and the bad guys, the natural performers and the natural duds. If you set up the right conditions, excellent performance is natural. About the people he ends up firing, he does not say they are bad performers. After trying a number of things, he concludes that he simply doesn't know how to arrange things so their performance will be better.

Philosophy bit number two is "Fix priorities." Decide which

tasks are important, and rank them. Bit number three is "If your job isn't fun, you're doing it wrong." "That means just what it says," Grady comments. "If every day is a pain in the ass, you're doing your job wrong! We define fun as the act of work being pleasant, or the result being a success."

The last bit is "Think breakthrough." "We call this the seagull approach," Grady says. It means going after new, higher, or unique goals, like Jonathan Livingston Seagull. For a salesman it might be setting his goal at 108 percent of last year's sales instead of the usual 104 percent. "That means you're going to have to change something. If all you do is set the goal, and tell yourself you will do it, while everything else remains the same, you're going to get 104 percent. You've got to change some approach or focus your effort on one thing. Kind of like managerial karate."

Behavior mod presents the businessman with an approach that is both radical and practical. Everything must be concrete and specific. Don't talk about the workers' attitudes; talk about their behavior. The employer buys a set of behavior from the worker. And that behavior will be good or bad, right or wrong, depending mostly on how the environment is set up. "Behavior that you thought depended on the individual really depends more on the environment," says Karen Brethower. "Before, you could assume that if you've got that bad performer, you could get rid of him and get rid of the problem. That's not true." That puts the problem of success or failure in the lap of the boss. Blaming the quality of workers is suddenly a very weak excuse. "There is the unsettling realization that as a boss, you are in control. That arrow that you're pointing down on subordinates gets turned right around. It boomerangs. You're the one that's setting the standards, communicating them or not. You're the one administering policies consistently or inconsistently," says Dr. Brethower.

Dan Grady puts it simply: "The issue of being a boss is this: number one, decide what the hell you want, precisely. Number two, when people are doing well, tell them how good they are."

In the classroom, educators used to blame failure on defective children. Under behavior mod, they can't get away with that. In business, it's the same for the bosses. The difference is simple: those with the power to do the controlling never believed they *really could* do much controlling. The mod squad has now pointed out that they have been controlling all along, mostly by accident. So they must accept the responsibility.

Another part of the plain practicality of behavior mod is dollars. Feeney emphasizes this. He talks about one video tape that was made in a customer service office to monitor performance. "The problem was that the customer service employee had to get up from her work area and walk across the room to get some papers. While she did that, the phones got busy, customers received busy signals, and a few eventually hung up. A group of people looked at that film and came up with twenty-nine different solutions, probably all of which would have solved the problem. Yet the problem had gone on for a year at this one office, and why? Because no one saw it. Problem-finding, not problem-solving, is the biggest hangup. . . ." When he says finding the problem, he doesn't mean finding *any* problem. He means finding the one that's costing money. "The trick is to find the few critical factors that have a big profit impact on a job or an organization."

At the bottom of the massive organization, with all its hierarchies, structures, requirements, places, and people, are small bits of behavior. Many of the bits don't count much. But a few of them are holding up great chunks of the business. Feeney once found a million-dollar pencil mark in the huge Emery organization. He declined to be very specific, for fear competitors would also find it. But he says, "On the loading dock, the man has thirty or more different tasks. Most of them he does on every shipment. He labels, sorts, and does paper work. And there is one little task he does on only 3 percent of the shipments. It only takes a minute—he marks the shipment a certain way. Our corporation does about $160 million business annually. A profit of fifteen or sixteen million. This *one* little task, that *one* of the workers does, *3* percent of the time, is worth more than a *million dollars* in profit!

This is leverage. . . . We got it up from 48 percent to 71 percent doing it correctly. We are working on getting it higher."

Mod squadders have not restricted themselves to the conventional in business. There have been a few off-beat answers from the behaviorists to the damned-ol'-assembly-line blues.

Tom Verhave began a paper on one of them like this: "Many operations in the inspection of commercial products consist of monotonous checking jobs performed by human operators. [Also] they require little manual dexterity . . . they require good visual acuity . . . they require a capacity for color vision . . . and they are extremely difficult to automate. There is however an organic device which has the following favorable properties: an average life span of ten to fifteen years . . . an extreme flexibility in adjusting to its environment . . . a visual acuity as good as the human eye . . . and color vision. The price for one such device is only (approximately) $1.50; the name of the device is Columba livia domestica. . . ."[1]

The man is talking about pigeons. Replacing workers on the assembly line with pigeons.

Verhave was in the employ of a large pharmaceutical company, doing research on the effect of drugs on animals. He took a tour of the drug plant some three years after he was employed there. He watched and was astonished by the problem of inspecting the twenty million gelatin capsules that left the company daily. The capsules were inspected by a squad of seventy bored women. Verhave says, "Seeing these women and their simple, monotonous task and knowing about Skinner's 'Pigeons in a Pelican,' I said to myself, 'A pigeon can do that!' Some time later I mentioned my birdbrain idea to a friend and fellow scientist . . . who supervised the electronics shop. . . . He almost fell out of his chair and choked in a fit of laughter." After the laughter subsided, the idea was booted around some more, and finally was set up as an experiment.

Verhave took his cue from a wartime project by which Skinner and his crew of pigeons hoped to do their part. Early in World

War II, the United States began developing a crude air-to-ground missile. It was a small, wing-steered glider. The problem with the device was that there was no guidance system. The guidance systems that had been developed were huge. They took up all the space inside the missile and left no room for explosives. So they called the developing missile the Pelican because it resembled the bird "whose beak can hold more than its belly can."

By the time the secret Pelican project was under way, Skinner had already learned that pigeons can steer a device toward a target quite accurately. By manipulating the schedules of food reinforcement of the pigeon, he could get perfect control of the birds.

During the first two years of the war, he devised a system by which a pigeon could ride in the nose of the Pelican, pecking at a screen, and guide the missile to its target. The front of the missile was equipped with a lens that projected onto the screen an image of what was ahead. The pigeon pecked at the target image on the screen. The movement of the screen from the pigeon's peck triggered the course corrections.

Skinner's guidance system worked perfectly. He demonstrated it again and again to scientists and military men. He had voluminous test data. They experimented in all kinds of conditions. But the scientists wouldn't buy it even after they had seen a perfect demonstration.

Skinner says, "The basic difficulty, of course, lay in convincing a dozen distinguished physical scientists that the behavior of a pigeon could be adequately controlled." He gave a demonstration to the scientists. "It was a perfect performance, but it had just the wrong effect. One can talk about phase lag in pursuit behavior and discuss mathematical predictions of hunting without reflecting too closely upon what is inside the black box. But the spectacle of a living pigeon carrying out its assignment, no matter how beautifully, simply reminded the committee of how utterly fantastic our proposal was. . . ."[2]

Knowing not only about Skinner's incredible guidance system, but also about the merriment and disbelief that greeted it, Tom

Verhave went ahead anyway. He set up a system by which the drug capsules passed by a window through which the pigeon watched. The capsules were lighted up, and the bird pressed either the "okay" button or the "defective" button. Verhave had no trouble teaching the pigeons which was which when the capsule defects were large. His first success caused a good deal of excitement among the company management and, he says, it "was a great source for jokes. There was talk about a new company subsidiary: Inspection, Inc. (company slogan: It's for the birds)."

Verhave eventually found a way for the pigeons to discriminate between good and bad capsules in even the most difficult situation—when capsules had two tops jammed on each other. On a tiny and clear capsule, even people inspectors have a hell of a time with this one. But Verhave found that if you shine a light properly, a capsule with one top reflects a single point of light at its peak and a capsule with two tops reflects two points of light. A pigeon could easily choose between the two if it was trained to watch for the reflection.

Eventually, however, the drug company higher-ups couldn't bring themselves to install the system. They were afraid of a bad press. Verhave writes, "One of them raised the question of possible adverse publicity. What about the Humane Society? More important, suppose salesmen from other pharmaceutical houses should tell doctors not to buy any of our products: 'Who would trust medicine inspected by pigeons?' "

When the company dumped Verhave's idea, he thought that would be the end of it. But no. The marvels of corporate America! After rejecting Verhave's inspection system, the company tried to patent it. "The poor lawyer assigned to the case almost developed a nervous breakdown. It turned out to be 'unpatentable' because, as the lawyers at the patent office put it (so succinctly), the method involved a 'mental process' which is unpatentable in principle. I tried to pin my lawyer friends down on what they meant by a 'mental process.' I suggested that the pigeon was merely an organic computer. However, I got nowhere. Lawyers apparently want no part of either physicalism or behaviorism."

Verhave is not the only one to have worked with pigeons as quality-control inspectors. William Cumming pulled off a similar feat when he taught pigeons to inspect diodes for defects. The birds performed remarkably well. In fact, during the early part of the experiment they worked too well for the humans in the experiment. To test the birds, a regular inspector checked each one of the diodes that the bird checked. The bird-man pair watched diodes together for an hour at a time in the beginning. To test the bird's durability, they upped it to four hours at a stretch. The bird tapped away accurately (less than 1 percent error) and without pause. But the bird's assistant "reported that for a human operator to examine these diodes for four hours caused the head to reel and the eyes to swim."

When the business of America was business, and not behavior, the issue of manipulation amounted to little. Attempts to abuse workers were obvious and crude. The issues were clearer. A technology of behavior make the issues fuzzier. It changes some of the rules.

As Dan Grady points out, attacks on the manipulation in behavior mod are usually misguided missiles. They aim at the wrong targets. "People say it's manipulative. They say, 'You're telling people they're good only so they'll get better!' Which is exactly why we do it. There is a fairness in that. If people enjoy doing things well, if excellence is a natural thing, then are you not just helping somebody enjoy a natural thing?" Some resort to the argument that it can't really work. "Some say it's sissylike. Big people don't like having their boss tell them they are good. I try to relate that to the stickers on football helmets. You know, a 280-pound tackle does a good job and he gets a sticker for his hat. He seems to enjoy that. . . . Others say, 'Well, can it work with people from the inner city?' You could just as well ask, 'Is it good with midgets?' It works with people."

Karen Brethower says that she felt it was important for her to face the issue of manipulation squarely before she could start teaching people to control behavior. Her thoughts, her worries, run like this: "We in fact control each other all the time. An employer controls an employee and has a contract to do so when the employee signs his contract. You are contracting for performance. If you are my employer, you and I are in collusion to try to get that performance. Insofar as my job is concerned, I have granted you a certain amount of control over me.

"So the issue is not between control and noncontrol. The issue is between *premeditated* control and . . . *unintentional* control."

She points out that the reason people have not worried about the control that has been going on everywhere, all the time, is that most of it was accidental. The employer Grady mentioned who forced his employees into lying and cheating did not know what he was doing. People have assumed that a person's behavior was actually being controlled mostly from within himself. But that is much less true than we thought. Now that we know that, and have some tools to do the controlling, control is an issue.

"We are not creating many problems that don't exist already," says Dr. Brethower. "The problem of control is important, but I think it's already there." Behavior mod simply magnifies the problem because it is so effective. "When you have control that is effective, what is a reasonable goal? You can get *anything* you want. What is it you *really* want?"

As it was for teachers in the classrooms, so it is for businessmen. They often want to change the things that irritate them most. Not the things that are important, or the things the worker or student would want to change. Perhaps workers would rather have their schedules quite flexible so their eight hours of work could be early, late, or spread out according to their own desires. Perhaps they would like to be judged only on output and performance, not on the hundred things employers seem to care about. Behavior mod in the hands of the workers might be a quite different thing from behavior mod in the hands of the executives. Who has the right to make the decisions? The issue is not being negotiated. The executive buys the services of the behavior modifier. He buys along with the services the power to make all the decisions.

6. Courtesy of the U. S. Government

Suppose, just for a moment, that beneath the bright exteriors of the young mod squadders there really are some hunchbacked-wart-infested-evil-scientist plots. Suppose a dozen controllers with that incurable twitch for power are meeting, now, in some secret mountain cabin. There, amid piles of rat-behavior charts, rows of cumulative recorders, and reams of human-foibles data, they are designing an environment. They are creating blueprints for a system that would produce the most terrible, violent, and antisocial people possible.

In the first few minutes of the job, the controllers would agree on a few basics. The environment should be populated by criminals. It should be a closed-in area, separated from all the natural reinforcements of the world. The environment itself should be stripped of reinforcing goodies like liquor and easy chairs. What privileges there are should be given to the inhabitants at the beginning, and then removed, one by one. Once the basic plan is set, the shapers would wire up the little world with payoffs for behavior that would drive the inhabitants to outrageous and bizarre behavior. From experiments with rats, pigeons, and mental patients, the shapers know that an environment can be maintained by punishment. And using punishment has side effects: avoidance behavior, such as lying and cheating, and aggression.

So in the perfectly designed destructive environment, the behaviorists would eliminate reinforcers and use punishment. Everything could be set in negative terms. Then the final coup would be delivered. Not only do you use punishment, but the aggression and avoidance that come from punishment would also be punished. With all those components, you have a first-class training school for terrible behavior.

Mod squadders don't have to sit down to design this worst of all possible environments. It already exists—in the nation's prisons.

Dr. Mike Milan is tall, but he doesn't look it as he slumps down in his office chair. He is a young man, and wears his light-colored hair in a great round bush, with matching thick mustache. He started his career in the mod squad working at Draper prison in Elmore, Alabama. He is now designing a token environment at a reform school near Montgomery. His work cubicle is on the reform school grounds, in an office building designed to look like a white-columned Southern mansion. The building lies on flat ground, stubbled with patches of trees and brush, a few hundred yards from the road, and about an equal distance from the "kids' " area.

Milan has looked at prisons from the inside for several years. The neatness of the terrible system impresses him.

"The prisons could not be any better designed to produce criminals than they are now. It's a beautiful system. It's like Nate Azrin and Harold Cohen and all those guys—if we all got together and said, 'Let us design the best possible system to breed crime, antisocial behavior, and maladaptive tendencies'—it's like we all got together and did it, rather than it just evolving and happening by chance.

"The system is magnificent! They do everything backward! They do everything they can to breed hostility. They *force* the offender to acquire new antisocial skills. What do they do? There are so many things, where do you begin? The man comes into the institution, and *every* potential backup reinforcer available is bestowed upon him. Everything! All the visiting privileges; he knows when he's expected to get out; mailing privileges; telephone privileges. Everything is given to him. And what happens? You give everything freely when the man comes into the system, you have only one kind of control procedure left. And that is to take things away. He fouls up? Well, we'll take away some good time. We'll restrict this privilege, restrict that privilege. That's a punishment model. The only reason people do anything is punishment."

In addition, he says, even the pure punishment model is maddeningly inconsistent. "There are no established criteria, so you're always in a state of flux. The officer who smiled at you when you did something yesterday is just as likely to write a disciplinary report when you do the *same thing* today. Who knows why? There is no way to predict when these bad things are going to happen. That breeds a lot of frustration. Some people can be written up for virtually nothing, and others can do virtually anything and not experience any consequences!"

Also, many systems, including Draper, have a real-money economy. The prisoners are allowed to have a limited amount of cash with which they can purchase items from a little store and a snack bar.

"Some people have a source of money. The family sends in twenty dollars a week. A lot of people don't have any source of money. So you've got the 'haves,' guys who are virtually immune to anything that goes on inside the institution because they have money. They can *buy* just about anything they want. *Anything,* except a woman. Then you have the guys who are the 'have-nots.' They have to go to some kind of a hustle, some money-making operation, which is frowned upon or illegal in the institution. Like voluntary homosexuality. It's the only way the guy can get half a dollar. So you have the 'haves,' who can go through virtually unaffected because of the power they have in their money, and the 'have-nots,' who resort to crime or degrading personal acts to raise the quality of their life. That's just shit!"

Milan, still slouching in his chair, pauses for a question. When punishment is administered carefully, he says, it works. But there are enormous hazards. "What are the side effects of a system that thrives on punishment? You breed inaction and passivity. And more important, you breed antisocial and aggressive behavior."

Milan sits up straight, leans over his desk, and pulls out a thick data book from the project at Draper prison. He opens to a page of graphs. "Here we are! Here is the example par excellence. Here are three complexes of behavior we were looking at. One is cleaning up the living area, making the bed, and personal appearance. This other one is work assignments: mopping the floors in the corridor, cleaning the commode, etc. These two kinds of things were not of great concern to me, but they were of great concern to the people who run the institution. They are the kind of things they employ the punishment model to maintain."

The two sets of jobs were not getting done; only about 40 percent were finished. The guards then used punishment systematically, applying it when the work was not done. Work done increased dramatically, up to over 80 percent.

But while this was going on, Milan and his crew were also measuring something else. They measured what they called "incidents," which were acts of aggression, insubordination, fights, destruction of property. The amount of aggression displayed by the inmates was low at the beginning. In a few weeks, there were only a couple of incidents. But when the punishment procedures were applied, the violent incidents popped up quickly. They began to occur more than once a day on the average.

"So on the things that the guards were concerned about, punishment worked," Milan says. They got much more work out of the inmates. Milan points to the violence chart. "Then we look over here, at the rate of fights, arguments, and destruction of property. When the punishment started, it jumped up immediately. When we *stopped* the punishment procedure, it dropped back down to normal. That looks like cause and effect to me. So that's the model! We are breeding antisocial behavior!"

Milan showed this interesting hunk of data to the guards. They looked at how well punishment worked, then looked at the increase in violence. They said, "Okay, let's punish them for the violence." "The answer they gave was to punish the things that are the *side effects* of the punishment model! And when you do that, I think, you get a riot. You have guards taken. You have people killed."

Punishing criminals by locking them up was an American reform. Public beating, branding, burning, and hanging awaited offenders before the nonviolent Quakers stopped it in Pennsylvania in the eighteenth century.

Like that of most reforms, the history of prisons is a curious one. It was clear very early that locking men up until they repented their acts was quite as cruel as earlier punishments. The caged men died or went crazy often enough that the prison approach had to be altered. The next step was hard labor, which grew a mass of abuses of its own, such as chain gangs. A combination of prison and labor gradually became the rule. Toward the end of the nineteenth century, another reform began.

This turn was to the treatment approach, which was based on the idea that criminals are by definition neurotic or psychotic. It was another humane step, but like earlier attempts it has so far failed utterly and smuggled massive new abuses into the system.

As Jessica Mitford says, "Recognition of failure dawns slowly in a bureaucracy, but dawned it has in California prison treatment circles." Prison psychiatrists in the California system, which is known for its progressive attitude, "admit that they now spend 90 percent of their time on paperwork, writing up reports for the Adult Authority based on perfunctory annual interviews with prisoners, that 'treatment' most often takes the form of heavy tranquilization of inmates labeled troublemakers. . . .

"Group therapy, once hailed as an exciting technique for trans-

forming the 'deviant personality,' is withering on the vine. Nor
have the treatment programs produced the anticipated docility in
the convict population; on the contrary, work strikes, hunger
strikes, and other forms of protest are now endemic throughout the
California prisons."[1]

Each successive wave of reform has rolled up, crashed against
the rocks of crime and prison, then receded. Each has left debris:
some sensible achievements, some cruel practices. A mixture of
punishment and confinement, hard labor, and treatment now slosh
around together in the American prison system.

But the system has come to an important pass. We are uncomfortable with, but have not given up, the view of prisons as the
place where society's righteous wrath is delivered to unfit men.
Echoing through our theories, ideas, and talk of crime and punishment is the muscular eloquence of Thomas Carlyle: "Caitiff . . .
we hate thee . . . not with a diabolic but with a divine hatred. As
a palpable deserter from the ranks where all men, at their eternal
peril, are bound to be . . . We solemnly expel thee from our
community; and will, in the name of God, not with joy and exulta-
tion, but with sorrow as stern as thy own, hang thee Wednesday
next."[2]

We are not ready to abandon Carlyle, but almost. He represents
the belief that each man operates as if he had complete freedom of
will. Caitiff freely chooses evil, and justice is done when he is
condemned and firmly punished. We would move from this position to a more modern one if somehow the modern approach were
practical. Edward Sachar sketches the modern view this way:
"The goals of the behavioral sciences are the understanding and
manipulation of behavior. For these ends, the concept of free will,
whatever its value in constructing systems of morality, is of no use.
On the contrary, it is necessary to postulate that behavior and the
thought of men are determined in accordance with discoverable
laws. . . . It may be that in many areas men have a largely free
and 'undetermined' choice, but the scientific exploration of behavior cannot begin unless that notion is excluded, just as in physics
the notion of the 'miraculous' is excluded. Knowledge of certain

aspects of behavior may be 'indeterminable,' that is, unascertainable. The laws of behavior become then, like all scientific law, statements of probability."[3]

This view of behavior, present in both behavior mod and other forms of psychology, is the way we would like to turn. But all forms of treatment delivered to the system so far have failed in the first step. They simply could not demonstrate that man's behavior *is* lawful. They have certainly tried, but could not find the causes of behavior, and could not change it. (Behavior in prisons has been changed, of course, with heavy doses of tranquilizer drugs. But this is essentially the same as applying a baseball bat to the prisoner's head. Nothing new here.)

Behavior modification grows up from the same scientific ground as other forms of psychology; it declares that man's behavior is lawful. More than that, the mod squad can demonstrate it and has done so. Behavior mod changes behavior. And has proof.

Behavior mod is the reform, then, that justifies all the talk of humane treatment and scientific approach. Forgetting our sad history of reforms for a moment, we should look at the pure theory of behavior mod. It is clear and logical. It begins with the question: What do you want? What do you expect to accomplish with prisoners and prisons? The usual answers are far too vague to be of any use at all. "When we look at corrections as a process which you subject people to," says Mike Milan, "it now has no objectives, nor standards. We don't know what the objectives are. We don't know when they have been met. We have some kind of fuzzy attitude about, well, he seems to be doing better, we'll let him out. The prisoner doesn't know what he's supposed to do. The staff doesn't know what he's supposed to do, either. The judges don't know what the institutions can and can't accomplish. The behavioral technology allows us to specify all these kinds of things."

There are three possibilities for criminals. The first is deterrent: Keep them from doing it again. The second is punishment: Knock the hell out of the bastards; they deserve it. The third is treatment: They're defective; let's fix them.

The behaviorists tell us we should forget the first one. Nearly all the data we have from hundreds of years' experience say that punishment does not deter crime. When punishments were most brutal and were done publicly, three hundred years ago, observers complained that public executions of thieves usually drew a squad of pickpockets who plied their trade while the horrible consequences were being displayed before their eyes. We have an enormous number of prisoners now who are punished once, twice, three times, and still don't give up their criminal behavior. The behavioral explanation of this is simple. The immediate consequences of behavior are the most powerful. If, each time a man stole, he were punished within seconds of the action, punishment would be effective. But if punishment is only occasional and is delivered weeks, months, or years after the offense, it cannot have an effect on most criminals. Dr. Milan's boss at both Draper and the reform school, Dr. John McKee, recalls a study from Holland:

"A few years ago, Holland announced to the world that it had a phenomenal change in the number of people in prisons. It dropped by half, and they maintained it over a period of a year or two. Correctional officials in other countries were just *amazed*. How in the world did they do that? It's great. We'll send teams over there to study that. Holland officials just wrote back, saying, 'Save your transportation over here. We can write you a few sentences and tell you what we did.' The judges all got together in Holland, and they decided that instead of giving long sentences, nobody would get a sentence of more than three or four years. No matter what he did. Most sentences were cut down to something under a year. They did careful studies of the consequences in the community. There was *no* increase in crimes. No increase in murder, or any kind of heinous crimes. No increases in robbery, burglary, grand larceny, and the like."

For those who follow Carlyle, and seek moral revenge, then the problem is of a different order. We may satisfy our sense of justice with punishment. But Carlyle could not see the mod squad's data. Using the punishment model, the criminal will get worse and the prisons will breed problems.

The third possibility is treatment, fixing the deviants. What information has been developed by the mod squad on this matter shows that whatever fixing goes on in our current system disappears when the prisoner goes home. Fixing the environment within the prison with behavior mod may make a crowd of nice, sociable prisoners. But when they are back in the street, their behavior is controlled by the payoffs of the street, of their friends, their work (if they can get it), and their families. There is not much chance that what behavior you fix in the prison will stay fixed. If you want to fix a criminal's behavior, you have to fix it where it counts. The criminal must be plugged into the right payoffs at home.

That's strike three. The way prisons are working now, no matter which of the three possibilities they choose, they will fail. Prisons cannot lower crime, cannot cure criminals, and can only create more problems with punishment.

The mod squad, however, has some ideas for a new system. Mike Milan offers one plan that would put the emphasis in the right places. His idea sights three targets: raise the standard of life for inmates within the prison; give the prisoner some skills that will increase his options when he gets out; and give the man his first good experience with a job, family, and social situation. The prison, he says, cannot offer much more than that. But if the prison can do that much, it will probably save a lot of broken lives.

He suggests a fixed prison term for nearly all crimes. Perhaps it would be one year. Perhaps three years. Beyond that limited time, prison helps no one, damages many.

After the fixed term, there would be an equal mandatory term in a halfway house in the man's home area. If the man is still not sliding easily back into the community, Milan's plan would offer another year of *voluntary* service to the prisoner and his family.

During the first stretch of the term, a minimum standard of life would be set and unchangeable. "A minimal standard means everything from the kind of food they would have to the kind of activities available to them to how many times they can go home.

What are the minimal standards? Perhaps the minimal standard is you don't go home at all. Perhaps the standard would be you go home once a month. But let's decide what they are. Let's make *that* the base quality of life. Then from there you can raise your quality of life in the institution based on your performance."

This is, of course, the reverse of the present system. There is no set standard of life in prison, and what privileges there are can be removed as a punishment. Milan suggests, instead of removing privileges, adding others. "The guys with high school degrees would have a shot at operating the kitchen, mopping floors, or assisting in educational programs. That's how they raise their quality of life. The fellows who don't have a high school diploma might raise their quality of life by participation in the academic programs offered."

Under such a system, the inmate would have the option of participating in the programs or simply sitting out his term. Milan adds, "Of course, the most difficult thing is encouraging a man to begin. To get those first bits of performance out of him is the most difficult task. How do we get the guy who has constantly failed in school to walk into the classroom? We would say, 'All we want you to do is come into the classroom and sit. Talk to the teacher. That's all we want.' " After he is pulled in with some good payoffs, the job of shaping him into a worker is easier. "If we can't design those incentives, a system that fosters participation of virtually all the people in prison, then *we* have dropped the ball. It's not the guy's fault. It's *our* fault."

So the first part of the fixed term served in prison would involve intensive academic and skills training, plus minimum privileges. These things will not make the man less likely to commit crimes. "These things are necessary, but not sufficient," says Milan, tapping on his cluttered desk. "Even if they weren't necessary, I would do it anyhow, because I think it's a goddamn disgrace that the people in here can't read a word, except stop on the stop sign. Even if giving them these things had no effect *whatsoever* on crime, I would say we *need* an intensive program just to raise the quality of their existence. But I think it *is* necessary. It will help on the outside."

But it won't help on the outside unless you have a good transitional program. "We have to have a program that makes sure they use the skills and the reading once we provide them. We're providing the guy with additional options. The man who can't read has fewer options than the man who can. The guy who doesn't have any employability skills has fewer options than the guy who does. But there's nothing that we can do *in* the institution to make sure that the guy will take advantage of these options and experience the natural consequences of them. We've got to work with him in the community."

So after the program on the inside, Milan wants to put the prisoner in a place where he can start feeling the natural payoffs of the straight life that keep most of us going. "Getting him a job isn't the whole thing. We've got to train the man on the job site to be a good employee the same way we train the guy in the education program to be a good student. We've got to shape the behavior we want. Reinforce approximations on the job."

This is the second part of the fixed term, the halfway house. The prisoner was given some skills and academics, and, says Milan, "I want him to exercise those options, by God! I really do. Only by exercising those options, and becoming proficient, does he experience the natural consequences. I want to get him started." The job is to get the criminal hooked on the payoffs of a normal life. Besides working on making the man a superemployee, Milan says the behavior mod techniques used for families can also be important. "How do you make the family a happier place? That's what we're concerned with. I want the offender spending more time with his family, because spending time at home with the wife and family is incompatible with being out committing a crime. Same thing with his circle of friends. I want to expose him to a new circle of friends, give him the skills he needs to be accepted, and to feel the payoffs offered by that circle of friends.

"Once I've exposed these people in these various settings, so the behavior is their own, and the consequences are natural, what more can I do? I've gone as far as I can go. If the natural consequences don't maintain the behavior, that's it. . . ."

There is still a third part of the program, and this part is voluntary. "After the mandatory stay in the halfway house, then for people who haven't gone as far as we would like to see them go, we contract with them for participation. We supplement their income, perhaps. Or if, for example, we have been really successful in providing some services to their family, there is every reason to believe they would want us to continue on and provide more services."

Milan's plan is nothing formal. It's just some ideas he's put together after working inside the system and seeing what's possible and what's not. Notably absent from his proposal is the usual cant put out by correctional psychologists about diagnosis and neurosis. By the behavioral analysis, criminals are not sick. They haven't got mental problems. In fact, there are often more "mental problems" among guards and administrators than among prisoners.

Milan's vision is ideal. But the tools to pull it off are all available, as we have seen in earlier chapters. There is plenty of evidence to show that *all* of it can be installed and operated quite successfully. Except that . . .

Mike Milan went straight from college to the Draper prison in Alabama. At Draper, several behavior mod experiments were started under the guidance of mod squadder John McKee. They trained guards to be behavior modifiers, set up two token economies, and ran academic programs with Skinnerian programmed instruction methods.

The token economy was divided into two parts, the first for fewer prisoners, and for only a portion of each day. The second was more complete, and included 125 prisoners who were monitored from 6 A.M. to 9:30 P.M. This second experiment lasted about four hundred days. Each inmate got a punch card with numbers every morning. As he moved through the day's activities, he earned points and the appropriate number was punched out. When he spent points, the punch hole was circled.

The system eliminated the need for guards' usual attention to failure and stopped most punishment. The points took care of it. Also, work could no longer be assigned as punishment.

The prisoners were paid points for three types of work: prison maintenance, self-maintenance (making bed, etc.), and academic performance. Some of the data reads: percent of inmates arising on time (sixty points possible) went from about 70 percent to an average over 90 percent; percent of beds made (sixty points) jumped from a range of 40–80 percent to a near-perfect record; percent of inmates passing inspection (sixty points) increased from 70 to 100 percent on nearly all days.

For all this work the inmates were earning access to the TV room, games of pool, free time, snacks, cigarettes, weekend movies, etc. When the prisoners were first plugged into the system, they were cynical. Prisoners in this age have become quite used to "treatment" programs, to dueling with psychologists. It's a game to the inmates. In programs run according to the mentalist schools of psychology, the inmates had little trouble with the shrinks. The shrinks talked to them, nothing more. So the inmates honed their con to perfection working on the innocent doctors. But in the token economy, they had some trouble. They tried to con the system by lying and cheating. "I put my points in the box." But they're not in there! "Well, I put them in there, goddamn it!" Sorry, but they aren't there.

The con didn't work out well for the convicts. The mod squadders ignored their verbal finesse, watching only their behavior.

The Draper experiments were the first behavior mod work with adult offenders inside a tough prison. They were demonstrating some powerful techniques in a difficult situation. And they succeeded. But after a change of wardens and some other problems, John McKee and his staff left. Not long afterward, the prison was back to normal. "It was as if we had never been there," says

Milan. "Like dropping a pebble in a lake." A few ripples, and it's gone. No effect. Beneath the surface of business as usual, the foolish and brutal way continues.

Even while the experiments were going on, they had a peculiar bent. After the guards were trained to use behavior mod, they were asked to perform little exercises in behavior-shaping. The exercises were intended to show the guards that the stuff really works. In the prison classroom, behaviorists had emphasized positive reinforcement. But in the practice exercises, none of the guards chose to use it. They used negative procedures. In one experiment, a guard got inmates to show up for work on time by making them work an extra two hours during their recreation time if they were late. Milan explains that the guards didn't have many positive reinforcers available to use. Also, they were accustomed to using punishment.

The behavior the guards chose to change was also telling. They often picked out bits of behavior that irritated them, thoroughly trivial items: cursing, making "inappropriate requests" of the guards, tardiness. The behavioral staff found no cause to veto the guards' choice of trivial behavior, especially since these items really irritated the guards and they would thus be more impressed if they could control them with behavior mod.

McKee and Milan noted in a report on the guard training that none of the guards used positive reinforcement, despite a heavy emphasis on it in class sessions. The effectiveness of it and all its desirable aspects were carefully explained to the guards. But still they used punishment. McKee and Milan commented that this kind of situation will effectively stop any attempts to make prisons models in the use of positive change. The punitive approach, they complain, is too thoroughly entrenched. So, even in their program, which was to be an enlightened one, behavior mod ended up bolstering the status quo. More punishment.

The token economies set up were also given a peculiar twist by the prison mentality. The token economy was built around "those aspects of inmate performance *of concern to custody personnel,"* the psychologists said. Those items that "custody personnel" worried about and wanted a program to shape up included the making of beds, rising at the appointed hour, cleaning the living area, and maintaining what was thought to be a presentable personal appearance.

Focusing powerful techniques on behaviors like that is the *problem,* not the solution. McKee and Milan themselves point out that the people who design such programs must choose whether they want to serve the correctional agency or the inmate. Most prison programs serve the administrative ends of the system, that is, they attempt to knock the inmates into line for the prison staff. "Placed in the wrong hands, behavior modification could compound this disservice rather than remediate it," McKee and Milan conclude.

The conflict between serving the prison and serving the prisoners was never more clear than in the recent controversy over a behavior modification program in the federal penitentiary in Springfield, Missouri. Prison officials there chose two dozen of what they said were the toughest and most uncooperative inmates and put them into the program. They were first put in "deadlock." That meant that each inmate would spend all his time in a dark six-by-ten-foot room, only to be let out two hours a week for exercise, and twice a week for showers. From this sullen existence they could earn their way to more privileges if they behaved properly. They could earn the chance to eat meals out of their cells, earn the chance to work in a factory, and eventually earn the opportunity to be put back in the general prison population from which they came.

The inmates didn't buy it. Said one, "There's nobody here who's going to modify me." When asked if he couldn't just fake cooperation, the inmate said, "It wouldn't be no act, it would be for real. They're trying to get a program going smoothly by bribing guys. If you are playing a game on them, you are playing it on yourself, because they want you modified, and they don't care what makes you do it. . . . I'm refusing to let them impose their will on me."[4]

The inmates in the program, with the help of the American Civil Liberties Union, eventually got a court test of the program. The program was dropped in January of this year. Unfortunately, most prisoners don't get the opportunity to fight back when prison officials slap a program on them designed to make life easier for officials, not for inmates.

The Draper experiments were intended to show the power of behavior mod techniques in prisons. They did. They also showed, inadvertently, the dangers of behavior mod in prison. Prisons could be more foolish, brutal, and rigid than they are now if behavior mod is installed without reforms to the whole punitive Them-Us approach. If we go back to the behavioral analysis of prisons, the pure theory, the first question was: What do you want? Well, we know what the prison people want. If anything is going to be modified, perhaps it should be that.

A half-dozen other behavior mod programs have popped up in prisons, and most of them rely on the token economy. Some have been purer successes, like one at the National Training School for Boys run by Harold Cohen and James Filipczak. Others have stumbled into the old punitive approach even more than the Draper project did.

The problems of behavior control that pop up in every setting are enlarged in prisons by the authoritarian atmosphere. And the extremes of behavior control in prison are likely to be severe. One behavior control procedure used in California prisons (which grew out of the same attitude that allowed Draper's guards to use punishment on trivial behavior) provides an example. The California treatment used the principles of behavior therapy, the Pavlovian twin to behavior modification.

Some eight or nine years before the California prison experiment, Anthony Burgess wrote his *Clockwork Orange* tale of a prison experiment. The terror therapy of clockwork orange and the terror therapy of the California prisons are alike, even down to some details.

Alex, the book's protagonist, was tossed in a state jail for his violent crimes. There he was jabbed with a fright drug that sent waves of terror and sickness through him. At its screaming peak, he was strapped down, his eyelids pinned open, and he was forced to watch films of violence. When it was over, Alex was shriveled, meek. He could no longer commit violence. In the real thing, more than 150 prisoners in two California state prison hospitals were jabbed with a drug that made them meek with terror.

The drug used was succinylcholine chloride, known by its trade name Anectine. The prisoner was strapped down and injected. The drug moved slowly. First the man felt growing numbness in his fingers. Soon he couldn't move his hands or feet. The deadness crept up his limbs, and he felt himself lose control. His arms and legs felt like dead flesh around him. Then his chest sunk to numbness, and his head lolled uncontrollably. He was paralyzed. Then, for two minutes, his diaphragm stopped pumping. He couldn't breathe. His muscles couldn't suck for air, and the horror of suffocation gripped his mind. At the fright's peak, the prison doctor was not understanding. He was commanding, authoritarian.

In a phone conversation with me some time ago, Dr. Martin Reimringer, who administered the drug at Atascadero State Hospital, talked about the fright treatment.

"It's a frightening experience for the patient. And you're quite authoritarian as you're talking to him, telling him what he must and must not do. Usually two or three treatments straighten out these sociopaths beautifully. Your assaultive patients, you know, and that sort of thing."

How many patients got it?

"Let's see . . . between ninety and a hundred."

About the consent from the patients . . . there is an issue there.

"Well, all our patients are court committed. So we really don't need consent."

I see. It's standard practice then; prior to using any kind of therapy, you don't . . . ?

"Succinylcholine has been used for many years in surgery and prior to giving electroconvulsive therapy. This is just a new application of the drug, that's all."

About the ethical situation . . . is there any discussion *beforehand* of the therapy?

"At times. And at other times, no."

When you had a discussion, what was involved?

"Well, we would talk to the patient and tell him he was going to receive the treatment unless he straightened up, you know. And then if he didn't, ah, then we would just go ahead and give it to him."

I see.

"You know, when you can't breathe, you're really quite receptive to what people are telling you. . . ."

I imagine I would be.

"Yes."

How did this affect the other patients?

"It had a very salutary effect."

They heard about it? And how did they react?

"They heard about it. And many of them saw it. It tended to cut down on the assaultive behavior and stealing and whatnot that go on in a place like this."

What has happened since the first experiments? Have you been able to get into it again?

"No. We haven't now for some time. Sacramento [the state capital] took a dim view of it. I don't know for what reason . . . but then Sacramento's always screwed up."

They asked you not to do it again?

"Right."

Did they give you any conditions under which you might be able to go ahead with it again?

"No. We haven't asked them for it again."

About the patients that you've dealt with so far . . . have you followed up on those to see how they're doing?

"Yeah; some of them are out of the hospital leading useful lives. Others again are here, but they're behaving much better."

Do you think the overall effect was satisfactory, or pleasing?

"I think it was very beneficial, really."

You don't have any plans to go ahead and try to give the therapy again?

"We may, later on. . . ."

Another prison medical facility, this one at Vacaville, also used the fright therapy on prisoners. Dr. Arthur Nugent, who oversaw some of the treatments, says, "I don't believe I would care to have it myself. I came close to drowning once as a small child. I know what a smothering sensation is, and I'm sure that's what they feel. So I have a personal aversion toward death by drowning." At Vacaville, there was more care given to the matter of getting a prisoner's consent. Almost all signed a paper authorizing the therapy. But later, when thirty-five of the patients were asked why they consented, eighteen said it was involuntary. Eleven said they signed because prison officials asked them to. In *A Clockwork Orange,* Alex signed a consent form, too. He did so because prison officials asked him to.

Vacaville's Dr. Thomas Clanon didn't worry too much about the ethics of the treatment or the damaging effects of the therapy on the prisoners. He says the human spirit is resilient enough to bounce back from it. He relates a little tale from a Midwestern veterans' hospital that encouraged his faith in humanity:

A treatment similar to the Anectine therapy was used to condition half a dozen men against drinking. The men were given a jab of the fright drug, and at the same time were allowed to curl their nostrils around the scent of their favorite liquor. After the therapy, any time the men smelled a glass of comfort, they would get frightened, their pulses would quicken, palms sweat. One day, the men got together and decided jointly that they'd had enough. They didn't like being scared of the bottle. To hell with this noise, the vets said, and they sneaked out of the hospital for the nearest bar. They stood at the bar pushing and jibing each other into drinking. And drinking. And drinking.

"They kept on drinking until they broke the conditioning," Clanon says, "which I thought was a triumph of the human spirit. It gave me confidence that people are not as suggestible as science fiction writers suppose."

The prisons are not the only field under government control that has got a dose of behavior mod. It is spreading rapidly, and a few critics have begun to assert themselves. Some of the critics, however, have misperceived behavior mod. The broadness of its name has led them to confuse it with other approaches. Jessica Mitford, for example, applies the term "behavior modification" quite generally to Skinnerian theory and a half-dozen other unrelated approaches.* These misunderstandings are natural, but in order to deal effectively with behavior mod, we must separate the theory from the chaff.

It is true that the serious abuses of behavior mod must be taken as part of the field. But the discussion must not stop with blatant abuses. Ben Bagdikian, in a review of Mitford's book, wrote this about behavior mod in prisons: "Astute manipulation of reward and punishment in most prisons means putting men in filthy cells without mattresses, giving them rotten food, periodic beatings, bathing in Mace, and then if there is an end to complaints at such treatment, the possible reward of a real stainless steel toilet, a mattress, regular prison food and other signs of the value of mutual human respect."[5]

Concentration on the more obvious "filthy cells without mattresses" may allow the subtler uses of behavior modification to slip by us. The issue is control of behavior, not just whether filthy cells or pleasant rewards are used. The issue of control goes deeper than brutality.

---

* In *Kind and Usual Punishment,* she writes, "However, the mental illness theory of criminality, and its concomitant, individualized treatment for offenders, find instant favor with all sorts of unlikely bedfellows: liberal reformers, prison administrators, judges . . . and those indefatigable experimenters, the 'behavior modification' experts." Behavior modifiers do *not* buy the mental illness approach. They are quite critical of it, and have battled against it for years.

This becomes clearer when you know that several mod squadders have conducted experiments in "attitude modification." They have begun to study how people make up their minds on an issue, and how to change their minds. The research is still a little thin, but the researchers are not timid.

The problem of control in its largest proportions may eventually come in the military. Since Eisenhower's presidency, the military has spent increasing money and energy on social and political research. It is no longer concerned only with hardware and problems of national defense in the strict sense. As we know from the army's surveillance of ordinary U.S. citizens, military men are now concerned with intervention *before* a war, revolution, or riot.

In the mid-sixties, the Defense Department embarked on a research program called Project Camelot. As Irving Horowitz pointed out in an article on Camelot, "Basically, it was a project for measuring and forecasting the causes of revolutions and insurgency in underdeveloped areas of the world. . . . [Its] aims were defined as: a study to make it possible to predict and influence politically significant aspects of social change in the developing nations . . ."[6]

A crew of sociologists, anthropologists, and others were hired to do the digging. Horowitz says that few involved in the project ever questioned the notion of the U.S. Army's halting revolutions and social change in other countries. They didn't ask whether some of those changes might be for the better. Finally, a Norwegian sociologist raised the questions. He found one thing especially difficult to understand: If the U.S. Army can mess in Latin American social and political change, how come the Latin American countries can't have programs to work on the innards of the United States?

Project Camelot eventually turned into a public debate, and it was halted. But the attempt at such a project makes clear the scale on which behavior modification might be a problem in the future.

Military psychologist Philip Sperling has written, "Guerrilla warfare of the last two decades has seen [our forces] heavily engaged in a variety of tasks in which the peaceful control of groups and the instilling of democratic institutions has been the ostensible motive. Military psychologists, along with other social scientists, are doing research on some of the problems relative to this effort. The valiant efforts of Theodore Vallance . . . which ended with Project Camelot, are well known. *It is the task of the American military today to try to assist the local military in the maintenance of political stability. . . ."*[7]

A report for the National Academy of Sciences begins: ". . . It has been properly stated that the Department of Defense must now wage not only warfare, but peacefare as well. Pacification, assistance, and the battle of ideas are major segments of the Department of Defense responsibility. . . ."

A survey among experts in weapons systems conducted by the Rand Corporation has projected as a major weapons system the behavioral control of mass populations. The techniques will be assembled and ready, the experts estimate, before 1980. Will Skinner protest?

While waiting for the behavioral cannon to go off, the military has done a few things with behavior mod already.

In a very crude program in Vietnam, the army paid villagers with a ticket in a lottery for learning some propaganda, and paid off children of the village with candy for digesting the material. Considerably more sophisticated work went into a training project here. It was discovered that in past wars, less than 25 percent of the men in combat actually fired their weapons. Psychologists of the Human Resources Research Organization set up training procedures to overcome soldiers' reluctance to fire frequently and effectively. Mod squadder James Holland comments about this: "The deliberate use of psychology to overcome a man's reluctance to kill seems hardly compatible with the aims of our profession. . . . can we expect to see this training transfer to the streets of America?"[8]

The military sometimes profits by earlier mistakes. During World War II, the brass may have turned down Skinner's pigeon-steered missile, but no longer. Using behavior mod's perfect control of animals, military men have trained pigeons to seek out Vietnamese in hiding.

Bruce Wallace, a professor of genetics at Cornell, told of another animal program: "Sea lions, pilot whales, porpoises, and killer whales are all being trained for various tasks by the Marine Life Sciences Laboratory, a division of the Naval Undersea Center in San Diego.

"Consider the use of armed porpoises trained as guards against enemy frogmen. Upon spotting a frogman, the porpoise sends a signal to a sailor in a nearby monitoring vessel. Should no friendly frogmen be authorized in the vicinity, the sailor radios back, 'Kill!' The porpoise then drives the knife that is strapped to its snout into the enemy frogman. Porpoises trained in this way were used not long ago in and around Haiphong Harbor. . . ."[9]

The animals have also been trained to carry explosives: they are live, sacrificial torpedoes.

It was during the Korean War, before behavior mod had got off the ground in the United States, that behavioral techniques were first used intentionally by a government. During that war, and just afterward, the great brainwash scare was stirring. Horror tales were circulating about what the Chinese Communists were doing to American prisoners of war. These tales were totally false, but they seemed at the time the only plausible explanation of the propagandizing and treasonous behavior of the captured Americans.

One army psychiatrist who was on a team that reconstructed the events in the prisoner of war camps in an effort to figure out just what the Chinese had been doing describes some of the panel's findings:

"More than any other American prisoners in any previous war (and we have a good deal of data about American prisoners of war), more than any others, these men seemed to be acquiescing to their Chinese Communist controllers. They seemed to be taking more part in Communist propaganda activities than Americans had ever done in the past; the things they were saying, the letters they were writing home to their mothers and the editors of their hometown newspapers begging them to band with other progressive members of the people and stop this senseless slaughter of innocent Koreans by the profiteering Wall Street warmongers. This kind of thing coming out of Korean prisoner camps, written by our Americans with perhaps an eighth or ninth grade education, led us to believe something strange was happening. . . . We expected to find evidence of mass executions and systematic starvation, the wiping out of large numbers of men. . . . we jumped hastily to the conclusion that these men had been subjected to a rather new phenomenon, a process that we had been hearing about, largely a Chinese invention, called brainwashing. . . . we assumed that they used drugs of some kind to influence the men. . . ."

To the complete surprise of the army psychiatrists, none of their expectations were confirmed. The men were not at all starved, beaten, drugged, or brainwashed. Nothing overtly horrible went on. In fact, the men were treated rather well. They simply went through an educational program that used the principles of Skinnerian psychology.

"It was basically an educational program, and called an educational program. In fact, the prisoners were never called prisoners; they were called students. . . . Rather than being kicked, and beaten, and spat upon from the moment of capture, which most of them fully expected, the soldiers were taken to collecting points right after they fell into enemy hands, and were introduced to a young Chinese, usually 25 to 35 years of age, who spoke 1950 U.S.-style English. . . . wearing no uniform and carrying no weapon of any kind, [he] would gather a group of these young and fearful men . . . and gave them a speech."

The speech was soft and considerate. Part of it went like this: "We hope you won't consider us your enemies. And to prove that we have nothing against you, we have a lenient policy for your treatment. We want to offer you a position—a deal. And the deal is very simple. From you we ask only one thing, your physical cooperation. Just don't fight us. . . . In return for this we give you the following things. No work—there are no slave camps here. . . . and secondly we'll give you the same food and clothing and shelter and medical care that we give our own people, the best we possibly can. We know it isn't as good as what you are used to, but it's the best we've got."

The army psychiatrist continues: "Now after a six-month period, the Communists started a formal educational program that had a printed curriculum. They taught seven days a week, all day, every day. . . . After the lecture the students were divided into small discussion groups. Each man was required to participate in such a group and to put into his own words the content of the lecture. . . . He wasn't penalized for disagreeing as long as he did so in a thoughtful and intelligent way. The only requirement was that he must participate, and if he didn't, the only penalty then was that the rest of his group of 10 or 12 men simply weren't allowed to go to supper until they convinced him that he ought to take part. . . .

"They had athletics. . . . If you wanted to pitch for the baseball team . . . you did so because you had demonstrated that you were a worthwhile and deserving member of the People's Democracy—which means you have the right attitudes, you're learning the right things, and you're taking part in the discussions in education. . . .

"And for those who weren't interested in any of these activities, but preferred art work, or this kind of expression, they had art classes and art groups which you could participate in as long as what you produced was art. Now, pictures of girls, that was not art. Pictures of Harry Truman with bloody dripping claws gathering up his exploited tools of the imperialist warmongers and throwing them into the claws of death in Korea, that's art. . . . Now if you could think up stuff like this, you could take part in the art classes, and not only could you take part in them, but you got paid for such productions. We found these productions showing up in Communist literature all over the world. . . ."

The same procedures held for other activities. Writing articles, for example. For the right material, they paid in cigarettes.

To control the relationships among prisoners, and to ensure that there were no conspired escapes, the Chinese developed an informant system. "We found that they encouraged informing publicly and promptly rewarding the man who informed, as long as he didn't inform in a vicious or nasty way. . . . And so, when you saw Joe Dokes swiping a turnip and eating the whole thing himself . . . you reported him purely out of your honest desire to see him helped to become a more worthwhile member of the people. Then you were in; then you got rewarded. Again, with cigarettes and candy and money and also with status and publicly given approval expressed by the Chinese in front of the other students . . . We can identify one American who was an informer out of every ten surviving Americans. We've never seen anything like this before. . . .

". . . they did the only protective thing they could do in such a situation; they began to withdraw from one another. They began insulating themselves against other people. . . . they began to withdraw, in a word, into the most magnificently constructed solitary confinement cell that any dictator has ever dreamed up. And in this one you don't have any steel or concrete floor, and it can't be fought like a steel and concrete confinement cell. And it's built by an expert; it's built by the prisoner. It's maintained by the prisoner. . . ."[10]

Don Whaley and Richard Malott comment about the Chinese techniques: "Many of our leading psychiatrists, physicians, and psychologists made wild guesses as to what fantastic means must have been employed to bring about the vast changes in behavior which were observed in our returning prisoners of war. . . . [But] the types of things which had been done to them seemed simple, almost humane, and had not appeared to be directed toward 'breaking' them or reducing them to the form of lower animals. Upon analysis, it was found that the techniques were basic and simple principles of operant psychology. Almost all of the important behavior changes were brought about by the use of reinforcement in the form of cigarettes, sweets, or privileges. These reinforcers were dispensed when the soldiers showed desirable behavior."

Whaley and Malott conclude their comments by comparing the principles of behavior to a gun. They say it is neither harmless nor dangerous, but is made so by its user.

But this argument passes over the fact that a man with a gun in his hand is no longer the same man. He has grown a powerful new appendage. That appendage has power and a purpose, and that fact to some extent modifies and directs the man's activities. When the spear was invented, man changed his pattern of life, his manner of hunting, his way of eating, to accommodate the new tool. Technology changes its user.

Whaley and Malott say that behavior mod is in itself not dangerous. This implies the hope that men will decide only to use it well, for moral purposes. History tells us this is a poor hope.

Among the recurring fantasies of the mod squadders is one about cops. Imagine, they say, a cop roaring up behind you in traffic and pulling you over. He stalks up to the car. He writes in a little book. Then he hands you a citation—for good driving. It's worth ten dollars and can be cashed at any bank. The cop smiles, and hops back on his cycle.

The idea behind the fantasy is that the role of policeman in America is the role of punisher. He spends all his time delivering hassle and punishment to citizens, because that's the way his job is designed. It is no wonder, say the behaviorists, that policemen are sometimes targets.

Why not design the poor policeman's job and fix some of the laws so he can deliver rewards at least as much as punishments?

Perhaps in an earlier America, when the policeman walked a beat in his own neighborhood, he was more than a punisher. He provided help in emergencies, counsel for the distressed, and friendly arbitration in disputes. But those things were not required.

Now that the policeman does not know most of the people he deals with, and does not live in the neighborhood he patrols (by car), he is a more distant figure. He naturally falls back into the strict requirements of his job, and leaves the extra services to the bureaucracies. The requirements of his job are drawn by the needs of the law: he must be a punisher. The law is an enormous list of don'ts, each one adorned with a threat. It's a pure punishment model.

The lesson of Pavlov's dogs fits here, say the behaviorists. To those dogs, the sound of a bell and a big dinner become so closely tied that the dog reacted to both the same way. For those who deal with policemen, it's the same. Hassle and punishment are so often paired with the blue uniform and the flashing lights that the two have become synonymous.

In prisons and Skinner boxes, punishment elicited aggression and fear. When those reactions get punished, you can expect violence. Perhaps the violence that trails policemen in America is explained by this phenomenon. The sight of a policeman, especially in some enclaves of our cities, automatically triggers some fear and aggression because cops are so often punishers. When the cop sees and hears this, he misunderstands it and reacts by punishing what appears to him lack of cooperation or a surly attitude. That punishment then triggers a whole scene: violence, charges of police brutality and insensitivity, and so on. Perhaps it also works in reverse: policemen have learned to associate certain types of people and characteristics with trouble. They react with fear and aggression, which get interpreted as cruelty and insensitivity. . . .

The cycle might be broken if the policeman's role were changed. But that would be difficult without some changes in the law. Can we have laws that reward people for proper behavior? Can we design a system of incentives?

The mod squad has already done it in at least one area. The problem that the mod squad took on was litter, which, like many another crime, has not yielded to burly policemen and tough laws. Mod squadders came in with attaché cases, charts, and graphs to solve, in two public theaters and in six national-forest campgrounds of the Northwest, a problem that had not been overcome by force.

In the theaters, they started by weighing all the trash found under the seats and in the aisles, and comparing it to the weight of trash deposited in containers. About .17 percent of the trash had been tossed in containers.

First, they doubled the number of containers. No effect. They began showing Walt Disney antilitter cartoons between features. Trash deposited rose by 5 percent. Next, they handed out litter bags to each person entering the theater. Deposits rose about 10 percent, but the doled-out litter bags themselves became part of the problem and the volume of trash increased.

Finally, they installed the behavioral program. They offered a reward of ten cents for each small bag of trash turned in after the show. Collected trash jumped to 94 percent.

Dr. Robert Burgess of the University of Washington was encouraged by the results of his theater experiment and decided to take the procedures to an open setting. In six park areas, the rangers were told to switch from policing litterers to handing out rewards to campground visitors for deposited trash. The program was aimed at children, and the rangers offered small prizes, Smokey the Bear badges, and gum for the bags handed in. The amount of trash collected jumped to about ten times what it had been. Immediately seeing the possibilities, one psychologist concluded, "Visitors to national forests will someday be lining up, litterbags in hand, to get their reinforcement from Smokey the Bear."

Besides getting the litter picked up quickly, the cost of the reinforcement program was tiny. The usual daily cost of cleaning the campground was fifty to sixty dollars and it required sixteen to twenty man-hours of labor. The reinforcement program did a better job, cost three dollars in prizes, and only two man-hours of ranger work.

In Utah, a similar experiment used a chance in a twenty-dollar lottery to lure adults into picking up trash.

The payoff approach to litter not only has succeeded, but tells us something about our other, expensive and foolish attempts to solve the problem—that they are expensive and foolish. Attempts to control litter have relied on tough laws, nearly impossible enforcement, local and national surveys, and ad campaigns. Keep America Beautiful, Inc., concluded in one of their reports that "publicity efforts led by Keep America Beautiful, Inc., and the state highway departments continue to offer the most practical approach to the problem of reducing litter. . . ." The report offered no evidence that publicity did *anything* to solve the problem. One quick look at the litter situation tells us that trying to change attitudes, levying fines, and dissecting the litterbug's personality simply haven't worked.

A dozen states are now beginning studies and programs based on the mod squad's work with litter. The studies also suggest that some of the social programs in the country could benefit from a behavioral analysis. The payoffs in the welfare system, for example, are delivered for all the wrong behavior. If two working parents cannot make a living, the welfare system pays off when the pair quit work and the father leaves the home.

One sidelight to the world of government and behavior mod has been provided by some creative behaviorists at the University of Alabama. It is a matter of common knowledge in Washington that congressmen tend to be lazy at the beginning of each session, and work feverishly at the end of each session. The Alabama behaviorists were intrigued by this phenomenon, so they decided to put some congressional behavior on the kind of charts Skinner used to monitor rats.

Paul Weisberg and Philip Waldrop counted the number of bills passed and the day of passage for eight congressional years. Congressional animals, they found, are like any other animals. They behave in a remarkably predictable way. The graphs for Congress match perfectly the graphs of a rat on a fixed-interval schedule of reinforcement.

When the reinforcers were given to rats at set times, the rats first worked lazily. Then, as the deadline approached, the rats began working faster and faster until the peak came at payoff time. The rats then took a break, and work began lazily once more. So it is with congressmen. The graphs of rats and lawmakers both describe a series of upward scallops across the paper.

For the rats, the payoff that precipitated all that work was a food pellet. At the same point in the scallop when the rat gets his pellet, the congressman gets his vacation break. The Alabama experimenters note that a number of other reinforcers are delivered to congressmen at the end of the session that may add to the importance of payoff time. For example, when they go home to constituents, they can talk about all the work done and bills passed.

The Alabamans noted in their study that they were only speculating about just what the payoffs are that get congressmen to behave on this schedule. They were reduced to speculation, they say, because Congress, unlike laboratory animals, is not "susceptible to experimental manipulation." Not yet, anyway.

Most of the anecdotes and cases cited in this book were funded by tax dollars. That includes the most terrible abuses. No one is now able to estimate the amount of public money that has been poured into behavior mod. I would guess that it is over fifty million dollars a year.

Part of the reason no one can make an estimate of how much the federal, state, and local governments are spending is that those who fund behavior mod projects many times *don't know* they are funding behavior mod projects. Since a number of phrases, such as "behavior mod," "operant conditioning," and "Skinnerian theory," have begun to carry some political dynamite on their backs, behavior modifiers have invented or cast about for other, fuzzier phrases to get their proposals past government grantsmen. Behavior modifiers are, of course, not the only ones who obfuscate in dealing with bureaucrats. It is simply a rule of survival in the bureaucratic tangle that plain English must not be used under any circumstances. It would expose too much fraud, fumbling, and uncertainty.

Obfuscation is more than just a pain in the ass. It is dangerous.

Behavior mod projects have been getting large sums of money from the federal government for a decade. But outside a few circles—educators, psychologists, and some bureaucrats—behavior modification is largely unknown. Whenever it has appeared publicly as an issue, it has been because B. F. Skinner has been bold. He has been speaking and writing mostly about philosophy and social policy. So critics typically respond that Skinner's ideas are horrible and wrong, and besides, they won't work. Pigeons are not like men. But these critics are writing about the state of behavioral science of two decades past. They are not aware that it works, it has been proved, and it has spread rapidly and been applied to practically every kind of human action. It has been installed on an enormous scale without any public debate over the real issues.

Montgomery County, Maryland, is a rich and well-educated county. The people of the county, which is bedroom to the nation's capital, are unusually alert to political and social issues. But a couple of years ago, a large behavior mod project was started in one of the public schools. Workshops to train teachers in the use of behavior mod were started. It was a year *after* behavior mod arrived in the school system that the school board and parents found out about it.

The large project had been approved under another name, and the board was caught entirely by surprise when a description of the program appeared in a news story in the *Washington Star*. After some quick shuffling and emergency visits to the school program, the board held public hearings. The disruption finally cooled, and the board determined that the program was valuable and was helping kids who were in trouble. They approved the project, which was already in its second year.

Perhaps this is the way of all new technology. The important questions are raised in the wake of its passage. But how deep into our harbor does it have to get before we ask the right questions?

We have always had at least crude ways of controlling people's behavior. We have refused to use most of them, and have regulated others. Why is behavior mod spreading so rapidly and unobtrusively? One reason is its subtlety. Controlling behavior with rewards and smiles is not as repugnant as controlling behavior with shotguns and lobotomies. We are hard to convince that control can be quite so serious a matter when the control is so soft.

Perhaps a more important reason than the fuzzy softness of the technique is the temperature of the times.

"We know one of the things going on is that this is the most crime-ridden period in recent history," says Dr. Daniel Robinson. "People want to be able to walk down the streets again. People would like to have some reason to believe their marriages will stay together; that their children won't be on drugs. They would like some reason to believe that the police force they hire will operate on their behalf. And when someone comes along and says, Look, we can get kids off drugs, we can get husbands off booze, we can get bed-wetters to stop wetting the beds, we can do lots of things; what is it you want us to do: we will do it . . . we now have a time in which many people will start saying, Do this, do that, do this, do that, do this! That's a long way from J. S. Mill, who says don't do a damn thing—it's none of your business unless you are *personally* threatened."

We noted earlier that behavior mod begins with the question: What do you want? Beginning with, that question plays to the urgency of the times. Beginning with that question allows us to skip over another question: Why do you want to control someone else's behavior; why do you think your way is better?

Consider two statements noted in a recent article by Stephan Chorover:[11]

"The average American is just like the child in the family. You give him some responsibility and he is going to amount to something. . . . If, on the other hand, you make him completely dependent and pamper him and cater to him too much you are going to make him soft, spoiled, and eventually a very weak individual." Richard M. Nixon

"There are people in our society who should be separated and discarded. I think it's one of the tendencies of the liberal community to feel that every person in a nation of 200 million people can be made into a productive citizen. I'm realist enough to believe this can't be. . . . we're always going to have our places of preventive detention for psychopaths; and we're always going to have a certain number of people in our community who have no desire to achieve or who have no desire to even fit in an amicable way with the rest of society. And these people should be separated from the community, not in a callous way, but they should be separated as far as any idea that their opinions shall have any effect on the course we follow." Spiro T. Agnew

Any behaviorist who would go to *these* two men and start with the question "What do you want?" is a dangerous individual.

Dr. Carl Rogers, the famous founder of non-directive therapy, put it this way: "Behavioral scientists, holding their present attitudes, will be in the position of the German rocket scientists specializing in guided missiles. . . . If behavioral scientists are concerned solely with advancing their science, it seems most probable that they will serve the purpose of whatever group has the power."[12]

So public money and government programs are training porpoises to kill frogmen, privates to kill less reluctantly, and prisoners to make their beds and stop cursing.

The mod squad is convinced that their technology can relieve suffering and make the social gears mesh more smoothly. They're probably right, but their enthusiasm moves them too quickly past important cautions.

Since government is already in the business of control, it is especially susceptible to urgent solutions. It also seems increasingly callous to questions of ethics. Behavior mod tucked in the social programs of fervent politicians is in its most dangerous berth.

We may feel comfortable about using behavior principles ourselves, perhaps at home. We may feel comfortable watching a behavior modifier give a retarded or autistic child a second shot at life. The power of behavior mod has its uses. But it is power. And perhaps we should not feel comfortable about seeing more of that in high places where the atmosphere is heady, and the understanding of power is light. Perhaps we shouldn't feel comfortable about it until we elect leaders who would begin their inaugurals something like this:

"People, I know that my work in office will be mostly to niggle in your lives. My government will muck about with your freedoms and your patience. Unfortunately, that's the job of government. You know this. But, people, I will do it with a sense of humor. I will apologize to you sometimes for it. And I will not tell you too many times that I am making a better, nobler world."

7. The Doctors

Some time ago I heard or read, I don't remember which, of a rat that had an electrode implanted in its brain. The fine wire was hooked up to the animal's pleasure center. In the animal's cage there was a lever on the wall, and each time it pressed the lever, the system turned on: the furry creature got a jolt of pleasure. As soon as the animal discovered this, it became quite attached to that lever. It began hammering away, sending jolt upon wave upon jolt of pleasure through its own body. It pounded at the lever for hours. Mealtime came and went; the animal still pounded. A female rat was put in the cage: no effect; the rat kept pounding in the pleasure. It did not eat, it did not drink, it did not groom or have sex. It didn't take long for the animal to curl up and die, presumably a pleasurable death.

Since the time I first heard that tale a few years ago, I have had a recurring fantasy concerning the future of man. It is a fantasy about what will happen to man when he has thorough control over his brain, when he is detached from the natural world that bore him.

It is an abstract fantasy. Absolute emptiness and loneliness of space. A man and a mirror are drifting, together, through the open, dark silence. The man is staring intently into the mirror, transfixed by an image. His head is bent slightly forward, his skull is opened, his brain exposed. His hands are fingering the soft gray folds, and with a small stylus he touches now this spot, now that spot. He is watching himself trip off thoughts, pleasures, images, watching them flood his mind. He is watching his face explode with a smile, then drop into a thoughtful gaze, then twist into a passion. . . . His brain is thinking and watching his brain being manipulated by his brain into moods that he watches and thinks about with his brain. . . . What will this man be like who can trigger a permanent bliss explosion in his head? Will he want to stop? What will food, love, moral sense mean to him when they can be turned off and on like great neon billboards?

When I had that fantasy, I thought it was one that could be the basis for a science fiction story set perhaps a thousand years from now. Perhaps that estimate was a little long.

Listen for a moment to UCLA researcher Michael Chase: "We assumed that the internal organs . . . the muscles of the heart, for instance, were beyond conscious control. Our assumption turned out to be wrong. Within the last six years, we have discovered that one can condition the processes of his internal organs, *and we now know that the brain can actually learn to control its own pattern of activities.*

"With simple conditioning techniques a person can learn to increase or decrease his rate of urine formation, to dilate or constrict his blood vessels, to raise or lower his blood pressure. This discovery fundamentally altered our perception of how the brain can be trained to control the function of other organs, and has suggested a new approach to brain research: *operant conditioning of the brain.*

"With this methodology, which applies the same behavioral principles that B. F. Skinner developed, we can teach the brain to alter its patterns of electrical activity. We can even teach it to fire one neuron and not to fire an adjacent neuron, or to alternate their firing in a complex pattern. . . ."[1]

Within the last few years, several techniques and bits of equipment have come together to allow researchers a foothold in brain self-control. First, there have been some developments in monitoring equipment and procedures that allow brain workers to trace accurately the electrical activity of the whole brain or single neural cells. Secondly, a new interest in self-monitoring of brain activity has been stirred, as evidenced by the bizarre craze in which people are buying machines to monitor their brain waves to produce the alpha, or drowsy, brain state. Add to these new turns the Skinnerian conditioning, and you have the beginnings of the field of brain self-control.

To begin with the blunter brain tool, the EEG, brain researchers have identified a few patterns of brain activity that seem directly related to behavior states. The EEG measures all the electrical activity of a large portion of the brain, and the machine's bouncing needle captures in pen strokes the rate of activity of a huge number of active cells. The cells together score the highest rate of activity when a person or animal is awake and active. This shows up on the EEG as small, rapid bounces of the needle. Theta and delta waves on the machine are taller, slow bounces of the needle, and usually occur during relaxed states. Alpha waves, the popular ones, are also related to a relaxed state, specifically a state in which the eyes are not active. When a person's eyes are closed, his brain is not processing visual information, and his body is in a relaxed state, his EEG would be expected to show the alpha pattern.

In conditioning EEG, very simple Skinnerian principles are used. As the rats in the Skinner box pressed a lever, got rewarded, and thus were more likely to press the lever again and again, so it is with brains. "The reward is the subject's feedback," says Dr. Chase. "It tells him that he is performing the task correctly. In the typical situation, both the investigator and the subject can see the response and feedback. In operant conditioning of the brain, the response, being an electrical pattern of activity, is invisible. So we hook the subject up to a machine that graphs electrical impulses. But these impulses occur at a rate of hundreds per second. Taken together, they result in complex electrical wave forms. We therefore need a computer, or 'black box' [biofeedback machine] of some nature, to ring a bell or flash a light to tell the subject when he has performed the desired response—that is, when he has performed the neural activity the experimenter wants. The bell or light provides the subject with feedback by telling him whether his performance has improved."[2]

By this procedure, a person can set his brain into any desired state of activity by self-monitoring. There are great possibilities for the use of such an ability. Dr. Chase has found, for example, that a distinct pattern of wakeful brain activity occurs during what he calls the state of inhibition. This is an EEG pattern that occurs when there is no movement of the body, when a person is in a thoughtful trance, perhaps daydreaming. When this nonmovement state occurs, the brain waves are a relaxed wobble on the machine, and other body functions also relax: muscles are limp, eye movements and heart rate slow.

Since this state is correlated with lack of movement, it might be useful in stopping violent movement, such as an epileptic attack. Some experiments to control epilepsy this way have already been carried out. "Also, if we can control the state of inhibition, it might be possible to control our responses easier. Rather than saying, 'I want to do that, but I shouldn't,' maybe by controlling the state, we can bring ourselves under more control. We might be able to prevent a heart attack if we are able to stop ourselves from getting so damn upset about something that we just fly off the handle," says Dr. Chase.

Monitoring and manipulating EEG patterns is a useful technique for controlling general states: excitement, relaxation, drowsiness. But it is a blunt tool. This makes it limited in the problems it can deal with. Its bluntness is also its danger. Change the general state of a general part of the brain, and the rest of the brain reacts, changes. The body follows suit. As Dr. Chase points out, we simply do not know enough about what these states are and what changes they bring overall to use the tool indiscriminately, as the alpha-wavers have. They believe the alpha state corresponds to a deep meditation that is the edge of enlightenment. It's a fantastic notion, and dangerous. Suppose it is just what it seems to the brain researchers—a sleepy, largely inactive state. Too much of it, then, could produce a lethargic, spaced-out, rather nonfunctioning person.

The brain researchers in recent years have gone to a much finer level of brain activity, and begun to control it with operant technology. They have worked with the firing of electrical charges from single nerve cells.

"This is done in animals principally, though it is sometimes done with humans in surgical procedures. You put an electrode into the brain next to a nerve cell. The electrode is just a simple wire that is insulated except for a tiny, tiny bit at the tip. When the nerve cell discharges, it gives off a little stab of electricity. The tip of the wire lying next to the nerve cell can detect this discharge. The wire then extends out of the brain and is connected to an electronic machine that will sense the discharge and turn on a light. When the light goes on—that's what the individual is trying to get."

Two kinds of rewards are used to get an animal to want to turn on the light (fire the neuron). One is milk, dispensed immediately after the light goes on. "The other reward, which is used just as much," Chase says, "is electrical stimulation of the brain. You stimulate his brain with an electrode already implanted in the brain. The point of stimulation of the brain is a nerve system, called the 'reward system' of the brain. It is incredibly pleasureful to have it stimulated. You stimulate this little pleasure center of the brain, and the animal has this most magnificent feeling—he will do almost anything to repeat it. So you can use this stimulation as a reinforcer to get him to do whatever you want him to do."

The brain men have found such a center in people as well as animals. Some pleasure jolting has been done to help get depressives out of their doldrums. "The human reports are that it's just the most wonderful, ecstatic, delightful . . . not quite sexual— they just feel better than they have ever felt in their lives. It's just like, wow!" says Dr. Chase.

Control of neuron-firing can be important because some nervous diseases, such as epilepsy, might boil down to just the misfiring of a small group of neurons. They might be brought under control with a little behavior mod on the brain. If single neurons can be controlled, it might also be possible for amputees to operate electric limbs in a manner very similar to the way a person controls his natural limbs—by firing neurons that activate muscles.

Another area of research that has grown out of this brain work is the direct control of the automatic functions of the body. The same feedback-reward system has been used to listen to and change heart rate, the production of urine, and blood pressure.

Though all of body and brain control research is in its first phase, it is now moving rapidly. Even now, says Dr. Chase, "With operant conditioning techniques, we can, in a sense, turn the electrical activity of the brain as a whole, or specific parts selectively, on and off like a faucet."

While the brain work continues in the medical labs, other mod squadders have begun practical work on hospital wards, untying a few of the knots in our health system. Among the more interesting work is that of Dr. Wilbert Fordyce with pain.

The feeling of pain has always been a mysterious event. Modern medical efficiency gets not much farther than the old philosophers in exposing it. It has never been effectively measured. We have tended in the past hundred years to associate it with physical injury or disease, but it appears at times when there is no such disorder. Sometimes it does not appear when there is. Even though it is elusive, it is quite important. Doctors diagnose and treat disorders after getting information about pain from the patient. It is sometimes the *only* thing doctors can use to figure out what's wrong and to treat it. But it is important to notice that the doctor is not dealing with the pain itself. He only knows what the patient *tells* him. The patient talks about pain, he grimaces, he makes motions. We recognize these activities as "pain behavior" because, normally, a person engages in such behavior only when pain is present.

What we know of pain comes from things other than the pain itself. We watch and listen to pain behavior, and assume that there is pain causing or eliciting the behavior. The pain and the behavior, however, are separate events. We know it is possible to have pain without the behavior, as Hollywood has shown us repeatedly with its stoical, stern-faced, long-suffering heroes.

But more important than the John Wayne syndrome is its opposite possibility: that sometimes a person acts as if he is in pain, when in fact there is little or no cause for it. This does not mean he is faking it. It is possible that pain feelings *and* pain behavior can be created or exaggerated without the patient knowing it.

A patient comes into the hospital. His doctor asks him frequently about his pain, the nurses attend to him when he has pain or discomfort. The pain behavior effectively elicits the attention and concern of those around him. In many cases, busy doctors and nurses are not much interested in other chitchat, not disposed to spend much time listening to a patient's talk about what he will do when he is well. So pain behavior, perhaps pain feelings themselves, are reinforced. Healthy behavior is extinguished.

"The behaviors making up most of the manifestations of pain . . . may be elicited by antecedent stimuli, for example, by the noxious stimuli of pathologic changes in tissue," says Fordyce, who works at the University of Washington. "However . . . pain behaviors *may* come under the control of consequences. They may come to occur only because they are followed systematically by positive consequences. Across the history of a patient's pain problem, his pain may have begun because of the presence of a noxious stimulus in the form of pathologic changes in tissue. If, however, his pain responses or behaviors were systematically reinforced during the early stages of his pain problem, it is possible those pain responses would continue to occur, if still being reinforced, even when the original noxious stimulus was no longer present or active—or was minimally active."[3]

Fordyce, who has spent several years studying pain from a behavioral point of view, says that doctors and hospital staff really have no way of telling the difference between pain caused by disorder or injury and pain or pain behavior caused by their own attentions.

In 1971, Fordyce began an experiment with thirty-six patients who had chronic pain problems. These were patients for whom all medical treatments were exhausted, but who still were bedridden and complained of much pain. Fordyce started from the assumption that while some pain is caused by physical disorder, other pain and pain behavior can be learned or conditioned by reinforcement. "When pain is treated as learned behavior, the focus is on the pain behaviors themselves. The measurement of treatment effects consists of measuring change in pain behaviors and 'well' behaviors. A patient would be considered to have improved if he displayed a decrease in specifically defined pain behaviors and an increase in the 'well' behaviors, which were the focus of treatment," Fordyce wrote in a report on the experiment.

The items counted and graphed for the patients were: the number of times physical activities were avoided because of pain; the amount of exercise done; the amount of medication taken; the amount of walking done; and the amount of time spent in social and work activities.

"The specific pain behaviors to be reduced or extinguished varied with each patient. The pain behaviors most frequently displayed were taking medication, moaning, gasping, or verbalizing the presence of pain by gesture or facial expression, walking in a guarded, protective manner, and interrupting or curtailing activities to recline or sit to ease pain.

"The activities to be increased (well behaviors) also were

specific to the individual patient. They can be grouped into certain classes common to all patients: one or more prescribed exercises in physical therapy, physically demanding tasks in occupational therapy (for example, weaving, operating a weighted hand printing press), walking laps in measured courses, and time in a work assignment at a job station. . . ."

The patients' spouses were trained at the beginning of the program in how to reinforce well behavior and extinguish pain behavior. The staff also was careful about what and when to reinforce.

Pain medication had been dispensed according to the needs of each patient; that is, each time the patient complained of pain and asked for a blast of pain reliever, he got it. So immediately following pain behavior two powerful reinforcers were delivered: the medicine that brought relief and the attention of the person giving the medicine. Fordyce changed this system so that delivery of medication did not come upon complaint. Recommended daily doses were determined for each patient, and the doses were delivered on a time schedule instead of after complaints. Over the period of the experiment, the doses were gradually decreased to zero without further complaints.

Pain had prevented the patients in this experiment from doing physical exercise, and kept them resting in bed nearly all the time. Attention is delivered for pain behavior while the patient is in bed. Also, any physical activity of the patient is stopped when pain behavior occurs, so that attention *and* rest keep the patients bed-bound. The first step to break this cycle is to administer attention regularly when the patient is not complaining, while trying to avoid responding each time the patient complains.

To increase physical activity, Fordyce and the staff first counted the amount of activity each patient usually put out before complaining of pain. They then set up activity quotas for the patients that were, at first, *below* the level at which the patient stopped and complained of pain. This way, the staff could deliver attention, praise, and rest for a finished quota rather than immediately after a pain complaint. Quotas were then gradually increased, with pay-offs still coming after completion and not after pain complaints.

Before the program, the patients had for months, in some cases years, been inactive some sixteen hours a day. After the weeks of the program, they increased their amount of time out of bed and active by several hours a day. Their pain complaints went down. The amount of dope they ingested for pain dropped.

In the conclusion of his study, Fordyce suggests that we need to broaden our concept of pain. It is apparently not caused only by injury or disease. It can be learned. And unlearned.

Fordyce expanded his behavioral analysis beyond matters of pain. In other projects, he analyzed the process of rehabilitation and exercise, which is sometimes difficult and seemingly endless. In an article for nurses, he explained his tack: "The way staff give attention to patients is as powerful as medicine, and should be planned as carefully. . . . Traditionally, nurses and other care-taking persons may be tempted, particularly when there are staff shortages, to give the most attention to the patient who makes the most noise. Many patients even prefer negative attention to having very little attention. . . . When sick behaviors are rewarded, patients can be predicted to display sick behaviors. . . . Without the patient or staff being aware that it is happening, the staff can train a patient to become sick, or to slow his progress."[4]

He described three examples, three patients who became hooked on sickness because the people around them accidentally encouraged the addiction.

One young nurse suffered a partial paralysis in her legs. Walking exercises were first attempted after her medical treatment was finished. But whenever the woman began walking, she felt dizzy and faint. Each time she was taken back to bed, and ministered to. After some time of trying the walking and always failing, the staff decided to try a therapy gadget. Since the woman could only tolerate being in a horizontal position, a tilting table was used that was gradually raised toward a ninety-degree angle. In a short time, the patient was able to tolerate being tilted up to a fifty-degree angle for about thirty minutes at a time. But no more. Week after week, she failed to get it much higher. At the end of a month of the tilt table, she still could not tolerate anything steeper than sixty degrees for short periods of time. The tilt-table sessions went like this: she was put on the table by a nurse, tilted up to fifty or sixty degrees, the nurse left for some time, the woman began to complain of dizziness and discomfort and then called the nurse, who talked with her for a moment, let her rest, then tilted the table again and left.

The nurse was then instructed in a new procedure. She was to stay with the woman throughout the time the table was being tilted up higher and higher, chatting amiably. As soon as the woman complained of dizziness or discomfort, the nurse was to cut off conversation, return the table to horizontal, and leave until the woman called her back for more table-tilting. After eleven days of this new procedure, the woman was up at ninety degrees for long periods of time. During the next twenty-one days, she began exercising on the parallel bars using crutches. She was discharged soon after she mastered the use of crutches.

Describing another common case, Fordyce detailed the problems of a woman who had injured her spinal cord. In order to aid recovery in such cases, patients must drink a large amount in order to produce 2500 cc of urine a day. The woman, like most such patients, had a great deal of difficulty getting herself to drink enough. When she didn't come up to the standards, the doctor and nurses began to talk to her about it often, trying to impress on her the importance of it. The woman still didn't drink enough. In fact, her drinking decreased a little. This brought a flurry of new attention, chiding, and advice from the staff. No effect. For four months, the woman managed to produce less than half the amount of urine needed. The more attention her failures produced, the more her performance declined. Then the procedures were changed. The woman was given a clipboard to record daily her intake of fluid. The staff said nothing to her about drinking from that point forward unless her chart showed an improvement. If it did, she was praised and encouraged. Under this system, within a month her intake jumped to over 3000 cc daily, sometimes even hitting more than 5000 cc.

Fordyce's third example was the case of a sixty-six-year-old woman who had a back injury. A back brace was prescribed to aid her recovery, but she refused to wear it. She said it restricted her motion and was damned uncomfortable. She had never had it on for more than a half hour. She was given a notebook to record the amount of time she wore the brace, and a graph was hung over her bed. The staff quit talking to her about the problem, except to make positive comments about her increasing tolerance for the brace and the increasing amount of time she spent wearing it. Within a short time, the woman was discharged from the hospital, and was wearing the brace an average of eight hours a day.

Dr. Mark Goldstein, a Florida mod squadder, has taken the next step in behavioral analysis of medical problems. One curious feature of the American medical game, he says, is that doctors and hospitals concentrate nearly all their money and effort on spot treatment, quick cures. A patient comes into a hospital needing surgery for a gastrointestinal disorder. He gets good care, a sophisticated operation, is cured and sent home. That's what we expect hospitals and doctors to do. But it's a miserably incomplete system.

There are now several careful studies that point out what's wrong with it. One of them studied a group of patients with chronic illnesses. In each case, after treatment was given, a board of doctors judged the quality of treatment given—the right treatment and medication, the wrong ones—and they included some patients who had no treatment at all. Then they kept track of the patients for many months to see the effects of differing qualities of treatment on the patients' problems.

They found that fine-quality treatment was just the same as no treatment after a few months. Some patients who had good treatment did not have trouble again; some did. Some patients who got no treatment improved; some got worse. Whether they gave the guy with kidney problems the right pill, the wrong pill, or no pill at all didn't matter; it led to about the same consequences in six months.

"Most docs wash their hands at the treatment door," says Goldstein. "We're finding out that while this doc can show his medical colleagues, 'Look, his kidneys are clear!' that has no relation to the patient's functioning on the outside. The patient could, within three days, generate it again. . . . If the stress in a man's marriage is great, the gastrointestinal distress he brings to the doc will not be resolved by the right diet or the right medicine or the right surgery. It will only be resolved by a new rate of response and reinforcement with his wife, plus the medicine. And the medicine may be less relevant than the gastrointestinal distress he suffers at the dinner table—during the screaming contests. One internist tells me, 'My God, I could treat these guys forever unless we resolve the major relationship struggle; they're gonna have surgery no matter what I give them.' A surgeon just came to me to do a behavioral analysis. He asked, 'How come I treat a seventy-three-year-old guy, cut out part of his lung, and he can't wait to get out and get back to screwing his twenty-three-year-old girl friend? But then I treat a fifty-five-year-old guy who's at the peak of health, who should have twenty years to go, and as soon as he gets out of here he croaks. . . . I know it's got something to do with his behavior in the environment.' "

So chronic illnesses—such things as cirrhosis, heart trouble, diabetes, lung ailments (like emphysema), high blood pressure, arterial problems—yield only very briefly to fine medical treatment. And our medical system is set up for the quickie treatment, a word of advice on how to avoid the problem in the future, and that's all. The patient is left on his own, to sink back into the environment and habits that gave him the disease in the first place. The problem is that to handle chronic illness, the patient must have some knowledge and control over his environment. If he doesn't, he'll be back, again and again.

"There's one study that shows the rarity with which diabetics follow their diabetic prescriptions," says Goldstein. "Here's this lovely diet therapy, they've been using it for years, and it doesn't work! Advising the diabetic on a diet doesn't get him to follow it. The question should be: How do you reinforce a person for following a set of behaviors, a diet? We stopped sending people to dieticians months ago. They have the answers to some problems, these docs and dieticians, but the behavior of the person following the diet is the only thing that matters in the final outcome."

With a large number of illnesses, then, all the fine treatment and advice amounts to little. Without the proper actions by the patient at home, the medical treatment is just a prescription scratched in the sand on a windy day.

Goldstein and his colleagues at the Veterans Administration Hospital in Gainesville, Florida, have studied the problem in their own hospital, watched the revolving door bring chronic patients back again and again. There are some 47,000 outpatient visits a year at their four-hundred-bed hospital. These are mostly the chronic patients, coming in once a month or less. These infrequent and brief visits do little for the patients' problems, but take up a great deal of hospital time nonetheless.

"They are continuous revolvers," says Goldstein. "They demand a disproportionate amount of time for no benefit or extremely little benefit to themselves. They consume enormous amounts of medication with no apparent benefits over time." The patients come in, wait in a long line to talk with the doctor, then try vaguely to recollect what's happened over the month. If their blood pressure is taken it's almost meaningless, because it's out of their home situation for one minute in a month. "There are 1,440 minutes in a day, times thirty days. That's 43,200 minutes. The doc sees him for twenty of those minutes, and has to make estimates about all the rest. The doc gives him advice when he leaves, about five to eight seconds of advice for each visit. That's supposed to last for a month. We've determined that the advice lasts about twenty minutes. No effect after that."

The problem, then, is to stay with the patient and monitor his health daily without putting him in a nursing home or some other institution. Goldstein and his colleagues have devised a system for this that combines the Fordycian medical analysis and self-recording procedures. Each patient is given a batch of behavior charts, and whatever equipment and simple training is necessary to monitor himself. He keeps logs, perhaps of heart rate, blood pressure, fluid intake, weight gain, urine analysis, exercises completed, etc. He then phones in his charting results daily to the hospital.

"We are saying, Hey, we want to know *every day* what activities you're engaging in, how much sleep you're getting. You call in each day, and our computer then generates some very sophisticated data. Each new point [on the graphs] goes in in a millisecond as we're talking to you. It instantly smooths out the whole curve statistically, tells where you've been, predicts where you'll be, and then tells us whether or not we should reinforce you. This is the point: 'Yeah, doc, I had thirty-one leg lifts and my knee seems to be getting better.' We look at the data, and we find that thirty-one isn't at all what it should be. We say, 'Okay, John, we'll call you tomorrow.' But if he says, 'Look, I had thirty-seven leg lifts!' the computer says reinforce that! He's definitely moving. That's a significant increment, that's where we want him to be. Then we say, 'That's great, John!' "

The total time of the phone contact is about seven minutes. The simple social reinforcement is based on the idea that the chronic patient comes into the hospital perhaps as much for reassurance as for pills and prescriptions. The patients like contact with the doctors.

Periodically, the reliability of the patient's graphs is checked to be sure he's not faking it. Several ways to check reliability have been tried. The most common method is to have a family member check on the patient's progress. "Wives and husbands are usually very good at checking on one another when both give permission and know what is going on. For example, number of beers in a cirrhotic. The wife will tell you how many empty cans pretty accurately," Goldstein says. For patients who need walking exercise, a pedometer that counts each step has been used. Goldstein has even tried measuring millimeters of shoe leather to see if he could estimate amount of walking by degree of wear. Essentially, Goldstein says, he looks for some checking system or device that will be accurate and will avoid the use of spies.

Of prime importance is the computer data and predictions. The computer projects an "envelope" around the data, a pair of lines that mark the low and high limits and project the direction and amount of change to be expected. "We set an envelope on the data to find out where we expect him to be in six months. We find out what would be good accurately, rather than just 'John, I want you to get more exercise, sleep a little better, eat less fats.' That typical Paul Dudley White stuff. It's all bullshit. Nice advice, but it doesn't work. We take a look at each one of these things, make it precise, and draw up a program on each man."

In some preliminary work on the system they found that they could shape the patients so that some 80 percent of their reports moved in the right direction on the charts, between 10 and 20 percent were static, and a small percentage moved in the wrong direction. The monitoring and reinforcement were able to cope with everything but social activity. Part of the treatment for alcoholism and cirrhosis, for example, is social outings with friends. The monitoring system, however, was not powerful enough to get much behavior change. Some 16 percent of the data moved in the right direction, 34 percent did not move, and 50 percent moved in the wrong direction.

Essentially, the whole system wires up the patient to the hospital. It provides extended service to add to the quick cure and treatment normally provided.

"The patient becomes the scientist of his own behavior," says Goldstein. "You have the consumer playing an active role in self-care, rather than robbing the data from him, which is the traditional way of doing it. We insist that all the data about his body be available to him, at home."

The hospital, like any social system, can make a good behaviorist despair. The consequences are all wrong. People accidentally get shaped into sickness and insanity when some simple attention to payoffs could create health. Dr. Israel Goldiamond of the University of Chicago got a close look at the payoffs arranged inside a hospital when he spent several months there after a car accident.

He described one patient who had come into the hospital with brain damage. The man was disoriented. He looked out the hospital window, saw factories and water, and asked, "What the hell am I doing in Panama?" He also had a habit of pissing on the walls of the hospital room. The room, Goldiamond noted, *did* look a little like a bathroom, with curtains like shower curtains between beds and bathroomlike tiles on the wall. But the hospital staff didn't see it that way. They confined him to bed. The man then refused to use the bedpan, and several times a day made a hell of a mess out of the sheets. Goldiamond observed that while the man often seemed disoriented, he was not always so bent out of shape. When it came time for meals in the cafeteria, the man functioned perfectly on his own. When the payoff for behavior was appropriate, he responded. Taking the cue, Goldiamond and a hospital attendant thought they might put together a little plan to aid in the man's urinary problem. Since he was constantly asking for cigarettes, they decided he could be shaped into proper urination if the payoff was in cigarettes. Each time the man delivered the full urinal to an attendant, he got a cigarette. The system worked well. Too well. The man, who was supposedly suffering from recent memory loss, had no trouble remembering the cigarette system. When he had a full urinal and the attendant was not nearby, he began searching for him in corridors and stairways to get his payoff. Unfortunately, while the staff appreciated his new urinary habits, they did not like his wandering. So they strapped him into a wheelchair. Instead of keeping up a urinary payoff program, they stopped it. The man went back to his old habits. The hospital staff then catheterized him. The man responded with rage, and seemed on his way to psychosis.

There was another patient, whom the staff decided to send home: the hospital had become too much of a good thing for him. To make it less of a good thing, they ignored him and removed his privileges. He responded, predictably, by finding a way to get his consequences back. He lay in bed all day on one side, and soon developed skin ulcers. These required frequent attention from the staff, and he thus got around the hospital's plan for his discharge.

Goldiamond consulted on another case, involving a man with a kidney ailment. His system had rejected a kidney transplant, and as far as his family was concerned, he was a terminal case. They were sure he would die, and were afraid that he would obliterate all the family's savings, home equity, and other financial security before going under. So when he arrived home after treatment, the family greeted him with the guilty hope that he would soon die. The man was back in the hospital quickly: he had drunk a six-pack of Coke, later a bottle of witch hazel. Goldiamond says, "The patient engaged in exactly the right behavior to get himself out of the home and back to the hospital, where people wanted him to live." The man need not have known or been able to explain his behavior, just as rats and pigeons don't know why they press levers. They just do it, and the consequences follow. Goldiamond adds, "We should classify him not as suicidal, but as highly desirous of life. It has occurred to me that this case would have been different in England. Because of the British health plan, the patient would not have threatened his family with bankruptcy. . . ."

Goldiamond saw incident after incident of payoffs for the wrong behavior. He wrote, "When critical consequences did not exist for a patient, or were not strong enough to maintain the difficult responses required to produce them, the patient was absent from the rehabilitation or lackadaisical while attending. One patient with nothing in particular to return to outside the hospital simply watched others, creating a social life of his own inside the hospital. Two others, who were involved in lawsuits where the size of the settlement would be determined by the extent of the injury, engaged in few recovery programs. Such cases puzzled the hospital staff. After all, people should *want* to get better, should *want* to stay alive longer. The staff knew how to make them better, so the patients should *want* to cooperate. When they did not, the staff would give them pep talks, and scare talks warning of the dire consequences of degeneration, show them movies, reason with them, etc. None of those tactics helped.

"The staff ascribed the negative attitudes of such patients to hostility, depression, or some other underlying psychodynamic problem. But none of these labels were relevant to the real problem, namely, the absence of consequences important enough to sustain the difficult responses.

". . . with current practices, institutions may actually be *programming* psychosis, deterioration, and debility."[5]

Behavior mod is only one of three sets of technology that, taken together, might be called psychotechnology. All three depart from the traditional psychodynamic way of looking at behavior. All three have been built up on a base of laboratory data, unlike the psychodynamic approach. Behavior mod is the only one of the three that is not essentially a medical procedure.

The other two parts of this triad are psychopharmacology and psychosurgery. Psychopharmacology is perhaps the most familiar; it uses drugs to alter behavior. Much has been written about the use and abuse of drugs by doctors, patients, and drug companies. Of the three, psychopharmacology is perhaps the crudest method of altering behavior, using as it does blunt physical states: tranquilized, hyped up, spaced out.

Psychosurgery is a newer and more refined technique for altering behavior. It is also thoroughly terrifying. Essentially, psychosurgery is a set of techniques for operating on the brain: cutting out, freezing, or melting spots that control certain behaviors.

The idea behind this is not new; only its sophisticated procedures are. As far as we know, the first people to think up the notion were the Romans, who observed that insanity might be relieved by a sword wound to the head.

Many centuries later, and with about the same sensitivity,

doctors learned that that sword wound should be placed so that it cut a set of nerve fibers in the frontal lobes of the brain. This, they said, allowed people to think, remember, and do most of what other people could do. However, the victims were usually quite numbed for life. Zombies, some called them. During the 1940s, a pair of doctors in Washington, D.C., found another bunch of brain stuff that could be cut up with the same effect. And they did so zealously. One of them, Walter Freeman, boasted that he personally performed the cerebral castration on some four thousand people. Wherever he went, he carried a gold ice pick in a velvet-lined box. After a little anesthetic, he jammed his gold pick through the thin bone in the upper part of the eye socket. A little wiggle, and the brain nerves were severed. Freeman zipped through this procedure anywhere that was convenient: the hospital, his office, the victim's home. Other doctors picked up the grisly Freeman technique, and it is now estimated that some fifty thousand people's brains were sliced up in this manner in the United States alone.

After the surge of interest in lobotomy, doctors discovered that drugs could apparently do the same job. Psychopharmacology quickly became a less messy way to produce the zombies, using heavy tranquilizers like Thorazine. It was later found that besides the mental blasting the victim receives with the tranquilizer, there are some serious side effects: blood abnormalities; occasional reactions opposite to those intended, like violent frenzy; and a thing called tardive dyskinesia, which means the victim develops permanent muscle spasms. This awful tranquilizing procedure is still in wide use, especially in prisons and mental hospitals.

But now there is a push back to psychosurgery. Doctors have found that behavior states can be controlled largely by dealing with the limbic system, the seat of emotions in the brain. They have also had much success in picking out targets that control behavior in this part of the brain. The pleasure center, for example, was mentioned earlier in this chapter.

In addition, doctors now have a good technique for their surgeries. They can cut a small hole in the skull and with a new optic device view a small portion of the brain as if it were great ranges of mountains. An extremely fine, almost invisible wire can then be inserted to perform the surgery. Under the viewing system, this fine wire appears huge. Since the patient is awake during brain surgery, the doctor can experiment with stimulating the gray hills to see what behavior he can elicit from the restrained patient. When he finds the right spot, he can melt, freeze, or remove that tiny offending gray matter.

While the techniques are refined, the results do not look a great deal different at times from the ice-pick-through-the-eye approach. The psychosurgeons cannot pinpoint a specific behavior and stop it. There is no good data to show exactly how much other behavior is changed by attempts to halt violent fits, for example. But the surgery is permanent. And worse, many doctors seem to have little desire to look for other means of treatment before proceeding.

Patients with a hand-washing obsession have been subjects of psychosurgery, even though behavior therapy has been successful in dealing with such obsessions. Psychosurgery has also been used on children who appear to be "hyperactive." Though almost nothing is known about "hyperactivity," though it may vanish by itself over time, though behavior modifiers have often been able to eliminate it by changing some consequences in the environment, some doctors have gone ahead and cut into the brains of children. One West Coast neurosurgeon has taken to performing psychosurgery on children as an office procedure.

That anyone in our society can perform such operations without quickly being thrown into jail or at least thrown out of the medical profession is a sign of our terrible and grasping desire to have a society that clicks like a Swiss watch. Our tolerance for people on the fringe of society is incredibly thin, and seems to be thinning more with each new powerful technique we shape.

Behavior modification is one of these powerful techniques. But with all its problems of power and manipulation, it is a pale threat alongside the butchery of psychosurgery and the personality distortion of psychopharmacology. In fact, looking at such things as hyperactivity, which has been attacked with each of the three psychotechniques, behavior mod seems the innocent, sensible, and humane treatment. At the least, it is not an irreversible physical disaster, a physical abuse, which the other two are.

In a century it will undoubtedly be clear that psychosurgery and psychopharmacology, while being technical advances, were used simply as means of torture and persecution of our unfortunate fringe souls. They are little more than new faces put on the thumbscrew, the rack, and the club. Perhaps behavior modification will fall into the same political trap. But perhaps not.

One of the problems psychotechnologists have failed to face is that of man's relation to society. A few, quite few, behavior modifiers have attacked the usual assumption that society has got everything in the right order. The experimenters who attempted to make teachers more tolerant of noise rather than children quieter, those who handed behavior mod over to the kids to shape their punishing teachers, have said something important to us about the possibilities for change. Maybe we ought also to try psychosurgery and tranquilizers on the doctors and teachers before using them on our more helpless citizens.

If psychotechnologies are really to be useful in making a civilized society, they ought to cut both ways. We need tools to afflict the troubled with normality far less than we need tools to make the normal more tolerant. Psychosurgery and psychopharmacology cannot be put into the hands of consumers, and they are unlikely to be used on the powerful. But behavior mod can go both ways, even though it does not do so very often.

There is a further difference between behavior mod and the other psychotechnologies that deserves mention. The foundation of behaviorism is that the environment and its contingencies are responsible for the actions of individuals. It looks for causes in the surroundings, in the society rather than in the person. This is important. It legitimizes social change. A behavioral analysis of the urban riots of the 1960s, for example, would look in the ghetto

environment for the contingencies that elicited burning and loot-
ing. It would assume that the rioters themselves are normal people,
behaving by the same laws of behavior as everyone else. But the
other psychotechniques begin by looking for abnormalities in the
rioters.

Stephan Chorover quotes a letter he found in the *Journal of the
American Medical Association* (1967) that passed over the social
causes of riots, and went on to suggest a search for "the more
subtle role of other possible factors, including brain dysfunction in
the rioters who engaged in arson, sniping, and physical assault.
. . . If slum conditions alone determined or initiated riots, why
are the vast majority of slum dwellers able to resist the temptation
of unrest and violence? Is there something peculiar about the
violent slum-dweller that differentiates him from his peaceful
neighbor?"[6] The letter suggested that brain disease might be the
problem, and proposed research to locate and identify the diseased
ones who might be prone to violence. Certainly these fringe people
would then be candidates for psychosurgery or tranquilizers.

We should acknowledge the better assumptions of behavior mod
over other psychotechniques. Then we must add that all psychotechnology has a weakness: it is used too often because of
expediency. The lustful desire to be quick and effective in curing
our ills takes a terrible toll among the helpless.

Goldstein's remote-patient care is an effort to remedy the disaster created by our overemphasis on quick and effective cures. It
is this sort of reform that we should expect from behavior mod.

8. Turn Yourself On

Behavior modifiers are, at first, hard to tell apart from regular human beings. But there is one characteristic of the modifiers that allows the layman to pick them out in a crowd. It is the "self-monitoring" syndrome.

The first identifying feature of the syndrome is audible: a series of metallic-sounding clicks. Locate the source of this sound and you are probably in the vicinity of a behavior modifier. The next step is to notice the wrists of those near the source of the clicking sound. On the wrist of the behavior modifier will be the certain mark that sets him apart from others: he will be wearing a be-havior counter.

It's a small (usually square and silver) metal box about the size of a wrist watch, most often attached to a watchband. Behavior modifiers wear two, three, sometimes four at once to count bits of their own behavior.

These behavioral physicians heal themselves, and nothing is outside the range of their counters. Some have counted cigarettes smoked, weight gains, and negative comments to friends. Some

171

have charted letters written, times teeth were brushed, hours spent working. Others have counted and graphed their sex lives: number of acts, number of orgasms (sex is apparently governed by the seasons as well as by romantic urges).

Ogden Lindsley, always out on the leading edge, has for some time been on a thought-counting binge. He's counted his sex urges, and got others to count theirs. "The first thing I found out about sexual norms and homosexuals was: My God, these people are *more* than homosexual. They're hypersexual! *And* homosexual! It was very common for these homosexuals to have 120 or 130 urges a day. These guys are in a frenzy! Eight, ten, fifteen, maybe forty, all right. But 120! Their real problem is not so much their homosexuality; even if they were heterosexual they couldn't cope. Their primary problem is the *hypersexuality!*"

Lindsley once charted near-future and far-future thoughts for a time. During the last couple of weeks of the charting he was in the hospital, and he noted that near-future thoughts rose and far-future thoughts stopped during the sickness. Lindsley disciples have left no chart ungraphed. "We've got charts of the effect of will," he says. "We've got charts of the effect of *prayer*. We've got charts of the increase in communication with God!"

One mod squadder said that the modifiers sometimes get a little overwrought with their clickers and charts. He told, only partly in jest, of a colleague who did a study of sex feelings and seemed especially interested in the charts of good-looking young women. The doctor would approach a young woman, saying, "I'm doing an experiment; would you like to help out? I'm counting sex urges." He might then invite the young lady up to his place some evening to go over the results. (You can just hear that pitch: "Let's see what your charts show. . . . Mmm hmm. . . . Yours are quite high compared to the men. . . . You have sex urges quite often. Your boyfriend [sentence drowned in muffled chuckles]. Your charts show a frequency of . . . Oh, that means you must be having a sex urge . . . right now! Oh!")

The techniques of self-control devised by the mod squad may be the most useful and innocent of all the behavioral technology. The tools are, by definition, in the hands of the behaver, not an outside controller. The tactics of self-control are a little different than those of most behavior mod, because some difficulties are encountered when the behaver must deliver rewards or punishments to himself. He can't very easily con himself; he could take the payoff anytime without putting out the required behavior. Giving himself the rewards or punishments on the right schedule requires some self-control, which of course was the original problem.

So, in self-control programs, behavior modifiers rely more heavily on two techniques: stimulus control and response-cost. When rewards and punishments are used, they try to rig a payoff system that works automatically without the self-control of the behaver being called up.

Dr. Donald Pumroy demonstrated the stimulus-control techniques with a musician. The musician complained that he spent a great deal of time trying to practice and worrying about practicing, but actually got very little practicing done. When the young man began graphing his practice time, he discovered that a minute percentage of it was spent in actual playing.

Most of the time was eaten up by distractions and other work. He had a cup of coffee, took a short nap, read the newspaper, worked on his tape deck, watched TV. He found both practicing and fooling around unpleasant because he felt continuously guilty about not getting enough done. Dr. Pumroy advised him to quit worrying. He suggested first that the musician should not expect so much of himself. He should specify a small amount of time each day that must be spent on practice, and consider the rest of the day free time. The young man decided forty minutes a day would be a good starting point, and he chose to do it in two twenty-minute sessions. Then Dr. Pumroy suggested the stimulus control.

He suggested putting one chair, the instrument, and a timer in the corner of one room. The chair should face a blank wall, and there should be *nothing* else in that corner. The idea is that objects and events are cues, or, in the behavioral jargon, discriminative stimuli, for certain behavior. A newspaper is a green light for reading, a humming TV is a cue for watching. Each item in the musician's line of vision and range of hearing presented itself as an opportunity for behavior. Together they were a chorus of distractions, and at various times, each one won out.

First, these other cues for behavior were eliminated from the practice area. The place where the young man customarily sat to practice might have been next to his stereo or near a set of books, so in that seat he could read, listen, drink coffee. Or practice. He did all of them. By putting the chair in the corner, and using it *only* for practicing, sitting in the chair became associated only with practice and not with other actions.

So the young man, twice a day, sat in the practice chair in the empty practice area and practiced. During the brief sessions, he could not do anything else—no coffee, no phone-answering, no naps. He ended up with much free time, and felt less guilty about it, because it no longer interfered with his work.

Dr. Israel Goldiamond worked with a young girl who could not bring herself to study enough. Goldiamond, who spent eight months carefully recording and modifying his own behavior—as well as observing fellow patients, as we have seen—after a crippling car accident, has perhaps the firmest grasp of self-control principles of any behavior modifier.

Goldiamond wrote, "The program with the young lady started with the human engineering of her desk. Since she felt sleepy when she studied, she was told to replace a 40-watt lamp with a good one and to turn her desk away from her bed. It was also decided that her desk was to control study behavior. If she wished to write a letter, she should do so, but in the dining room; if she wished to read comic books, she should do so, but in the kitchen; if she wished to daydream, she was to do so, but was to go to another room; at her desk she was to engage in her schoolwork and her schoolwork only.

"This girl had previously had a course in behavioral analysis and said, 'I know what you're up to. You want that desk to assume stimulus control over me. I'm not going to let any piece of wood run my life for me.'

" 'On the contrary,' I said, 'you *want* that desk to run you. It is you who decide when to put yourself under the control of your desk. It is like having a sharpened knife in the drawer. You decide when to use it; but when you want it, it is ready.'

"After the first week of the regimen, she came to me and gleefully said, 'I spent only ten minutes at my desk last week.' Did you study there? I asked. 'Yes, I did,' she said. Good, I said, let's try to double that next week."[1]

A second procedure used in self-control projects is response-cost. In plain English it means putting obstacles in the way of behavior. You want to smoke? Okay, but it'll cost you some rigmarole first. Maryland's Dr. Roger McIntire used the idea with a heavy smoker. The woman had tried many other tactics, but hadn't been able to quit. Dr. McIntire decided not to confront her will to smoke, but to make an end run around it. He first instructed her to record the number of cigarettes she smoked each day. When she was getting a good record, he suggested that she record each cigarette at the time she smoked it. She was also to record the time and place she lit up. Later, she added to this procedure by recording the time she started smoking each weed, the time she finished smoking it, and any companions while puffing.

Next, she had to record the smoking behavior fully, *and* save each cigarette butt in an envelope. Already the procedure had become awkward and embarrassing in some situations, such as parties. Her smoking dropped off.

In the next step, the woman was to start quitting cigarettes in certain places. She began by eliminating the places she smoked least—in the car, at the supermarket. Very slowly, she knocked off one area after another. Each room in her house gradually became off limits. Finally, she was down to a single room—the one where most of her smoking had occurred. She could still smoke as much as she wanted, but it had to be in that room. Still she hung on to the last few weeds.

She then limited herself to smoking in one favorite chair in that smoking room. She could not do anything else in that chair—no reading, no TV, no talking. Only smoking.

She then delivered the final blow to her habit. At Dr. McIntire's suggestion, the favorite chair was moved from the living room to the basement laundry room. She could still smoke there, but she never did.

"One of the nice things about this approach to quitting cigarettes is that we never directly confronted the woman's will to smoke. She could always smoke, but we built up obstacles."

The same response-cost principle was demonstrated in a factory in an experiment to get steelworkers to wear protective goggles. The company had had many accidents because the men were not wearing the goggles. The company urged workers as strongly as they could. No result. The problem turned out to be that the workers had to go to a storage room and sign out a pair of goggles, and then check them in after use. Many just didn't bother. When the company put the goggles out in buckets near the work site, the workers all picked them up. The company lost more goggles because they were not checked out, but the problem of wearing them was solved.

The mod squadders are fond of rewriting conventional wisdom. On self-control, Dr. Israel Goldiamond suggested the revision: "The Greek maxim 'Know thyself' translates into 'Know thy behaviors, know thy environment, and know the functional relation between the two.' . . . If you want a specified behavior from yourself, set up the conditions which you know will control it. For example, if you cannot get up in the morning by firmly resolving to do so and telling yourself that you must, buy and set an alarm clock. . . . Although the relation between an alarm clock and waking up is a simple and familiar one, other relations are neither this simple nor this familiar. There have, however, been developed in the laboratories of operant behavior a body of known functional relations between behavior, and programs and other procedures which can alter even more complex behavior systematically."[2]

Among the most common self-control projects reported by the mod squad have been those to control smoking, overweight, and getting organized.

Besides the response-cost system outlined by Roger McIntire, a number of other procedures for stopping smoking have been used successfully. Perhaps the simplest relies on punishment: The smoker keeps a graph of cigarettes smoked, then sets small goals for cutting down as he goes along. For example, a puffer who uses thirty cigarettes a day might set twenty-seven a day as his goal during the first week. If he fails to make the goal, then the punishment is delivered. In order to avoid the problem of self-punishment, the behavior modifiers suggest recruiting a second party to hold the consequences over the smoker's head. Perhaps the most popular punishment is this: The smoker writes out a series of checks, perhaps ten of them. These checks, perhaps twenty-five dollars each, are made out to a cause that the smoker loathes. For some it might be the American Nazi Party; others might choose the Communist Party of the United States. After the checks are made out, each is put in an envelope, addressed, and stamped. The batch is then handed over to the second party. After each week, the smoker's graphs are reviewed. Each week that he fails to make the goal, one envelope is deposited in the mailbox. If the goal is made, the smoker gets his check back and can spend the money on himself. A more personal punishment, favored by Richard Malott, is that each time he puts a contract out on himself, if he fails to meet a goal he is forced to give away a favorite article of clothing.

The strength of punishment and reward in this method can be adjusted according to the enormity of the smoker's urge.

Another method for quitting the habit was designed by Nate Azrin and Jay Powell. Their system was simpler, but it required assembling a mechanical cigarette case. Using an inexpensive timer and latch placed inside a case just a little larger than the usual cigarette case, they were able to make the case self-locking. After the case was closed, it remained locked for a set length of time. Azrin and Powell wrote, "For about one week, the cigarette case was locked for only 6 minutes after each opening of the lid. Since the duration was about equal to that needed to smoke a cigarette, the period allowed the subject to become accustomed to the case and its associated stimuli without interference with his smoking. Subsequently, the duration for which the case remained locked was increased. The experimenter contacted the subject every 3 days by phone or in person and asked whether the subject wished the duration increased. The change, if desired, was made on the same day that the subject requested it. . . . each increase was limited to 5 minutes and was made no less than three days since the last change."[3]

The smokers averaged about thirty-four cigarettes per day at the beginning of the study. After approximately nine weeks, all the smokers were down to about ten a day. The experiment ended before the smokers reached zero.

Another mechanical device used to try to limit smoking was a cigarette case that delivered an electric shock to the smoker whenever he opened it. The shock was gradually increased from a mild buzz to a painful jolt. The experiment broke down, however, when the smokers dumped their cigarette cases after they became too painful.

Dr. Don Pumroy and others have also begun to experiment with a new thought-association procedure. It's called P-therapy, and Pumroy told of one experiment that he conducted to see if it would have any effect on smoking. He worked with several young men, instructing them to write out and memorize six statements. Three were to be statements in their own words on the benefits of quitting the habit. Three were statements of the damaging effects of continuing the habit. He wanted the young men simply to repeat these statements to themselves several times a day. The idea was to build up an association between the statements and the smoking.

At first, he found that there was some difficulty in getting the young men to repeat the statements to themselves. They tended to get busy with everyday things and forget about the statements. So Pumroy decided to pick a set time of day when the men should practice their self-thought control. He wanted to pick a quiet time, when the men could concentrate on the ideas. He finally came up with a good one: when the men were relieving themselves in the bathroom, they were to practice the P-therapy.

Pumroy's tactic was effective. As the men propagandized themselves in the bathroom daily, their smoking dropped off. When they thought of smoking, the phrases popped into their minds.

For the pudgy among us, the mod squad has an even greater range of techniques that have been tried and found at least partially successful. Overweight is a much more difficult problem to tackle than smoking, because it involves a large collection of behaviors with different controls. "Almost anything can be a stimulus to eat," says Pumroy, "and it is difficult to control all the stimuli. If someone drops by, you want to offer them coffee and pie. During breaks at work, you want something to drink and maybe something to munch on. Talking, reading, watching TV can all be cues for eating."

Israel Goldiamond dealt with this problem when he worked with one heavy young man. "The stimulus for overeating is normally not food. In our culture, food is normally hidden; it is kept in a refrigerator or cupboard. In the cafeteria, where it is in the interests of the management to get people to eat, food is exposed.

"The initial strategy for slimming the young man was to bring his eating behavior under the control of food alone, since food is normally not available as a stimulus. He was instructed to eat to his heart's content and not to repress the desire. He was, however, to treat food with the dignity it deserved. Rather than eating while he watched television, or while he studied, he was to devote himself to eating when he ate. If he wished to eat a sandwich, he was to put it on a plate, and sit down and devote himself to it. Thus, reinforcing consequences such as watching television or reading would be withdrawn when he engaged in the behavior of preparing food, eating, and cleaning up. . . . Television, studying, and other stimuli would lose their control of initiating the chain of behaviors and conditions that terminated in eating. Within one week, the young man cut out all eating between meals. 'You've taken the fun out of it,' he said to me."

After straightening out the problem of multiple cues for gorging, Goldiamond moved on to other parts of the problem. He worked with the young man on what he ate as well as when. "He stopped attending sessions. I met him about three months later; he was considerably slimmer and remarked that he needed neither me nor the clinical psychologist to solve his problems. He could handle them himself," Goldiamond says.[4]

The steps taken by Goldiamond in this study have since become common in weight-control projects: separating eating from other behavior and then controlling the content of the diet. Additionally, weight and calorie count records are often kept, and punishments and rewards are delivered on the basis of those records. The behavioral approach, not unlike some other diet approaches in many ways, points up the greatest failing of most diets. They prescribe proper foods and exercise and suggest cutting out eating except at meals. But they fail to deal with the problem behavior in any detail. Diets then become blind exercise of will. The dieter doesn't have enough information about his problem to analyze it and deal with it.

Another tactic sometimes used when there are special problems of overeating is an item called "covert sensitization." Like P-therapy, it depends on thought associations. One example was given by Don Pumroy. If part of your weight problem is an apple pie fetish, the behaviorist would sit you down and ask you to imagine a large piece of delicate apple pie. He would spend some time describing the marvelous aroma, the fresh apples, the still warm crust. He would have you imagine now dipping your fork into the crust, and lifting it to your mouth. When you got it in your mouth and were beginning to savor the taste, he would shift gears. It tastes terrible! Like cardboard covered with shit! he would say. It's a sloppy gooey mess of revulsion.

If the scenario is repeated enough, apple pie simply doesn't have the same attraction it used to.

Dr. Richard Stuart, a behaviorist who has specialized in self-control procedures, did an experiment some time ago with eight overweight women, and used all the procedures mentioned above, and a few other little bits. The work began with the women taking records of the food they ate and their current weights. These records were voluminous and were taken carefully several times a day. Stuart also asked the women what special fears were connected with their overweight. For some it was the fear of heart attack and early death. For others it was social disaster.

The food and weight data you would expect the modifiers to collect. But those other two bits of data were used in interesting ways. Stuart wanted to find out some of the reinforcements the women were getting for activities other than eating. "For some, activities such as reading, talking to friends, watching television, or reading the newspaper are readily available. [But] for those suffering from a 'behavioral depression' eating may be the only readily available high probability behavior. It may be necessary to help the patient to cultivate a reservoir of positively reinforcing responses."

That second bit of extra data collected about fears was used in covert sensitization. During the sensitization, each woman "is trained to relax, then imagine she is about to indulge in a compulsion, then to imagine the occurrence of an aversive event. [One woman] found considerable difficulty in controlling the eating of a particular kind of cookie at specific times during the day. She was first trained in vivid imagery, and then instructed to imagine eating her favorite cookie . . . taking it from the package, bringing it to her lips, hearing her teeth crunch as the cookie crumbles, tasting its sweetness . . . and she was finally instructed to immediately switch to the detailed image of her husband in the process of seducing another woman—a great fear which she had identified during the initial interview. This process was highly successful. . . ."

Stuart met with the women in the weight project several times over the period of a year. The first step was beginning the recording of weight and food information. In the second step, each woman was "instructed to remove food from all places in the house, other than the kitchen . . . [and] to keep in the house only those foods which require preparation." These things cut down on the compulsive eating between meals of which the women were often unaware.

Step three was to make eating for the women "a pure experience." They were instructed to "pair eating with no other activity, such as reading, listening to the radio . . . talking on the telephone or with friends." This is stimulus control.

Step four was to require the women to eat more slowly at meals: biting and chewing were to be followed by putting down the fork for a moment before swallowing. Step five was to get the women to do something else that is reinforcing at a time when they would normally eat. Step six was the covert sensitization. Over the next six months, the earlier procedures were practiced, and Stuart watched progress and spent some time reinforcing good work.

During the whole procedure, the women worked on losing about a pound per week. The eight women averaged thirty-seven pounds lost during the project. The treatment was aimed, and succeeded, at "building the skill of the patient in being his own contingency manager. This is a self-control procedure which is reinforced through the patient's experience of success in the control of his own behavior. . . ."[5]

We have already seen the examples of the mod squad's getting people to organize themselves to work more effectively. The control the young musician and the student used were just stimulus control. In most problems of getting organized, that's the central issue. But for some tougher problems of self-control, consequences for behavior must be installed. Two mod squadders who were writing a book exercised some stimulus control; but the fruition of their work was so far away (more than a year), procrastination was a bigger problem. So they decided that they should work five hours on four nights every week. For each night they failed, they had to donate thirty-five dollars to their university.

A young graduate student of behaviorism at North Texas State

University put all the counting, controlling, and self-rewarding together about a year ago. Dan O'Banion had done a little self-management on his study behavior and other habits. He and a few friends traded contracts on each other, one holding the consequences for the other. "Like we would give each other money. But then if we failed, we could always talk the guy into giving it back. Or if a guy couldn't talk his friend into giving it back, he got all pissed off at him. So then I just kind of flashed on this idea—a company! Wow! They could write contracts and hold the consequences. Fantastic!"

That was in January of 1973. He set up the office of his Behavior Contracting Service in a behavior clinic at Denton, Texas. And he started writing contracts. One of his first and most consistent customers was mod squadder Don Whaley, who worked under a weight-loss contract and a guitar-practice contract. "In the weight program my consequence was that if I didn't meet the goal, they would come into my office and take out my air conditioners. And let me tell you, that's very aversive," says Whaley.

The business is a simple one. Anybody interested in increasing or decreasing a behavior comes to the company and negotiates a contract with O'Banion. The company agrees to monitor behavior and deliver consequences, while the behaver agrees to stop or to put out some behavior.

"The person would put up so much money or some valuable he thinks he would really like to keep. I hold it until you do such-and-such. You lose it if you don't," O'Banion says. Most people put up money, ranging from $25 to $150, but some put up rings, clothes, tennis rackets, cherished mementos, and some have even put up other behavior. One girl who was trying to lose weight agreed, if she failed in her contract, to put on a bikini and walk across campus. She never missed a goal. "You know, people can put up the most trivial little things and really work their ass off to save it," O'Banion says, "but there are other people who will put up fifty dollars and just blow it like it meant nothing to them. You have to evaluate the reinforcers carefully."

The contracts he puts out are tough little documents. They have to be. In one of the first contracts put out, on Dr. Whaley, Whaley slipped through loopholes three times before the contract was tight enough. O'Banion now writes them cautiously, and leaves nothing to chance. On weight contracts, he has a scale to monitor performance. For cigarette smokers, he uses a lie detector to be sure they've quit. To those trying to increase work or study time he gives a stopwatch that records the cumulative amount of time on a job, and then he backs that monitor up with a lie detector test.

He has put out about 170 contracts since the company began. There is a small fee for the monitoring work done by the company; it usually amounts to three or four dollars a month. Right now, his operation is not a legally established company, and there are no profits. What isn't paid in salaries to workers goes into equipment, though there is rarely anything left over.

In all but a handful of the 170 cases, his contracts have been fulfilled. He takes the responsibility for *all* failures. He sets up the contingencies in the contract, and if they don't work, he figures he set them up improperly. Any trouble with contracts he has run into over the past year has been a result of collecting too little data, he says. So now he requires more information.

In weight programs, for example, "If I leave it up to the person what diet to use, or what to do to lose weight, with me just consequating it when he comes in, I don't have nearly as good a program. I try to take a lot of measures to see what's happening. What does he *do* to avoid losing such-and-such? Most people, if you just weigh them in once or twice a week, they wait till the last minute and starve themselves."

So now he structures the weight loss more. He gets the behaver to keep track of a number of items. Where do you eat? What time? Who's there? What other things are you doing when you eat? After getting the data, he suggests a tactic for weight loss so that it can be consistent and regular rather than quick starvation. The same data and structuring go for all the contracts he now puts out.

"The data is very important. When people take data on themselves they become aware of what they're doing. They find out just exactly what the problem is. In fact, sometimes just taking the data can help. One chick came in and started taking data. She lost six pounds just by taking the data before we started the contract, just by looking at what she ate and how much she ate. It's a way of teaching people self-control," O'Banion says.

Beyond the service group he's running now, O'Banion sees large possibilities for a behavior holding company as a real profit-making outfit. "People spend hundreds of dollars going to psychologists trying to get these things straightened out. Shit, it would be great! You could demand a fairly large service fee, and people would pay it. It still wouldn't be as much as going to a psychologist. And the results—they're fantastic!" And unlike most psychological services, he would take the responsibility for failure, not blame the patient's neurosis.

Marriage might be a considerably different, and more successful, institution if good self-control were the rule among mates. But alas, it's not so. Dr. Goldiamond has worked with some married couples to build self-control skills. One couple came to him when their marriage was about to break up. The twenty-nine-year-old man (called X here) told Goldiamond that his "wife had committed the 'ultimate betrayal' two years ago with his best friend. Even worse, it was [X] who suggested that the friend keep his wife company while he was in the library that night. Since that time, whenever he saw his wife, [X] screamed at her for hours on end or else was ashamed of himself for having done so and spent hours sulking and brooding," Goldiamond wrote.

Some changes were made, beginning with a "program of establishing new stimuli. . . . [X] was instructed to rearrange the use of rooms and furniture in the house to make it appear considerably different. His wife went one step further and took the occasion to buy a new outfit. . . . Since it was impossible for [X] to converse in a civilized manner with his wife, we discussed a program of going to one evening spot on Monday, another on Tuesday, and another on Wednesday. 'Oh,' he said, 'you want us to be together.' 'On the contrary,' I said, 'I am interested in your subjecting yourself to an environment where civilized chit chat is maintained. . . .'

"Since, in the absence of yelling at his wife, [X] sulked, and since the program was designed to reduce yelling, [X's] sulking was in danger of increasing. [X] was instructed to sulk to his heart's content, but to do so in a specified place (stimulus control). Whenever he felt like sulking, he was to go into the garage, sit on a special sulking stool, and sulk and mutter over the indignities of life for as long as he wished. When he was through with his sulking, he could leave the garage and join his wife." The young man kept a graph of sulking. In about three and a half weeks, it dropped to zero.

". . . Since the bedroom had been the scene of both bickering and occasional lapses, the problem was presented of changing its stimulus value when conjugality was involved. If this could be done consistently, eventually the special stimuli might come to control such behavior. The problem was to find a stimulus which could alter the room entirely and would be easy to apply and withdraw. Finally, a yellow night light was put in, was turned on when both felt amorous, and was turned off otherwise. . . .

"One of the notions [X] held very strongly was that his wife's behavior stemmed from some inaccessible source within her . . . 'my wife doesn't need me as much as I need her.' The . . . message was that he had no control over his wife, but I chose to ignore this message in favor of a didactic one on the behavioral definition of needs. He was asked how he knew what his wife's needs were. Was he an amoeba slithering into her tissues and observing tissue needs? Was he a mind reader? . . . He redefined the problem behaviorally; namely, that his wife behaved a certain way less than he did. . . . What were these behaviors? They apparently included such dependency behaviors as asking him to do things for her. 'When was the last time she asked you to do something for her?' . . . He replied that the previous day, she asked him to replace a lightbulb in the kitchen. Had he done so? . . . No, he said. . . . He was then asked to consider the extinction of pigeon behavior, and took notes to the effect that, if he wished his wife to act helpless, he should reinforce dependency by doing what she asked. . . ."

This line—the old idea that the woman is really the boss around home but at the same time is quite dependent—has a familiar ring.

In another Goldiamond project, a couple was aided in facilitating their sex life. The two had no functional problems, but they did not make love very often. A couple of procedures were employed. The husband was usually quite tired by the time they got around to making love at night. The woman tried romance and fondling. She gave him a copy of *Playboy* to read before bed, but he fell asleep reading it. He was a rising young executive, and often had a full appointment book during the day and many nights. The pair finally decided that he should make an appointment twice a week with his wife to make love. And the contract included a punishment for failing at the appointment. Both of the pair were well groomed, she going to the beautician once a week and he to the barber as often. They decided that each failed appointment should require cancellation of their grooming sessions until the appointments were regular again. After a few missed sessions with the barber and the beautician, the sex appointments began to click.

So, says the mod squad, one good answer to marital discord is to put a contract out on your mate. Get the behavior up on a graph, control some stimuli, and throw in some payoffs. Some situations require a number of careful procedures, others require some graphing and payoffs, or graphing and stimulus control. Some situations, in fact, can be handled by graphs alone.

Lindsley estimates that about 30 percent of the behavior problems he encounters can be handled just with graphs. They provide some new information about your problem, and the excitement of watching the jagged line drop to zero is sometimes enough to make it work.

Don Pumroy had a problem with sleeplessness and tried just counting. He wore a wrist counter to bed. As soon as he got into bed, he closed his eyes and started counting slowly to five. Each time he reached five, he clicked the counter. He used the same procedure when he woke up in the middle of the night. Each time, he kept on counting and clicking, counting and clicking, until he fell asleep in the behavioral version of watching sheep pass by. In the beginning, his graphs showed that he was getting forty or fifty clicks before he slept, but gradually the number dropped down to very few. Soon, he was able to drop off almost upon hitting the mattress.

For Ogden Lindsley, the matter of self-management and self-monitoring is of a different order of magnitude. To most behavior modifiers, it is one among a fistful of tactics to solve problems. But to Lindsley it is the core, the essence of behavioral science.

To begin, he says that measurement is the base of science. Other sciences got a handle on their measurement early. But with human behavior, the explorers of psychology got bogged down in the "medical model," inferring imaginary organs of personality and diseases these organs might get. The attempts to measure things became descriptions of the measuring tool rather than real measurements. The measurement began when Skinner discovered frequency. Then a couple of things happened. First, many behaviorists saw that actions could be measured easily, but there seemed to be no certain way to deal with thoughts, emotions, urges, will. So they abandoned the inner stuff. They decided the "inner man" was a nearly hopeless concept, and they chucked the old philosophers.

When some of the results of work on humans were in, it also became clear, at least to most modifiers, that the man who holds the charts holds the power over behavior. Most of the mod squadders, feeling as other professionals do about themselves, held on to the power. They designed programs, set goals, and made sure the count of behavior was "reliable."

Lindsley wrestled, boxed, and fenced with these issues for years. He had a lot of doubts. He hammered at them. And bit by bit, some answers came loose. What he came up with was a radically different kind of behavior modification.

It is a behavior mod that sees self-recording as the key tool, that plays down the importance of the behavior modifiers, that thinks the "inner works" can be dealt with, and it is a behavior mod that may redeem the old philosophers.

Lindsley's case for putting the power of the charts in the hands of the people begins with the notation that people monitoring themselves is an inexpensive system. When you bring in machines, and behavior watchers, it becomes expensive. Also, people counting themselves produce charts that are sufficiently accurate. Even retarded kids, who may miss the accurate numbers by a long way, get the *proportions* right. When the real count goes up, their inaccurate count shows an increase. When the real count goes down, their count shows a drop. The proportions are most important, Lindsley says.

And then there is the matter of trust. "If you have two procedures of equal effectiveness for counting behavior, and one trusts the child and one does not, you're much better off with the trust one," says Lindsley. He is sitting on the rug of his large modern home in Lawrence, Kansas. There are charts strewn on the floor. There are heavy tones in his voice; this stuff matters to him. "I think one of the major criticisms of using external measurement and external decision-making is trust. Not that these things don't *involve* the child in changing his behavior, but that they don't *trust* the child.

"Okay. If I ask you how much money you have in your pocket, and you answer me, 'Twenty-eight dollars,' and I say, 'Let me see it. Let me count it,' I've increased the accuracy of the count, perhaps—but—then I've gone even further into eroding trust," he says. And of course that's exactly what is going on. Mod squadders don't trust people's counts of their own behavior, and will take great pains to get a count of their own. This is also true of making decisions about what behavior to change and how.

"You know," says Lindsley, "the whole testing movement in schools in the early 1900s (and it's now with us larger than ever) was based upon mistrust of teachers and children. I've looked for data. Did they have teachers and children who were caught wrong?

Did they get into trouble because what they had was unreliable? No! They just *assumed* that a person could not accurately evaluate his own performance. So they put in external measures."

In the hierarchy of a behavioral project, there is the behavior manager who works with the behaver, there is also an adviser who checks periodically with the manager and oversees his work, and finally there is the supervisor, who runs the project and never deals with the behaver at all. "Unfortunately, charts are usually in the adviser's hands, the records are in the manager's hands, and the behaver is just an object. He might as well have been a tree or a mouse; he wasn't involved at all! Also, the change decisions are primarily made not even at the adviser's level, but at the supervisor's level, by the Ph.D. in discussion with the adviser. The adviser would share the charts with the supervisor, and they would say, 'Well, let's put him on time-out.' This is extreme manipulation. It's not only manipulation, but it's bureaucratic! Most of the decisions have been made on the basis of testing academic theory: 'Let's see if we can demonstrate the effect of time-out,' rather than 'What does Tommy most want to experience this week?'

"He might not want to experience in-the-closet this week. He may want to experience stand-on-his-head-for-three-minutes. I don't know what kind of punishment Tommy digs this week!"

Professional considerations have kept the power from the hands of the behaver. The behaver gets changed, but doesn't do the changing. Lindsley has attacked the "professional" assumptions that underlie the practice, and has come up with another answer: self-management, or the closest possible thing to it, is the best approach.

Lindsley also blasts the assumptions that have been made about inner events. Skinnerian behaviorism began by measuring the physical activity of animals. There wasn't even a suggestion of measuring animal thoughts. When the work began on people, the same bias was applied. Outward behavior was measured; inner behavior didn't matter. Most assumed that inner behavior was uncountable, vague. No one made the attempt.

But Crazy Og had more faith in frequency charts than most. He felt that Skinner's measuring stick was a major step forward in learning about man, and its use should not be limited by premature biases. "When you get into feelings and so forth, everybody—Wundt, Titchener, and all these guys—just bombed trying to measure the nature of, the quality of, the type of experience. All of structuralism and mentalism fell on its face. Behaviorism was a reaction against all that.

"But now, if you take Skinner's discovery of frequency, and then put it once more back into mentalism, the data are beautiful! It's very easy for you to count the number of headaches you have. But if I ask you to rank them on a scale of intensity, or tell me which were the complicated headaches and which were the simple ones, which were the headaches composed of three parts and which were composed of two parts, you'll just blow your mind!

"Frequency is just a fantastic record of behavior. It looks like it might be the *best* way to compare anxieties across a group of anxious people. You're not analyzing the anxiety, or analyzing the headache. What you're measuring is the effect. You're working, and suddenly, *pow!* There it is! You've got a headache. . . . When you measure thoughts, you're not measuring their quality or anything; it's just a thought intrusion."

So, he says, the combination of measuring effects and using frequency to record them might reopen the whole world of inner life.

"It's almost like God was a joker. He put the solution to [Carl] Rogers' and Freud's problems in Skinner's hands! He said, 'All right, you bastards, as long as you fight, do not combine and share. . . . You're gonna stew in the juice of ignorance!' "

Thus Crazy Og has arrived at another outrageous conclusion. For more than a hundred years psychologists, and for hundreds of years before that philosophers, have strained and pained and bent themselves into verbal knots trying to get a handle on the inner life of man. Behaviorism came along and chucked all that work in the garbage. Look only at behavior, it said. And here comes Lindsley, saying that the greatest measurement tool for inner life was put in Skinner's hands. The mentalists, the humanists, have got the concern, and the Skinnerians have got the tool. Lindsley is now trying to be the bridge; he's trying to reopen the road to the insides with a Skinnerian pick and shovel.

Crazy Og has disciples self-recording their behavior, but he also has them recording anxiety flashes, sex urges, trust frequencies, anger, feelings of freedom, feelings of freedom violations, and so on. "We found these things easier to count than outer behavior . . . and the results have the same variability and predictability as the counts of outer behavior. . . . When we worked with retarded children, we first made the mistake—we thought that they would find it easier to count the effects of their behavior or the behavior of other people, rather than their own feelings. It isn't true. . . . When we offer retarded children the opportunity to count their feelings or their external behavior, more of them do the feelings. When I discovered this, I stopped, and went back to my clinical experience. I thought, Of course! How many times have I inter-acted with a beautiful schizophrenic or retarded or multiple-labeled child, and had him say something like, 'Doccuh Linnly, yuh mek me mad!'

"I'd say, 'Freddy, what's the matter? Tell me what I did that made you mad and I won't do it anymore. Because I love you, I'm trying to help you.'

" 'Yuh makin' me madduh!'

"That's almost par for the course. What's he telling me? 'I don't know what in the hell is going on outside of me! I don't know what you're doing! I just know, goddamn it, you're hurting me!' Once you look at it this way, it's obvious. He can count mads easier than he can count mad producers. A lot of courting couples get hung up on this. The chick says, 'You're hurting me.' The guy asks for an external referent. She's asking for some acceptance; she doesn't know what it is that hurts. He's saying, 'I can't do a goddamn thing until you tell me what I did.' One interpretation of that is that the complaining person is able to count the feelings easier."

Lindsley says that it's possible to take an approach just opposite the usual one of behavior mod. Behavior modifiers say: Let's not worry about the feelings. Let's change the behavior first; then maybe we can talk about feelings. It may also work this way: Since we can count feelings, sometimes the feelings should be counted first and changed first, and then maybe worry about the behavior later. Both procedures would still be Skinnerian modifications of behavior. But one works on the outside alone, one on the inside alone.

"It is beginning to look, to the behaver, like things like anxieties, spacey feelings, put-ups, put-downs, human rights violated are *easier* to count and deal with than external behavior," says Lindsley.

The Lindsley approach has led to some wild work and possibilities.

He has charted the behavior of some organizations. For example, one young woman student was considering a career as an educational administrator. She wanted to work in her home state of Missouri. So Lindsley suggested getting data from the past thirty years in the state school systems. When all of it was laid out on Lindsley's special logarithmic behavior chart, the situation became clear. Female principals were being hired less and less, female superintendents were being hired less, female assistant principals were being hired less. The only category in which more men and more women were both being hired was curriculum supervisor. Lindsley's advice to her was: get credentials to fill any of the jobs, then go looking for work as a curriculum supervisor until another opportunity opens.

"You can chart the behavior of organizations. But you can also chart the *feelings* of organizations," he says. There are many tactics for doing this. A system that seems to work is putting two boxes in a prominent place, one for positive feelings about anything related to work, the other for negative feelings. This is a simple and somewhat crude procedure, but it will yield data for a chart.

A school administrator introduced a series of new programs, and was working on getting a more positive attitude. He put some feelings boxes in the hall. There were twenty-seven teachers in the school. At the beginning, between ten and twenty positive notes were dropped in the box. Some six weeks later, the teachers dropped an average of fifty positive notes in the box. Negative feelings, charted from notes dropped in the other box, also went up a little.

One interesting thing Lindsley has run across several times is the fact that, in charting feelings, whenever positive feelings go up, the negatives don't usually go down. In charting feeling between mates, he says love seems to increase positive feelings enormously. But negative feelings also go up. When a couple gets married and, after some years, the positives drop down, the negatives are left up there.

The administrator who had his teachers register positive and negative feelings also had them chart the number of decisions made, and the number of times they shared information and ideas with each other. He charted his own positive and negative feelings, his decision-making, and his idea-sharing. Among all the graph paper, there was one chart called "Feels Lonely."

Lindsley pulls out the chart. "Here he feels lonely. That's very characteristic of administrators. I've never known an administrator who didn't feel quite lonely in his job. His chart shows lonely feelings at between two and twelve a day. First it decelerates, then goes up . . . an average of about ten a day overall. Once we do lots of charting of this kind, we can find out what is par for the course. If you're an individual who can't stand ten lonelies a day, your probability of surviving the job of school administrator would be practically zero, because the average is ten a day. Or conversely, do you dig loneliness? If you can handle twenty, thirty, forty a day, 'Beautiful,' you can say. 'I have found a place where my meshugana, my craziness, will fit.' "

When stopping cigarette smoking, Lindsley suggests counting not only the number of cigarettes smoked, but also the urges to smoke, "because there are ways to quit smoking cigarettes that will make the cigarettes go way down and the urge go up, so that you are a bedeviled nonsmoker. Like the guy who has a very stable habit, smoking forty to forty-five cigarettes a day, every day, no matter what. If he drops it immediately to zero, the urges may go from forty-five to sixty."

One of Lindsley's disciples, a feminist, decided to measure feelings of freedom and feelings of freedom violation. She had several women and several men measure these feelings. Both groups had about the same number of freedom feelings. The women, however, had more human-rights-violated feelings.

To back up his venture into the inner life of man with behavioral tools, Lindsley tells a little tale. When he was working with Skinner some years ago, he needed to hire someone to help him with experiments on dogs. Skinner and Lindsley looked at one candidate and his qualifications. Lindsley says, "Fred's [Skinner's] first question was: Can you trust him? Now if *that's* the *first question* in hiring a person, then why isn't it in our supposed all-encompassing approach to human behavior?"

Lindsley has put it in. He says that he has just begun to explore the inner life with Skinnerian techniques. He doesn't know much yet. "We don't know a lot. We haven't had a thousand people record human rights violated yet. All we know is: these things are countable. This microscope can look at things like that and see things that you don't see without the microscope."

Crazy Og's voyage into feelings and self-control has given him a new sense of his science. "It looks like we're getting very close to the possibility of building a science of the person, in which his feelings and external behavior and everything will have equal status and equal play," he says. And the new technology need not be some tyrannical manipulation, if care is taken to put the tools in the right hands.

Behavior modifiers have explored and expanded one great branch of Skinnerian theory by observing and changing outward behavior. Crazy Og has begun the exploration of another great branch of Skinnerian theory, the inner trip, and the two come together naturally in the techniques of self-control.

9. An American Reformation

Kenneth Clark, the rear-view-mirror spectator to the unfolding of civilizations, tells us we are plunk in the middle of a Heroic Materialism. "Imagine an immensely speeded up movie of Manhattan Island during the last hundred years," he says. It would look like "some tremendous natural upheaval. It's godless, it's brutal, it's violent . . . but in the energy, strength of will and mental grasp that have gone to make New York, materialism has transcended itself."[1]

It produces miracles to match any of those retold in religious stories. It has its central figures of belief—doctors and scientists in white coats—to hold the power of priests. Revelation and great works are their trade. Seventy-five years from that first brief moment of flight over the North Carolina sand, we have seen a squadron of craft circling the moon and men bouncing through its dust. In the same flash of time, a hundred other awes have been set before us.

What we got from the physicists, chemists, and engineers, we also expected from the psychologists. After all, they were wearing the same white coats as the scientists and speaking the same language as the doctors. They talked about organs of personality, symptoms and breakthrough cures. They seemed to be part of the same successful game. So we went along, and perhaps believed even more ferociously than some of the European creators of the psychology. Though it never seemed to live up to its promises, for want of an alternative this organic psychology was installed alongside the other institutions of our Heroic Materialism. Its ideas became articles of social canon. We used them to give us the power to scoop up and forcibly hold half a million people in "hospitals." We have used them to nullify Guilty verdicts in court, and to weed out thousands from our best classrooms and jobs. We have used them to justify an enormous Naugahyde-couch-and-good-advice industry whose main result is bank deposits for doctors.

But as a science, it still remained the bastard. It could not come up with the right answers when we needed them. Into our political doctrine we wrote, "All men are created equal," like a scientific statement. $E = mc^2$. Of course. What else? But the psychologists could not supply the right numbers for the equation. If all men are created equal, then it must be their environment that shapes them into what they are. Maybe, said the psychologists, but we really haven't figured out how the environment might work on people. Their "organs of personality" were fitful, elusive, and quite personal.

Behaviorism was the American reaction to this European transplant that had never quite fit. It went back to the laboratory for some harder answers and for some numbers to put in the environmental equation that we always wanted to believe. The bloom of behaviorism—behavior modification—finally appeared after the Second World War. It is another burst of the sort of faith H. G. Wells had before it was punctured by the war. As Anthony Burgess put it, "Science and education, said Wells, would outlaw war, poverty, squalor. All of us carry an image of the Wellsian future—rational buildings of steel and glass, rational tunics, clean air, a diet of scientifically balanced vitamin capsules, clean trips to the moon, perpetual world peace. . . ."[2] Behavior mod fits nicely that Wellsian image, that American notion. It strips us all down to clean bundles of behavior, to social atoms.

Behavior mod is now challenging the older psychology's notions of behaving man. It is challenging the legal, social, and almost religious dogmas that have built up around those notions. In making the challenge, behavior mod has also grown into a social phenomenon that is part science and technology, part business, part religion. It has bumper stickers (THINK BEHAVIOR) and colored advertising brochures. It has hierarchies, built-in biases, rebels, and a typical behavior modifier (a fairly young man, liberal, frank, hair on the fashionably long side). It has a lecture circuit, ranks of consultants, and a collection of inside jokes. There are even behavior mod sweat shirts and wall posters (BETTER LIVING THROUGH BEHAVIORISM).

The behavioral thinking is grounded in thousands of laboratory and real-world experiments. But as a social movement it must do more than explain *itself* with data. It must revise the past by undoing old beliefs and providing new explanations for old cases and documents. It must also revise the future by redrawing the maps of where psychology can and will take us.

The work of revising the past is carried on, in one form or another, by nearly all behavior modifiers. In lectures, papers, and books, the comments pop up: "It used to be that . . ." "We no longer believe that . . ." "The reason the old way doesn't work is . . ." We have already seen one example of revision of the past in Chapter Two. Freud's proud "cure" of Little Hans's horse phobia was neatly picked apart. There are many other examples of this sort of archaeology, and one of the most important involves Dr. Carl Rogers.

Rogers is one of the giants in the old psychology. His particular brand of psychotherapy is called the "nondirective" approach. The therapist, he says, does not take an active role in the cure of a patient. He merely provides a comfortable setting and a sympathetic ear for important talk by the patient. The patient, using the therapy as a foil, cures himself.

Behaviorists say that change is very unlikely to happen that way. They say that a good therapist probably reinforces some behavior of the patient, or there would be no change at all. They see the therapy situation simply: The patient comes in and talks about his confusion and distress. During therapy, the confused and distressed statements drop out of his verbal repertoire gradually, and are replaced with more optimistic and accurate assessments of his own behavior. This change takes place by the verbal reinforcement of the patient's "healthy" talk and the extinction of the "unhealthy" talk.

Rogers doesn't accept this behavioral analysis; he believes and teaches that the therapist is nondirective, that is, he is just warm and open, and does not lead the patient in any direction, healthy or unhealthy.

Dr. Charles Truax put Rogers' ideas to a test to find out whether the Rogerian therapist does or does not shape his patient's verbal behavior. Truax studied therapy sessions from the best Rogerian of all—Carl Rogers. He took tapes of sessions between Rogers and a patient, and had them analyzed and judged by a panel of five psychologists. The five were given transcripts of statements from the therapy, and asked to decide which statements by the doctor were warm and accepting, which were neutral, and which were cool. They also analyzed the patient's talk during therapy to separate the healthy and optimistic statements from the negative and anxious statements. The judges did not know what the experiment was about or that they were looking at material from Carl Rogers' therapy sessions.

When the panel was finished sorting and judging, the results were fairly clear. Rogers *did* react quite differently to the healthy and the unhealthy statements. He was more affirmative to the healthy ones, more neutral and cool to the ones he thought unhealthy.[3]

Thus, say the behaviorists, the patient gets reinforced for the right verbal behavior. He gets friendly comments when he's optimistic and clear. He gets nothing when he's not. So gradually the patient's verbal behavior gets healthier. He carries his new view outside the therapy room, and gets a good reaction from friends and relations. More reinforcement. He has put on a new personality and it fits, so he buys it. Eventually, he may be getting enough reinforcement for his happier ways so that he can stop seeing the shrink.

For the mod squad, then, the new definition of a good therapist is "someone who is good at verbal reinforcement." Rogers, for example, is quite good at it, notwithstanding the fact that he doesn't believe in it. Under this new definition, it is clear that almost *any* kind of therapy can work occasionally as long as the reinforcers are present.

One of the mod squad's favorite targets in the older psychologies is the unbearable vagueness of them. This showed up in a study by Ray Jeffrey, who went to court records to see what sort of expert witnesses psychologists make. He reproduced some bits of testimony: [4]

> Q: You then asked Kent to draw a tree. Why?
> A: We have discovered that a person often expresses feelings about himself that are on a subconscious level when he draws a tree.
> Q: And what does this drawing indicate about Kent's personality?
> A: The defendant said it was a Sequoia, 1500 years old. . . . The tree has no leaves and it leans to the left. This indicates a lack of contact with the outside world—the absence of leaves.
> Q: Don't trees lose their leaves in winter, doctor? If you look out the window now, in Washington, do you see leaves on the trees? Perhaps the defendant was drawing a picture of a tree without leaves. . . .

In cross-examination, some of the dialogue was as follows:

> Q: You gave him the Wechsler Adult Scale?
> A: Yes. . . .

Q: Now you asked the defendant to define blood vessels, did you not?

A: Yes.

Q: And his answer was capillaries and veins. You scored him zero. Why? Aren't capillaries and veins blood vessels?

A: I don't know. The norms don't consider that answer acceptable.

Q: What norms?

A: You see, these tests are scored on the basis of norms secured by administering the tests to thousands of people.

Q: On the comprehension section you asked Kent: "If you found a sealed, addressed, stamped envelope on the street, what would you do with it?" and he answered, "Turn it in." Why did you give him a one? Why not a two?

A: Because of the norms. A 2-answer would require more—something like "mail it" or "take it to the post office."

Q: You asked him to define "sentence," and he said, "A group of words, as a noun and verb." Why did you give him a 1?

A: A 2-answer would include the notion that a sentence expresses an idea.

Q: You asked him "What is a sanctuary?" and he said "protection." Why did you give him a 1?

A: According to the norms, a 2-answer includes the notion of a place or a building.

Q: You asked Kent to define "calamity," and he said "A bad thing." You gave him a zero. Isn't a calamity a bad thing, doctor?

A: Bad is not an acceptable answer in terms of the norms. . . .

Q: You asked him to draw a house?

A: Yes.

Q: And what did this tell you about Kent?

A: The absence of a door, and the bars on the windows, indicate he saw the house as a jail, not a home. Also, you will notice it is a side view of the house; he was making it inaccessible.

Q: Isn't it normal to draw a side view of a house? You didn't ask him to draw a front view, did you?

A: No.

Q: And those bars on the window, could they have been venetian blinds and not bars? Who called them bars, you or Kent?

A: I did.

Q: Did you ask him what they were?

A: No.

Q: What else did the drawing reveal about Kent?

A: The line in front of the house runs from left to right. This indicates a need for security.

Q: This line indicates insecurity! Could it also indicate the contour of the landscape, like a lawn or something?

A: That is not the interpretation I gave it.

Q: And the chimney—what does it indicate?

A: You will notice the chimney is dark. This indicates disturbed sexual feelings. The smoke indicates inner daydreaming.

Q: Did I understand you correctly? Did you say dark chimneys indicate disturbed sex feelings?

A: Yes.

Jeffrey's examples go on and on. They show supposedly professional men confessing that incredible trivialities like those above are what get people labeled psychotic. The logic of the tests is simple: If you don't give the answer that the majority of people give, then you're weird. Weird people are psychotic, and should be put away. Part of the mission of behaviorism is to discredit this sort of "professional judgment."

In other revisions, some mod squadders have suggested that hypnosis is a special form of role-playing rather than a state of consciousness. Superstitious behavior is actually "accidental conditioning." One of Skinner's pigeons, for example, turned around once just before getting a reinforcement. The bird then began spinning around more often, and a few more times the spinning occurred just before the payoff. There was really no relation between the spinning and the payoff, but the bird accidentally was conditioned to spin, believing there was a connection with the payoff. Black cats, broken mirrors, and good-luck pieces earned their connotations from just such accidents.

Under the new rules, love is essentially reciprocal positive reinforcement. A successful marriage, then, does depend on love. Each partner must provide enough payoffs without providing too much aversive behavior for the match to work.

Along with these revisions of the past—Carl Rogers' reinforcement of his patients, the case against psychiatrists in court, and other items—the mod squad has also begun to recast the future.

Skinner's *Walden Two* was the first full-blown behavioral fantasy about the future. He followed up that fantasy with more speculation and more details in *Science and Human Behavior,* and later in *Beyond Freedom and Dignity.* For later behavior modifiers, the vision of the future has been expressed in odd assorted places and packages. For Mark Goldstein, the vision pops up in the dry puffed language of a grant proposal to experiment with new systems of health care. For Don Whaley and Richard Malott, it appears as a brief chapter at the end of a lively textbook. They speak of a streamlined system of education that is at once more effective and quicker than the present twelve-to-twenty-one-year stint students suffer.

In rural Virginia, one experiment in behavioral futurism came straight from the pages of *Walden Two.*

In the back scrubs of Virginia farm country, an hour's jaunt from Richmond, there is a red-dirt-and-clay farm called Twin Oaks. As one drives up the rutted road, the first building in sight is expected: an old white farmhouse with pocked and weathered board siding. A tree swing hangs limply; hammocks are pegged between sturdy trunks. But across a patch of grass and a pool of mud from the familiar farmhouse is a long, low wooden building that looks like an office building transplanted from some California suburb. It is no rude or haphazard farm building; its double-sweeping roof and panels of glass had their origin on an architect's board. Over another patch of mud and earth a few yards away, there are other buildings clustered, shed and barn, and another California-office-building transplant. Out past the cow pasture, over a hill, and into the woods, there is a concrete building that can't be seen from this cluster. This Twin Oaks farm is a commune, a Skinnerian commune. It houses the usual crew of young people looking for an alternative, and has the usual biases of such a narrow group. But it has something else, which has allowed it to survive when a hundred others have split and fallen.

It began with the vision and plan borrowed from Skinner's *Walden Two* commune. Kathleen Kinkade, one of the community's founders, has written, "It was in an extension course in philosophy that I ran into *Walden Two,* recommended by the professor as 'sinister' and 'dangerous.' *Walden Two* for me was a brilliant flash of light. I cannot exaggerate the excitement I felt as I read it. The community it depicted was everything I had ever wanted, everything I had ever believed in, everything I needed to be happy. It was impossible to believe that there was no such place in real life. . . ."[5]

Two years after her brilliant flash of light, Kinkade and a handful of others were on the land with Skinner's fantasies for blueprints. After a few bouts with the total-freedom approach to getting work done on the farm, they first ventured into Skinnerian design. Skinner's novel had mentioned with only sketchy detail a labor plan by which everyone got to do the work he wanted for the most part.

With this idea in mind, the Twin Oaks people ran through a few systems before they found the one that is still in force there. There is basically one credit given for one hour worked. An average of forty hours per week is required from each member, although this changes according to the needs of the community. Some jobs are preferred, some loathed, and each member has his preferences. So each of the fifty or so community members writes out his job preferences, and gives each job a credit rating. A job that is enjoyed by many members of the community will not keep its one-credit-for-one-hour value. People will take the job for .8 or .5 credit. The miserable jobs, washing dishes being the most hated, will go for more than one credit. Each hour washing dishes might earn 1.5 credits. The jobs are doled out by a labor-management team that tries to fit preferences as closely as possible. Under this system, it is possible for two people to be working side by side in the latrine with one earning twice his co-worker's credits. The system also allows a worker to build up excess credits easily and take a vacation.

The community has established the job of behavior mod manager to give advice to those trying to change their behavior and to work out community-wide behavior changes. Twin Oaks also prints its own special graph paper and has a regular operant-conditioning class. Over the years the group and members have gone through dozens of behavior-shaping programs. In order to cut down on community smoking, the members limited smoking to roll-your-own. They then took the can of tobacco and moved it to places progressively harder for the smokers to get to.

In order to lure more workers into the hammock-making shop (their most profitable enterprise), they once delivered a big reinforcer to hammock-makers on a random schedule. For the weary workers, every now and then, a tray of fresh-baked chocolate-chip cookies would appear. Such treats are among the greatest delights of the subsistence community.

Some community members found that behavior change is its own reinforcement; others found that just a graceful downward line on a neat graph was payoff enough to change behavior. For others, there have been social payoffs: back tickles received for avoiding nasty remarks, or cutting off talk to a member who hasn't performed his work.

One young man became a chart addict. He plastered his room with behavior dots on graphs: times he avoided an argument; amount he jogged; letters answered; times he had sex; pages read; times he initiated conversations. He graphed his toothbrushing, giving seven dollars to a girl friend and getting back a dollar each day he brushed. In the end, he even had a graph on how often he filled out his graphs before breakfast.

In the beginning, the Twin Oaks crew rejected the psychologists' and designers' view of a utopian community. They didn't want to take the time and money to create a totally engineered society.

Instead, over the years, they have moved gradually from the usual commune to a more designed society. "The old-culture habits are very strong," says the current behavior mod manager, "but we are now getting more behavior-oriented. We are consciously moving in that direction."

The biggest challenge to their behavioral utopia is represented by the building under construction in the woods. It is a nursery. The community is now planning to raise children by the Skinnerian method. The children will be taken away from their biological parents in the first year to be raised communally. The parents will then have no more control or special relations with the child than any other member. "We don't want the children to grow up with their parents' hangups," runs the Twin Oaks argument. The children will be cared for in the nursery by members designated "metas." "That's to get away from the sex bias of mother and father," the argument continues. The metas will be trained in behavior mod techniques of child shaping, and will know how to operate Dr. Skinner's baby box.

There are at least a half-dozen other Skinnerian communes, which have branched off from Twin Oaks as it grew, or have started on their own. The communities are growing and dividing and growing much as Skinner described the growth of his Walden Two communes. They are structured enough to be sensible, open enough to attract utopian dreamers. They are working out, in their own nonscientific manner, the future as seen by the mod squad.

Out in Lawrence, Kansas, there is another experiment in living that sketches out a chunk of the behavioral future. Where Twin Oaks has been designed bit by bit spontaneously, the Kansas experiment was a heavily sculpted environment from the beginning. The Kansas experiment is a way to deal with problem kids, juvenile delinquents. It is a supersaturated thick-payoff behavior mod machine that is an example of how the behaviorists want to handle the nation's problem youth in the future. It is also a design for living and raising children, which, mod squadders say, might apply to any home.

It is called Achievement Place, and began with a little bundle of federal money and the purchase of a beat-up house in Lawrence.[6] The house was renovated and furnished, and the behavioral blueprints were laid out by Lonnie and Elaine Phillips, Dean Fixsen, and Montrose Wolf. The Phillipses were installed as overseers (called teaching-parents) to a dozen and a half hard-nosed kids who were to live in the home for about a year.

The kids had been angry, disruptive flops in school, and had left or been booted out. At home, in what little time they spent there, they were belligerent and difficult to control. They roamed the streets and "were known as dirty, dishonest nuisances whose primary mode of greeting was to 'flip you the bird.' They were regular patrons of the Kansas courtrooms and police stations."

When these kids first arrive at the Achievement Place home, they are immediately wired up to an hourly system of reward and punishment transfusions. For the tiniest signs of good will and appropriate behavior, they earn points. For noncooperation and belligerence, they are docked points. Every hour or two, they are allowed to use the points earned to buy some payoffs: TV, snacks, leave time to go to town, and spending money. When the kids have figured out the wrinkles of the system and appear to be getting hooked on it, their payoffs are shifted to a twenty-four-hour system in which each day's points are the next day's currency. After that has taken hold, the payoffs start coming on a weekly basis. Points are totaled and spendable at the end of each week. The final stage is the merit system. All the good behavior displayed to earn points is expected to continue, but the behavior now earns only positive comments and encouragement, no points. The payoffs that had to be earned now come freely.

Failure at any of the payoff levels can ship a child back to an earlier level. After making it successfully through each stage, and finding no trouble at the final one, the youngster is gradually weaned back to his own home.

There are eight categories of items that youngsters can buy with their behavior points, ranging from the "basics" (sold as a package of privileges for five thousand points and including use of tools, telephone, radio, and recreation room) to the "specials" (youngsters can negotiate a price for any privilege they can think up). Hundreds of behaviors are under the control of payoffs: brushing teeth, making beds, sulking, not responding when spoken to, improper language, greeting each other, proper pronunciation, schoolwork and school behavior, slamming doors, making excuses, having your fly unzipped, sloppy posture, saying good night, self-deprecating statements, boasting, and so on. . . .

The point of it all is to resocialize each kid completely, from his minutest behavior on up. The program has had striking successes, and homes designed on the Achievement Place model have begun popping up all over the country. At other juvenile institutions in Kansas, more than half of the youngsters, within two years of their release, were back in court on another charge. Two years after treatment at Achievement Place, less than 20 percent had come back to court. By the third semester after treatment, 90 percent of the Achievement Place youngsters were still in public schools. For the other state systems, less than a third were still in school. Of those attending school, the children from other institutions had 40 to 50 percent of their number passing. Achievement Place had 90 percent passing.

Another of the behavior mod visions of the future comes from Don Whaley and Richard Malott. They have taken a look at our public school system, and have drawn up the plans for a new one, the "accelerated educational program." "The graduate of an accelerated education program is eleven years old and has a Ph.D.," they say.

These two behaviorists argue that an eleven-year-old Ph.D. would not necessarily be more immature or less knowledgeable than our current twenty-six-year-old Ph.D.s. Their program is this: The child enters school at three years old. Behavioral studies suggest this is a good age to start, that all the material taught in first and second grades can be handled at this age. In some behavioral work, six-year-olds are achieving at the sixth-grade level. The rapid learning is easy, using behavior mod techniques and a little machinery, such as the "talking typewriter." On this machine, whenever the child hits a key, the letter is typed in a huge script while a soft voice repeats the name of the letter through a loudspeaker. After the child gets used to the idea of the machine, the system is changed a little. A letter appears on a screen above the typewriter. Then the only key that works and produces the voice is the one pictured on the screen. After the child gets used to this system, it is changed again. This time, a whole word appears on the screen, with an arrow pointing to the first letter. When the child makes it through the word in the usual manner, the loudspeaker then repeats the whole word. Children seem to enjoy the typewriter game, and learn some letter and word discriminations quickly.

In these accelerated schools, the teaching would be year-round, thus reducing automatically the normal time it takes to get to the Ph.D. It normally takes twenty-one years; with just a change in the school calendar, it would be cut to fourteen years. Add Saturday schooling, and it comes down to 12.2 years. They expect improved technology to reduce the twelve years to eight, and suggest that children start school at age three.

The new schools would be working only on behavior. They would not improve the child's mind or increase his knowledge. These are really fictitious notions, mod squadders say. Schools are in the business of changing behavior. A little physical training goes on (learning to write) and much training of verbal behavior goes on. So the first thing to do for every course in school is to specify what behavior you want each child to have when he leaves a course. Those courses that cannot give precise goals get dropped. Grades, of course, will be superfluous in this system. The school will train various kinds of behavior in each class, and when the child has learned those behaviors, he moves on. Thus, there would be no grade elites here. Every student passing through a course would have mastered it. The advantages of the accelerated education, say Whaley and Malott, are economic. "Since the child would

attend school eight hours per day starting at three years, the
mother would be freed of her custodial duties sooner, and would
be able to earn an income earlier. In spite of the increased amount
of schooling per student, the absolute number of years of schooling
per student would not be increased, and the absolute amount of
facilities per student would not be increased. . . . This program
would provide a means of breaking the vicious cycle of the slum
child whose potential is geared toward becoming a slum parent
and toward breeding more slum children. Once he has a Ph.D., and
the values that usually accompany that degree, he will probably
not return to the slums. . . . The imminent possibility of a society
of accelerated students so staggers the imagination that the challenge to develop the program must be accepted."[7]

Not the least of the benefits of the behavioral system would be
the elimination of the haphazard, punishing, and "ability-oriented"
system now used on students.

On the matter of the maturity of an eleven-year-old Ph.D., the
mod squadders say that maturity seems to be a function of experience, not of age. They think it would be possible to condense the
normal range and variety of experiences a twenty-six-year-old goes
through into the eleven-year-old's schooling. Some of these experiences could be given vicariously, some could be arranged. If the
system seems too highly organized and rigid, then some sur-
prises—"planned spontaneity"—could be arranged.

Whaley and Malott raise other problems, posit other answers.
Essentially, they are saying that the reason the process of education takes as long as it does now is simply that it was not designed.
It grew casually, with no knowledge of how people learn and
behave. Our system is an accidental one, formed two hundred
years ago. When the system is designed carefully, they say, what
you end up with is eleven-year-old Ph.D.s. We now have the tools
to make such a design.

We have already seen the case for licensing of parents, and the
behavioral training of fathers and mothers. We have also seen
behavioral designs in business, prisons, hospitals, and seen a few
ideas for a more effective government.

Among Ogden Lindsley's prime contributions to behavioral futurism, he believes, is a standard behavior chart that he has devised. We now have a single way to measure all behavior, inner and outer—by frequency. In order to make this tool effective and usable on a national and international scale, there should be a common recording device for frequency. If we had a single recording device that could handle all kinds of behavior—from the very frequent "blinking of eyes" to the very slow "orgasms"—then information could easily be stored in computers and shared.

What Lindsley has with his sophisticated chart, he believes, is this universal measuring device for behavior. We have universal measures in chemistry and physics, and standard devices to measure with; now the behaviorists have such a device. Since the chart is not too complicated, and it deals with things far more interesting to most of us than atoms and chemicals—human behavior—Lindsley imagines the chart becoming a common household item. Like the thermometer. Or the gas meter.

Take together the universal behavior chart, the accelerated educational system, the dreams of Twin Oaks and Walden Two, the behavioral designs for new hospital, prison, and corporate organizations, and you have a sketch of the mod squad's attempt to recreate the future. The mod squadders say it, again and again, in conversations, in lectures, in books and scientific papers: Let's not let things go the way they have. Our world if far too accidental. Let's design it a little. They know they are asking for a revolution. Mark Goldstein, when he finished detailing his plan for hospitals, commented that what he was really after was a complete remaking of the hospital system in America. He acknowledged that this was a tall order, but he added, "That's the only way to stay turned on! Take on more than you can possibly finish. That makes it exciting!"

Before making a final examination of behavior mod, there is one more element of this social movement, which, perhaps, plays more light on the nature of it than anything that has gone before. It is the special humor of the mod squad. It is a dark humor. An

element present in nearly all of it is the play on the idea of control
and manipulation. Behavior modifiers don't like to talk much
about these issues. They like to keep their debates intramural, for
fear that their work will be rejected by a frightened and unin-
formed society. But their humor always circles back to the manipulation, as in an offhand quip by one mod squadder. The talk was
about porpoises that have been reinforcement-trained by the Navy
to be live torpedoes. The mod squadder imitated what the porpoise
might say after he has struck a ship and is blown up out of the
water: "My God! This isn't the way it's supposed to be! I'm
supposed to get reinforced!"

B. F. Skinner writes with a sober voice. In his discussion of
behaviorism, when a line calls out for an obvious quip, he usually
passes it up. Even in his novel, the humor is slight. But about ten
years ago, he did write one bit of behavioral humor. It was a skit
to be put on at Christmas time for the Harvard psychology
department. In it, he spoofed himself and his science. One scene of
the skit is set in the office of Professor Skinneybox. A student
interested in taking graduate psychology courses comes in to talk
with the professor about his interest and his choice of courses. The
professor sits him down in a wired-up chair, and proceeds to shape
the student's ideas into the professor's mold.

> (*Professor Skinneybox at his desk, reading a copy of* Esquire.
> *Barrelbottom, a new graduate student, enters and clears his throat
> two or three times as Prof. S. goes on reading. Prof. S. sees him,
> puts down* Esquire, *takes a form out of his drawer, and starts to
> write as he asks questions.*)
>
> PROF. S.: Your name?
> BARRELBOTTOM: Barrelbottom.
> PROF. S.: Sit down, Barrelbottom. (*Barrelbottom sits
> down, lets out a terrific yell, and jumps up
> again.*) Oh, sorry. (*Prof. S. adjusts a switch on
> his desk.*) Didn't know it was on. Sit down. It
> won't hurt you now. . . . Now, Barrelbottom,
> we are here to learn psychology, right?

BARRELBOTTOM: Right.
(Prof. S. turns a switch, and the vending machine makes a noise.)

PROF. S.: It's quite all right, Barrelbottom. Peanuts. Help yourself. *(Barrelbottom takes a couple of peanuts from the vending machine and eats them.)* You want to be a graduate student in psychology, right?

BARRELBOTTOM: Right. *(The vending machine operates and Barrelbottom takes another peanut.)*

PROF. S.: What are your interests?

BARRELBOTTOM: Well, sir, I want to be a psychologist.

PROF. S.: You want to be a psychologist, right?

BARRELBOTTOM: Right. *(The vending machine makes a noise; Barrelbottom looks in, but finds nothing.)* I guess it isn't working, sir.

PROF. S.: That's what you think! Now, what particular branch of psychology?

BARRELBOTTOM: Well, I'm sort of interested in clinical—*(Prof. S. pulls a switch on his desk and Barrelbottom lets out a terrific whoop as he jumps into the air.)*

PROF. S.: Sit down, Barrelbottom. Sit down. Now let's see, what are your fields of interest?

BARRELBOTTOM: Well, sir, I've always thought education was kind of—*(Lets out another yell and jumps up again.)*

PROF. S.: Sit down, sit down, Barrelbottom.

BARRELBOTTOM: Then there's what they call this experimental psychology. *(The vending machine makes a terrific noise, and Barrelbottom eats about five peanuts.)*

PROF. S.: Good, Barrelbottom, that's excellent. You're making progress. Now I am going to make a little change in the situation. *(Carries a typewriter over and puts it on a table in front of Barrelbottom.)* So far, you've been talking to me, but that's expensive. It costs a lot to pay me to stay in this office. You don't really need me,

BARRELBOTTOM:

PROF. S.:

though. The whole thing can be done by machine. Can you type?

Well, a little bit.

Now I'm going to put a paper in this machine and I want you to type out the next answer. What particular field of experimental psychology are you interested in?

(Barrelbottom pokes about seven or eight letters. . . . Then he jumps up a bit and says, "Sorry" moves the carriage back . . . then he types another word, jumps up again, and says, "Sorry." Then types a third word, whereupon the vending machine rattles and he eats a couple of peanuts.)

PROF. S.: Fine, fine. Now you see we are getting along famously. Now I'm going to put a new sheet of paper in the machine there. It's got a lot of questions on it, and they are all punched in code. All you have to do is to type in the right answers. I'll just leave you to yourself, and you can begin to see what graduate study in psychology is going to be like around here.

(Barrelbottom settles down to typing answers. . . . At each answer he either jumps a bit and hurriedly strikes out what he has written, or he gets a few peanuts. After a few moments of this, the Prof., who has been reading Esquire, *goes over and says:)*

PROF. S.: Fine, fine. That's doing very well, Barrelbottom. *(He takes a rubber hose and puts it into Barrelbottom's mouth. The hose connects with the vending machine. Barrelbottom now starts to type, rather hesitantly. . . . Occasionally he bounces off the chair; occasionally he stops to chew a bit. Prof. S. goes back to his* Esquire.[8]

Skinner plays with the extremity of manipulation in this piece. Since control implies a controller, reversal is also a staple sort of behavioral humor. Perhaps the most reprinted cartoon in all behavior mod journals and books is one that pictures two rats in a Skinner box. One is leaning nonchalantly against a wall, the other is smiling, with his paw on a food lever. The one with paw on lever is commenting, "Boy, do we have this guy conditioned. Every time I press the bar down, he drops a pellet in."[9]

One tale, which was nonfiction before it turned into a humorous rumor, involved a stodgy professor of behavioral science and this young psychology student. One recent version of the yarn has Skinner as the professor and Lindsley as one of the scheming students. Lindsley says it sounds like something he would do, but denies having done it.

The professor taught behaviorism to his young class with an emphasis on the practical. He took pains to point out how the principles could be applied. The students got the message, but they were also a little perturbed by a curious classroom habit of the professor: he spoke almost entirely from the far right-hand corner of the room. One student put the two things together in a brilliant vision. Why not make the classroom into one great Skinner box? The student would play controller, and the professor, of course, would play pigeon. The scheming student began by taking data in class. During the hour of lecture, he found that the professor spent all but a handful of minutes in the cozy right-hand corner of the room. He wandered to the left only when he had to—to get a book or write on the blackboard.

Before the next class period, the student arranged a rendezvous with his classmates a few minutes before class time. He laid out the data and the plot.

When the innocent professor entered the room, he quickly zipped to the favorite corner. He stood there, droning for a few minutes. A great concert of yawns, bored looks, downturned eyes, and nervous shifting was begun. The professor went on, a little puzzled. In a moment, he moved to the blackboard, and as the board's right side filled, he was forced over to the uncomfortable left-hand side of the room. As soon as the teacher crossed the border, a chorus of attentiveness was awaked. The students sat up, leaned forward, and nodded aggressively. The professor became pleased with himself, thinking that his bits of wisdom were finally getting across. After a moment he paced back over to the favored corner of the room. Heads dropped, backs slouched, books closed. Over the next few moments, the professor unconsciously began pacing back and forth across the room, from hot to cold to hot reactions. He finally settled in the left-hand side of the room for the rest of the period. In the next class period, the students drove him deeper into the unfavored territory.

When the students finally confessed their perfidy to the scholar, he first was angry, then a little pleased. He admitted that he had been an excellent pigeon, and hadn't had the faintest idea that he was being shaped in his own behavior-shaping class.

With all its humor, evangelism, and social ideals, behavior mod is an American reform. It grows naturally out of the purely American pragmatic idealism. It proposes plain solutions and quick results, a formula attractive as apple pie on Thanksgiving. It speaks frankly of manipulation, proposing that people controlling each other is the normal state of life, and we should face it. That way we can manipulate each other consciously and not con ourselves. This sort of frank talk about controlling people has disturbed the sleep of many. But, as Stephen Yafa points out, "The ethics of the mod squad are the ethics of a conscientious whore, and the ethics of a conscientious whore—despite all that we have read in books and heard from pulpits—are often more pure and noble than those of the God-fearing forces that salute flags and kill others in the name of religion or political ideology."[10]

Yafa is perhaps right. For the moment. We can appreciate what so far has been an unorthodox and refreshing break from the cant and cruelty of other psychologies. But we must expect that, sooner or later, the mod squad's arteries will harden and behavior mod will become an institution: The Behavior Control Industry. Reforms stop being reforms; candor gives way to policy.

10. Clowns

For some reason, we believe that our society is more humane and free than others. We think of freedom, and quickly we talk of our government and our laws. But we cannot measure our freedom the way a medieval man did, counting the tyrannies of his government against him. Since we now have created means to alter or abolish tyrannical governments, we must weigh our freedom in a different balance.

A perceptive history teacher a century from now might begin a class on the freedom in our era by reading about life in a mental hospital, perhaps this bit of Ken Kesey.

> "That's the Shock Shop I was telling you about. . . . The EST, Electro-Shock Therapy. . . ."
>
> "What they do is"—McMurphy listens a moment—"take some bird in there and shoot *electricity* through his skull?"
>
> "That's a concise way of putting it."
>
> "What the hell *for?*"
>
> "Why, the patient's good, of course. Everything done here is for the patient's good. . . . EST isn't always used for punitive

measures, as our nurses use it, and it isn't pure sadism on the staff's part either. A number of supposed irrecoverables were brought back into contact with shock . . . just as a number were helped with lobotomy. . . . Shock treatment has some advantages: it's cheap, quick. . . . It simply induces a seizure. . . ."

"What a life," Sefelt moans, "give some of us pills to stop a fit, give the rest shock to start one."

Harding leans forward to explain it to McMurphy. "Here's how it came about: two psychiatrists were visiting a slaughterhouse . . . and were watching cattle being killed by a blow between the eyes with a sledgehammer. They noticed that not all of the cattle were killed, that some would fall to the floor in a state that greatly resembled an epileptic convulsion. 'Ah, *zo,*' the first doctor says. 'Ziz is exactly vot ve need for our patients —zee induced *fit!*' . . . It was known that men coming out of an epileptic convulsion were inclined to be calmer and more peaceful for a time, and that violent cases completely out of contact were able to carry on rational conversations after a convulsion. . . . If they were going to knock a man in the head, they needed to use something surer and more accurate than a hammer; they finally settled on electricity."

"Jesus, didn't they think it might do some damage? Didn't the public raise Cain about it?"

"I don't think you fully understand the public, my friend; in this country, when something is out of order, then the quickest way to get it fixed is the best way."[1]

This bit of conversation tells us more about freedom in our society than all the civics classes and Brownie meetings of a decade. John Stuart Mill told us, 115 years ago, that not governments, but the *people* "may desire to oppress a part of their number, and precautions are needed against this." Social tyranny, he said, is more formidable than political oppression. We must protect our misfits from being forced to dress, talk, and behave according to the prevailing fashion of the majority. The majority can take care of itself, but the misfits cannot protect themselves from the attacks by the majority.

So this is the way we must judge freedom in America. How are our misfits faring? Does the law protect them enough?

Well, it seems that in America we have suspended our laws so that we can seek out and crush misfits. It is illegal to deprive a man of his property here, except when the man is declared "unfit to manage his affairs." It is illegal to detain people in prison for fear that they *might* commit a crime, except that those laws are suspended when it comes to people judged "mentally ill." It is now estimated that 300,000 students who were behavior problems to their teachers have been drugged to keep them from being "hyperactive." It is common to employ "personality tests" on job applicants to make sure they will be the right sort of employee.

The key to all this is that we now have a formal set of jargon to justify, even legally, our punishment of misfits. We call them mentally ill, and that is supposed to let us know that our persecution of them is not political. We have seen enough of traditional psychologists and their ideas to know that they haven't the faintest idea what "mental illness" is, or how to treat it effectively. They just know that there are some people who are *deviant* and who must be dealt with so they don't offend us with their odd behavior. Some used to call such deviants witches. They have also been called heretics and traitors. Our pseudo-scientific label for them matches our scientific times.

So on the matter of freedom in America, we have certainly devised a system that prevents some of the excesses of government. But we have not stopped any of the social excesses, the social tyranny. We have new words for it. In fact, we have devised quite fascinating new scientific methods to blast our misfits: the electroshock, the brain surgery, the drugs.

Now comes behavior mod. It effectively throws a thick cloud around the legal and social issues we have discussed. Traditional psychology can be seen quite clearly as a political instrument to enforce conformity in our society. It takes pains to define what a "normal" person is, and what a "neurotic" or "disturbed" person is. All you need to know to see the evil of traditional psychology is that it tries to tell us what "normal" is. There is obviously no such thing as a normal person, except, of course, to those interested in forcing some prevailing fashion of life on people they don't like.

But behavior mod makes no attempt to figure out which people are normal. Behavior mod is humane reform. On the other hand, behavior mod is claimed to be a "morally neutral technology." Its power can be used for good or evil purposes, the behaviorists say. The net effect of that belief among behaviorists is simple: behavior mod will be used to enforce the prevailing beliefs of society. And here we arrive back at John Stuart Mill. He believed that we must foster differences among people, and fight at every turn against enforcement of the prevailing attitudes of society. He spoke of protecting the minority through law.

But Mill was speaking of the things his age could comprehend. He might have opposed the jailing of people who use drugs: that is their personal right, the majority's distaste for drugs notwithstanding. He opposed the notion of declaring people "mentally ill" and putting them away. The McCarthy era's abuses would have given him fits, as would some of the attacks on those who opposed the Vietnam war, and the restraints on people who wear long hair. Mill spoke of those sorts of things.

But he could not foresee something like behavior mod. It is a soft technique for changing people who are misfits. It can be a far more effective way to deal with "communists" or "hippies" than jail or ostracism was. Mill's arguments were not prepared for, as Dr. Daniel Robinson put it, "the institutionalization of friendly persuasion, utterly successful persuasion." Some of the fashionable behavior that Skinner would like to "persuade" people into is instructive. In *Beyond Freedom and Dignity* he worries that "students . . . drop out of school, possibly for long periods of time, they take only courses which they enjoy or which seem to have relevance to their problems. . . . Many young people work as little as possible. . . . a serious problem arises when young people refuse to serve in the armed forces and desert or defect to other countries. . . . what must be changed are the contingencies which induce young people to behave in given ways toward their governments." Though the behaviorists pretend to neutrality, they are not neutral. In fact, behavior modifiers shape just about any behavior dictated by the man who pays the behavior modifier's salary. We know who those people will be.

Mill proposed that we should defend the minorities and the misfits. How do we defend them against "designed environments" and positive reinforcement? In considering this, we must also think about an important fact: though behavior modifiers know their techniques are effective, they *do not know why*. They have no theory of man; they do not understand why schedules of reinforcement are so powerful. So the modifiers are not operating like a physicist or a chemist, who has a body of knowledge upholding his work. The modifiers are out shaping behavior every which way, without being certain what would happen to a Poe without his drug abuse, to a Van Gogh without depression, or to a Leonardo without his homosexual urges.

The defense against designed environments must begin with an ethical question. It is the question most often ignored by behavior modifiers, the one that makes them fall back on rote answers and shift uneasily in their chairs. Now that we can control a lot of behavior, what behavior *should* we be controlling? An office, a factory, a classroom, a home are certainly different places if we can carry out our fantasies of control.

Anthony Burgess raised the issue in *A Clockwork Orange,* most clearly in a conversation between the young thug protagonist and the prison chaplain:

> ". . . One thing I want you to understand, boy, is that this is nothing to do with me. Were it expedient I would protest about it, but it is not expedient. . . . Do I make myself clear? . . . Very hard ethical questions are involved," he went on. "You are to be made into a good boy, 6655321. Never again will you have the desire to commit acts of violence or to offend in any way whatsoever against the State's Peace. I hope you take all that in. . . ."

"Oh, it will be nice to be good, sir. . . ."

"It may not be nice to be good, little 6655321. It may be horrible to be good. And when I say that to you I realize how self-contradictory that sounds. I know I shall have many sleepless nights about this. What does God want? Does he want goodness or the choice of goodness? Is a man who chooses the bad perhaps in some way better than a man who has the good imposed upon him? Deep and hard questions, little 6655321. . . ."

To make his point, Burgess clearly preferred the violence of the young thug to the cold, clinical conditioning of the thug into meekness. The conditioning was a kind of calculated violence by the state, as he saw it. The thug's violence, at least, was senseless. When it comes to the choice of what behavior to shape, Burgess doesn't like the idea of shaping *at all*.

Skinner recognized that massive chunks of technology that come whomping down on society from the blue can create problems. Unready for them, we cannot limit or guide them properly. In *Science and Human Behavior,* one of his landmark books on behaviorism, Skinner noted some of the difficulties: "The technologies based upon science are disturbing. Isolated groups of relatively stable people are brought into contact with one another and lose their equilibrium. Industries spring up for which the life of a community may be unprepared, while others vanish leaving millions unfit for productive work. . . . Science has made war more terrible and more destructive. Much of this has not been done deliberately, but it has been done. And since scientists are necessarily men of some intelligence, they might have been expected to be alert to these consequences."

Despite those lines, Skinner does not seem to understand what hazards lie in the implementing of *his* chunk of technology. He has written much about freedom and the technology of behavior, but strangely enough, he has not dealt with the problem of deviance from normality and persecution. He says only that differences among people are accidental, which is bad. We should have some diversity, but it should be *planned* diversity.

Skinner has consistently and massively underestimated the problems of power and control, as have his followers, the behavior modifiers. Skinner has written extensively about the philosophical aspects of behaviorism: what the ideas and ideals are, what a perfect behavioral system for the world would be. He has created a debate about behaviorism at ethereal levels. The critics have leaped in at these levels. Arthur Koestler wrote about sixteen pages of attack on Skinner and behaviorism, saying essentially that the jargon of behaviorism is silly and circular, and that it will never work with people because people are not rats or pigeons.[2] Reviews of Skinner's *Beyond Freedom and Dignity* said the same things, in some cases adding that if it does work it's a terrible idea. So Skinner's philosophical writings led critics right past the issue. He set up a colorful straw man, and the critics tackled and thoroughly savaged it. The real issues of behavior mod were left standing, barely touched by the fight.

The issue is not whether behavior mod works. It is not whether behavioral jargon is silly. Thousands of mod squadders have been out shaping behavior for ten years, largely unaffected by the aerial battle over terminology. In my office I have thick piles of case studies of behavior-shaping. A fairly large percentage of them are shapings that never should have been carried out. Behavior modifiers freely admit that there is much bad practice in their field, that they have shaped such things as "on-task" classroom behavior in children without first finding out whether that's a good idea. They admit that behaviorism has sometimes been used cruelly and stupidly. And many will even admit that the power of behavior mod, a possibly revolutionary tool, has fallen into the same hands that gave us incarceration in mental hospitals, and other wonders.

The technology of behavior, an experimental technology, is being pushed too fast and hard. It is, in fact, being *advertised* and *sold* by some modifiers, something that should clearly not be done with experimental procedures. The rush to install a technology of behavior has caused the blurring of subtle lines, the dismissal of sensitive questions.

For example, the modifiers in most cases make a point of informing the shaping subjects of what will be done with them, and how it will be done. The subjects of behavior mod are mostly voluntary.

But then we must ask: Do the subjects know enough to realize what is going on? Parents might be told that their children will be encouraged to cooperate with teachers, and given small incentives to be attentive in class. They will get affection and other rewards for being good students rather than always being punished. Parents might agree to that. But then, if they were told that this shaping of on-task or attentive behavior really has no relation to academic performance, it only makes the student more docile for the teacher, how would parents react? And further, if they were told that the modifiers do not know whether the youngster's newly learned docility will make a problem in other parts of his life or prevent him from being assertive when he should be later on, how would parents react to that?

We know that people are shockingly willing to cooperate with authority, even when that authority asks us to do something that is clearly wrong.[3] People have an enormous capacity for trust of authority. Behavior modifiers as psychologists and "scientists" are authority. How much difference does it make that a figure of supposed knowledge and authority is making the request for control and behavior change? How voluntary are decisions made under those conditions?

Further, we are familiar with situations in which one person or group attempts to compel others into unfair or exploitative relationships. We most often think of the means used to compel as punishing or cruel: the landlord who forces tenants to put up with poor maintenance and high rents because no other housing is available, or because a blackball system prevents the tenant from moving; the boss who enforces a strict dress code, timetable, and unpleasant working conditions because he holds the power to punish uncooperative workers in many ways. The situation of coal miners in a company town is classic.

But what happens when unfair relationships are compelled not by punishing means, but by quite pleasant ones? Skinner offers one example: prisoners who are invited to volunteer to be guinea pigs for experiments, in return for which they will get better living conditions or shortened sentences. Skinner says, "Everyone would protest if the prisoners were forced to participate, but are they really free when positively reinforced, particularly when the . . . sentence to be shortened was imposed by the state?"[4]

Skinner cites another interesting case: In the 1930s, the Agricultural Adjustment Act was passed, and it provided payments to farmers who cut their production. It would have been illegal for the government to compel the farmers to reduce production. The Supreme Court, recognizing the compelling power of positive reinforcement, ruled that the "power to confer or withhold unlimited benefit is the power to coerce or destroy." Compelling by punishment or reward is still compelling. But the court later reversed itself because the earlier decision could "plunge the law into endless difficulties."

Exactly. Behavior mod is the total master of the soft, positive art of compelling change. Its soft force does pose endless difficulties on the question of control. A woman who has some doubts about being trapped into housewifery is gradually shaped by big doses of reinforcement from her husband into doing dishes, meals, and cleaning. Then the reinforcers slow down. Has she been exploited? The employee in a nonunion shop who sees the need to bring in union soon finds himself enjoying his situation more. Comments from the boss, warm and friendly, for the right sorts of behavior. Little manipulations in the right places, without his awareness, and he never gets around to talking and planning about the union anymore.

In earlier chapters, we heard awed behavior modifiers tell us what an enormous amount of behavior they can get out of people and animals by offering the tiniest rewards. We heard about schedules of reinforcement by which people and animals can first be lured into behaving a certain way by heavy doses of reinforcement, then their behavior can be maintained *at a high rate for long periods of time* with quite skimpy rewards. How many people have been induced into becoming behavioral addicts to gambling by such schedules of reinforcement? We know that the relationship between a gambling house and its patrons is a grossly exploitative one. But now behaviorists have found the key to that exploitation, and new ways of employing that key.

Positive reinforcement, then, can serve to create and disguise unfair relationships. Skinner notes the problem in *Beyond Freedom and Dignity*: ". . . a system of slavery so well designed that it does not breed revolt is the real threat." Where do we draw the line on inducing and compelling behavior? Sorting out these issues is quite difficult. But behavior mod rushes along, debating only with itself over these problems, when there is debate at all.

There is another problem that behavior modifiers sometimes encounter in their work. Praise as a positive reinforcer is among the commonest of consequences employed by the mod squad. As Dr. Paul Graubard found out in his study that had children shaping their teachers, the matter of sincerity is interesting. Trust is an important factor in human relations. The kids, when insincere, could create distrust with their contrived praise and reinforcement. The teachers could often detect it, and began to mistrust the children. But the children could be, and were, trained to be successful in their fraud. They practiced their con artistry with mirrors and tape recorders, until their false praise sounded and looked real.

Behavior modifiers say that sincerity is the best policy. But praise and warmth *are* sometimes contrived in their work. That can create either the destruction of trust, or a con artist. What happens to the people who learn to distrust warmth and praise? What happens to the con artist when friends or others find out that he has sometimes used warmth or praise only as a manipulator?

We are, at the moment, vulnerable to the evangelism and the excesses of behavior mod because they pose problems that are not familiar. When friendly persuasion is inept, as billboards and TV soap ads, we laugh and dismiss it. Their effect on us is minimal. But dealing with "utterly successful persuasion" is another matter. Are we really so desperate for quick and simple solutions to our problems that we cannot tell the behavior modifiers to slow down until they have more answers to the problems they raise? Mill suggested that the misfits and the minorities need protection against the prevailing fashion of the majority; so do we all need some protection from the prevailing fashion among scientists.

"Man is being abolished," says C. S. Lewis.

"Good riddance," says Skinner.

"How like a god!" says Hamlet of man.

"How like a dog!" says Pavlov.

It is as if we were a crowd at the circus. The lights are dim, the great blue beams of light spot a small performer in the ring. He is dressed in a billowy suit, dotted with red and orange and green. His toes curl up into a bright-blue tassel that jiggles when he dances. His straw hat grows a bright, waving daisy. His face is a painted smile and painted twinkling eyes. We laugh at his little dances and the little battles with himself that he always loses. He is puzzled and cheerful through all his foolishness.

Someone in the crowd notices that the grease paint on his face stops just below his chin. His neck is pale, and it droops with wrinkled skin. Someone in the crowd notices that his back is bowed slightly, and that when his hands are not juggling, they are a little shaky. Someone in the crowd shouts out, "It's an *old man!* It's just a *sorry* old man!"

So it is. He is really not a jester, a sprightly fool, a magician, or even a simple clown. He is just an old man with paint on his face. But a thousand people laughed and cheered and were caught in the illusion.

The someone in the crowd is perhaps B. F. Skinner. We have painted a face on man, he says. We have been fooled, he says.

When time has passed, and the debates are over, we will probably find that Skinner and the mod squad were right about many things. Their perception will be of great use. But we will also find that they missed something, something about the painted face of man. . . . There is more than meets the Skinnerian glance.

We have always had, effective or not, repulsive or palatable, means of controlling behavior. W. H. Auden said it: "Of course behaviorism 'works.' So does torture. Give me a no-nonsense, down-to-earth behaviorist, a few drugs and simple electrical appliances, and in six months I will have him reciting the Athanasian Creed in public." The problem of control is not simple, and we should not let the enthusiasm or sales skill of the mod squad resolve it for us.

In the final analysis, behavior modification is a small invasion of science into the territory of man. Though it seems a major step forward, though it could spawn a massive technology, though it easily surpasses other fields of psychology in its grasp of behavior, it is still a small piece of science. It is small not by comparison to previous attempts to understand and shape man, but it is small, infinitesimal, compared to all there is to know about man.

Behavior modification raises, but cannot answer, the most fundamental questions about man and society. Men have for long submitted to control by governments, economies, institutions. Behavior modifiers now suggest making those systems work more efficiently. But they suggest it without first asking: Why control? What in man makes it necessary or unnecessary? The proper role of the behavior modifier is to begin answering fundamental questions. The proper role is not to offer tools and control systems before the fundamental questions have been answered.

Aldous Huxley once pointed out that all the political, social, and industrial revolutions through which man has passed are as nothing compared to the behavioral revolution now beginning. Behavior modifiers should provide some small light into that darkness ahead, not lead us, blindly running, into it.

Source Notes

CHAPTER 1. THE CONTROLLERS

1. John B. Watson, *Behaviorism* (Chicago: University of Chicago Press, Phoenix Books, 1958).
2. B. F. Skinner, *Beyond Freedom and Dignity* (New York: Bantam/ Vintage, 1972).

CHAPTER 2. THE IDEAS

1. Bertolt Brecht, *Galileo* (New York: Grove Press, 1966).
2. B. F. Skinner, *The Behavior of Organisms: An Experimental Analysis* (New York: Appleton-Century-Crofts, 1938).
3. R. Vance Hall, *Managing Behavior,* vol. 2 (Lawrence, Kansas: H&H Enterprises, 1971).
4. Reprinted in Hall's *Managing Behavior.*
5. D. Whaley and R. Malott, *Elementary Principles of Behavior* (New York: Appleton-Century-Crofts, 1971). The anecdote is shortened and paraphrased.
6. *Elementary Principles.*
7. Described in *Elementary Principles.*
8. *Elementary Principles.*

9. Personal interview with Dr. Michael Milan.
10. H. J. Eysenck, *Fact and Fiction in Psychology* (Baltimore: Penguin Books, 1965).
11. *Elementary Principles.*
12. Richard Evans, *B. F. Skinner: The Man and His Ideas* (New York: Dutton, 1968).

CHAPTER 3. THE CHILDREN

1. James Johnston, "In Support of Human Behavior," *Art Education,* October, 1969.
2. B. F. Skinner, *Science and Human Behavior* (New York: Macmillan, The Free Press, 1953).
3. Schmidt and Ulrich, "Effects of Group Contingent Events Upon Classroom Noise," *Journal of Applied Behavior Analysis,* Fall, 1969.
4. Lloyd Homme, *How to Use Contingency Contracting in the Classroom* (Champaign: Ill.: Research Press, 1970).
5. Elizabeth Goetz and Donald Baer, "Descriptive Social Reinforcement of 'Creative' Block Building by Young Children," paper delivered at University of Kansas Center for Research in Early Childhood Education.
6. *Science and Human Behavior.*
7. Details of the Miami state school program were gathered from a personal interview with Dr. Todd Risley, who investigated the incidents, and from the *Miami Herald,* April 1 to April 26, 1972.
8. Paul Graubard, Harry Rosenberg, Martin Miller, "Student Applications of Behavior Modification to Teachers and Environments or Ecological Approaches to Social Deviancy 1, 2."

CHAPTER 4. FAMILIES

1. Roger McIntire, "Parenthood Training or Mandatory Birth Control, Take Your Choice," *Psychology Today,* October, 1973.
2. Gerald Patterson, *Families* (Champaign, Ill.: Research Press, 1971).
3. Roger McIntire, *For Love of Children* (Del Mar, Calif.: CRM Books, 1970).
4. B. F. Skinner, *Walden Two* (New York: Macmillan, 1962).
5. For further information see Nathan Azrin and Richard Foxx,

Toilet Training in Less Than a Day (New York: Simon & Schuster, 1974).

6. Hawkins, Peterson, Schweid and Bijou, "Behavior Therapy in the Home: Amelioration of Problem Parent-Child Relations with the Parent in a Therapeutic Role," *Journal of Experimental Child Psychology,* September, 1966.

7. Stephen Yafa, "Zap! You're Normal," *Playboy,* March, 1973.

8. "Dr. Thomas Szasz, Penthouse Interview," *Penthouse,* October, 1973.

9. Roger McIntire, "Can Society Find Happiness Beyond Freedom and Dignity?" (Unpublished paper.)

10. Daniel Robinson, "Therapies: A Clear and Present Danger," *The American Psychologist,* February, 1973.

CHAPTER 5. THE CORPORATE CONTROLLERS

1. "The Pigeon as a Quality Control Inspector," in *Control of Human Behavior,* ed. Ulrich, Stachnik, and Mabry, vol. 1 (Glenview, Ill.: Scott, Foresman, 1966).

2. B. F. Skinner, "Pigeons in a Pelican," *The American Psychologist,* 1960.

CHAPTER 6. COURTESY OF THE U.S. GOVERNMENT

1. Jessica Mitford, *Kind and Usual Punishment: The Prison Business* (New York: Alfred A. Knopf, 1973).

2. Edward Sachar, "Behavioral Science and Criminal Law," *Scientific American,* November, 1963.

3. *Ibid.*

4. *Washington Post,* December 16, 17, 1973; *New York Times,* February 10, 1974.

5. *Washington Post,* October 14, 1973.

6. Irving Horowitz, *The Reinforcement of Social Behavior* (Boston: Houghton Mifflin, 1971).

7. Philip Sperling, "A New Direction for Military Psychology: Political Psychology" (address to meeting of military psychologists, 1967). Italics added.

8. James Holland, "The Science of Behavior in Support of War (paper presented at meeting of Eastern Psychological Association, 1970).

9. Bruce Wallace, "Conscription at Sea," *Saturday Review of Science,* March, 1973.
10. From Whaley and Malott, *Elementary Principles of Behavior.*
11. Stephan Chorover, *Psychology Today,* October, 1973.
12. Quoted by Leonard Krasner in "Behavior Control and Social Responsibility," *The American Psychologist,* 17, 1962.

CHAPTER 7. THE DOCTORS

1. Michael Chase, "The Matriculating Brain," *Psychology Today,* June, 1973.
2. *Ibid.*
3. Fordyce, Fowler, Lehmann, De Lateur, Sand, and Trieschmann, "Operant Conditioning in the Treatment of Pain," *Archives of Physical Medicine and Rehabilitation* 54, no. 9 (September, 1973).
4. Wilbert Fordyce, "Operant Conditioning in Chronic Illness," *American Journal of Nursing* 44 (1969).
5. Israel Goldiamond, "A Diary of Self-Modification," *Psychology Today,* November, 1973.
6. Stephan Chorover, "Big Brother and Psychotechnology," *Psychology Today,* October, 1973.

CHAPTER 8. TURN YOURSELF ON

1. Israel Goldiamond, "Self-Control Procedures in Personal Behavior Problems," in *Control of Human Behavior,* ed. Ulrich, Stachnik, and Mabry, vol. 1 (Glenview, Ill.: Scott, Foresman, 1966).
2. *Ibid.*
3. Nathan Azrin and Jay Powell, "Behavioral Engineering: The Reduction of Smoking Behavior by a Conditioning Apparatus and Procedure," in *Control of Human Behavior,* vol. 2 (1970).
4. *Control of Human Behavior.*
5. Richard Stuart, "Behavioral Control of Overeating," *Behavior Research and Therapy,* no. 5 (1967).

CHAPTER 9. AN AMERICAN REFORMATION

1. Kenneth Clark, *Civilization* (New York: Harper & Row, 1969).
2. Anthony Burgess, *The Novel Now* (New York: Norton/Pegasus, 1970).

3. Charles Truax, "Reinforcement and Nonreinforcement in Rogerian Psychotherapy," *Journal of Abnormal Psychology* 71, no. 1 (1966).

4. Ray Jeffrey, "The Psychologist as an Expert Witness," *The American Psychologist,* no. 1 (1964).

5. Kathleen Kinkade, *A Walden Two Experiment* (New York: William Morrow, 1973).

6. Achievement Place, final report for National Institute for Mental Health grant, No. MH 16609.

7. Whaley and Malott, *Elementary Principles.*

8. From "A Christmas Caramel," reprinted in *The Wormrunner's Digest,* August, 1963.

9. From the *Columbia Jester.*

10. Yafa, "Zap! You're Normal."

CHAPTER 10. CLOWNS

1. Ken Kesey, *One Flew Over the Cuckoo's Nest* (New York: Viking Press, 1964).

2. Arthur Koestler, *The Ghost in the Machine* (Chicago: Regnery/ Gateway, 1971).

3. See Stanley Milgram, "A Behavioral Study of Obedience," *Journal of Abnormal and Social Psychology* 67 (1963).

4. B. F. Skinner, *Beyond Freedom and Dignity.*

Index